The Drummer Drives!
Everybody Else Rides

The Musical Life and Times of Harry Brabec,
Legendary Chicago Symphony
Percussionist and Humorist

by Barbara Brabec

Visit **www.TheDrummerDrives.com** website for feature articles illustrated with rare music photographs and memorabilia from the Brabec scrapbooks. (Details on page 276.)

ISBN 978-1-4507-0915-6

Published by Barbara Brabec Productions, Naperville, IL
www.BarbaraBrabec.com

Printed in the United States of America
by Lightning Source, Inc.

Library of Congress Control Number: 2010903692
Library of Congress Subject Headings:
Memoir
Biography
Music Profession
Self Employment
Percussion Books
Christian Books

Cover photos: Harry Brabec during his big band days in the 1940s, and when he was performing with the Chicago Symphony Orchestra in 1965.

Cover design, book design, editing, and typesetting by the author.

for Bonnie Jo Brabec

Contents

Acknowledgments

This book would have been lacking in interesting historical detail and colorful anecdotes if not for the special contributions made by several of Harry's Morton High School chums, relatives, former students, and particularly professional musicians he worked with through the years. My heartfelt thanks go out to each and every individual who shared even a few words for this book, but especially to the following:

• **Joel Cohen,** for helping me locate still-active musicians of Harry's era, for updating me on how the Chicago music scene has changed over the years, and especially for his special contribution of information about playing *A Chorus Line*;

• **Gordon Peters,** for remembrances of his and Harry's school days with Louis Blaha, for Chicago Symphony details and anecdotes, and recommendations for musicians I could contact for additional information;

• **Sam Denov,** for allowing me to reprint two Harry-Reiner stories from his book, *Symphonic Paradox: The Misadventures of a Wayward Musician,* and for helping me with details related to some photos, music, and recordings related to the Chicago Symphony;

• **Frank Kaderabek,** for telling me about Harry's life as a jobbing musician in high school, and particularly for details about Harry and Fritz Reiner that were a revelation to me;

- **Bob Robertson,** for connecting me to so many of Harry's school chums at J. Sterling Morton High;

- **Loren Binford,** for helping me find several musicians who were active in Chicago's jingle and recording business in the forties and fifties that knew or worked with Harry in those days;

- **Everett Zlatoff-Mirsky,** for his invaluable contribution of information about Chicago's recording studios in the fifties, and his Fritz Reiner stories;

- **John Melcher,** for connecting me to musicians Harry worked with at Disney World, and especially for the story about the "76 Trombones" recording Harry made while there;

- **Rich Sherrill,** for his special remembrances of Harry as a teacher and friend, his behind-the-scenes view of the life of a Disney World musician, and especially for his personal encouragement as I wrote this book;

- **Fred Lewis,** for his warm conductor's remembrances of Harry, and especially for giving me permission to include some of his playing with the Bensenville Band on the book's companion website;

- **James Dillehay,** for his invaluable graphic arts assistance in converting my book's cover design into the required digital format for printing, and then generating the necessary PDF cover and text documents for the printer. His patience with me was unending as I struggled to get everything just the way I wanted it.

Finally, I'd like to thank my younger sisters, **Mary Kaufmann** and **Mollie Wakeman,** who have given me lifelong encouragement and support, with special thanks to Mollie for her keen editing help on the book's sensitive personal content and for being my second pair of proofreading eyes.

Preface

T he title of this book is a famous quotation by rhythm and blues drummer Panama Francis* that hit me dead center when I accidentally stumbled across it on the Web. It seemed to sum up Harry's life in a nutshell.

A good drummer always drives a band, and all the other musicians simply ride along. Francis' comment spoke to me not only about how my Harry could carry a band with his rock-steady beat, but how he lived his entire life. He was always the bold leader, always the one saying "Follow me, I know the way." He figured younger musicians should take his advice and follow his lead since he'd "been there, done that," and since he had ten years on me, he expected me to do the same. I did follow him everywhere he wanted to go, but not always without protest.

Harry was quick on his feet and always ready to lead even when he didn't know the way; always willing to take chances for something he hoped to gain, or simply as a matter of principle. He dared to be different, even when he risked financial loss. His foolhardy nature often worried me and sometimes caused me distress, but more often than not, it simply made life with him interestingly unpredictable and exciting. As is true of most marriages, ours was not always a bed of roses. Harry gave me large measures of both supreme happiness and heartbreaking grief in our nearly 44 years together, yet we were perfectly suited to one another, and I loved him with all my heart. He remains the most complex, frustrating, interesting, and amusing person I've ever known, and the excitement, color, and drama he brought to my life cannot be conveyed in mere words.

This autobiographic narrative and biography places emphasis on that period of time when Harry was making both a personal comeback after a devastating divorce and a musical comeback after losing his job as Principal Percussionist of the Chicago Symphony Orchestra. Beat by beat, I've described the jobbing life of a percussionist in Chicago in the 1960s, as well as what the music business itself was like in those days when the city was so vibrant with all kinds of musical entertainment.

Lest you imagine that this memoir is the result of an old widow's fuzzy memories, think again. It is based both on Harry's letters and scrapbooks as well as my own lifetime of letters, journals, and scrapbooks. In them, I documented my own brief career as a musical entertainer before I met Harry, the stories he told me, and the most interesting and amusing musical experiences I had as I watched him perform and mingle with others backstage.

Through excerpts from Harry's reminiscent and informative letters in the last ten years of his life—dictated to me because handwriting and typing were then too painful for his arthritic hands—you'll learn much about his life and the Chicago music scene in the forties and fifties before I met him. Here are his remembrances of the days when he was fresh out of J. Sterling Morton High School and playing with the big bands and doing recordings in Chicago; his comments about many of the musicians, entertainers, and conductors he worked with through the years; his thoughts on being Czech; his love of good food, fine books, record collecting, band music and the circus; and how he felt about getting old and being forced to lay down his sticks because of ill health. In speaking with several of Harry's school chums, relatives, former students, music buddies, and a couple of conductors he worked with, I picked up a wealth of revealing information about his past and delightful stories about him I had not heard before.

Without question, Harry was an exceptional musician—a percussionist and virtuoso snare drummer many other musicians looked up to and admired, not only for his talents as a musician, but for his keen sense of humor and gutsy approach to life. He was a risk-taker in both his professional and personal life—a daring improviser who lived for the moment and rarely worried about the future. Impetuous, gregarious, and sharp-witted, he always saw the funny side of any situation and was quick to share his humorous quips with me or anyone else who happened to be within earshot. In fact, his humor was as legendary as his musical ability, and I thank God I had the foresight to capture much of it in writing.

Early in our marriage when I realized I was married to a very funny fellow, I started what I called "My Funny Book." In it, I recorded Harry's silly day-to-day utterings for posterity, figuring that if they made us laugh once, they'd make us laugh again later. Near the end of Harry's life when he was very ill and in great pain, I began to read some of his best jokes aloud to cheer him up. At one point after he stopped laughing at something he had said years before, he paused thoughtfully for a moment and then quietly said with humbleness, "I *was* pretty funny, wasn't I?" Funny how he had always taken his sense of humor for granted.

So now I hope you'll lean back in your seat and get comfortable, because the lights are dimming, the curtain's going up . . . and my musical story is about to begin.

---

*Panama Francis (1918–2001) became the first musician to be recognized by the Rhythm and Blues Foundation in 1993 and to be inducted into the Smithsonian National Museum of American History. His drumsticks are on display at the Rock-n-Roll Hall of Fame to commemorate his musical artistry and lifelong contributions to twentieth-century American music.

CHAPTER 1

Beginning Again

Just look for a guy with a rose in his teeth wearing baggy pants and looking like one of the last Mohicans. —Harry

I got my first glimpse of how Harry operated as a jobbing musician the day we went downtown to pick up our marriage license at City Hall. Afterward, Harry stopped off to see Bill Walker, a music contractor he had gotten jobs from in earlier years, just to let him know he was back in town and available for work. The guy was so busy he practically shoved Harry out the door. We had no sooner left his office than he hollered out, "What is it you play?"

Everything.

"Got four timps?"

Sure!

"Okay, be at Universal at nine on Monday."

Wham bam. Just like that.

"But you don't have one drum, let alone four," I said with pre-wifely concern.

"Yeah," he grinned, "but I know where to get them. If I'd been totally honest, I'd have lost the job."

Off we went to Franks Drum Shop, which was owned by Harry's old music buddy Maurie Lishon. Musicians in town called this place Percussion Central. It had every instrument imaginable for rent or purchase, and it drew a steady crowd of both local and out-of-town drummers, which made it a great networking headquarters. Within minutes, Harry had the four timps squared away for delivery to the job site at the proper time. I learned a lesson that day that I would later relate in one of my business books when I was speaking about the importance of creating an "illusion of success." Basically, there's a difference between lying and just leaving out a few small details. If we really want to be successful, looking as if we already are is a good way to start. Harry was always very good at that.

A Whirlwind Courtship

I met Harry on a blind date in front of Fourth Presbyterian Church on the near north side of Chicago on Sunday, August 8, 1961 after our mutual friend, Gordon Peters, suggested he call me for dinner.

"How will I know you?" I asked when he called. "Will you wear a rose or something?"

"In my teeth, maybe," he said with a sexy chuckle. "Just look for a guy wearing baggy pants and looking like one of the last Mohicans."

Well, that was certainly different, I thought. I could hardly wait to meet this fellow. He was on time, waiting for me in front of the church steps as I came out. His back was to me, and a dozen thoughts rushed through my mind as I started down the steps: *What will he look like? Do I look all right? Will he like me?* To his back I said, "Are you the Mohican with baggy pants I'm supposed to meet?"

He turned around with a smile that warmed me to my toes. Even without the rose in his teeth, there was no mistaking him. Very tall—six foot and then some. Brown hair with a crew cut so short it almost made him look scalped. Black suit with baggy pants and a jacket that hung loosely from his skinny frame. Interesting face with smiling hazel eyes.

An exchange of hellos and then, "Barbara, I want to take you to the best restaurant in town . . . but I have a little problem."

With just 22 cents and a paycheck from the Chicago Symphony in his pocket, he had taken a risk by inviting me to dinner in hopes that I could find someone on a Sunday night who would cash his check. He had tried several places to no avail, so he was visibly relieved when I told him I just happened to have an acquaintance with the owner of a nearby grocery shop. It took a little coaxing, but he finally cashed Harry's check and we set off to have dinner at Ballentine's restaurant on Dearborn Street.

In just ten minutes' time over a dinner drink, I knew Harry was impatient like me, blunt and to the point, delightfully charming, witty, and very sentimental. "Look," he said, "I'm going to level with you right from the beginning. I know we're going to be good friends."

By the time the main dish arrived, we were speaking very personally, slowly drawing one another out until we found ourselves sharing very personal details of our lives by the time dessert arrived. Over coffee, after telling me a bit about his divorce, my heart fell a bit when he said he didn't think he would ever marry again.

It was a beautiful evening, so we decided to take a walk after dinner. When I hooked my arm in his, he said he was the proudest guy in town to be walking down the street with me. As we passed a flower shop he suddenly said, "Time out," and quickly ushered me inside. In a commanding voice to the florist he said, "Give me the most beautiful rose in the shop for the most beautiful girl in the world."

The florist seemed indignant that Harry was buying only one rose instead of a whole bouquet, but I was absolutely entranced. No one had ever bought me a rose before, let alone call me beautiful. From there we walked over to Rush Street, Chicago's famous nightlife and entertainment center. Harry wanted to hear Bob Scobey and his Dixieland Band at Bourbon Street, where Art Hodes, a friend from his days at NBC, was playing piano. We spent a couple of enjoyable hours there, with Harry chatting with Art and the other musicians when they were on break.

On leaving the club, we talked nonstop as we slowly ambled our way back to the Three Arts Club, a women's residence on North Dearborn where I had a midnight curfew. I was literally in a daze by the time Harry dropped me at the door, gave me a gentle hug, kissed my forehead and said, "You're gonna bug me. I'll call you for lunch tomorrow."

I practically floated up the four flights of stairs to my room.

For the next three days, in between Harry's work schedule and my short-hours' secretarial job at the Harding Restaurant Company, we spent many hours together talking nonstop and learning many new things about each other. In a cab as he was taking me home on Wednesday night, he knocked me for a loop when he casually interrupted the conversation to say, "Incidentally, I'm going to marry you. You might be thinking about it a little bit."

"You're nuts!" I said with both excitement and amazement.

He gave me a grin and said, "You might as well get used to it."

When Harry phoned my dad the next evening and formally asked him for my hand in marriage, Daddy just chuckled and said it was fine with him, that he knew better than to tell me what to do. Mother wasn't as understanding; she was sure I was moving too fast and making a big mistake since Harry was both a divorced man and one who was ten years older than her precious daughter of 24 who had never dated much. But when Harry met her on the following Sunday, gave her his wonderful smile, said "Hi, Mom" and hugged her, she just melted. He was easy to love.

Although I felt as though I'd known Harry forever as a soul mate, at this point I knew very little about his earlier life and music career; only that his divorce had been very traumatic, that he had been out of the music business for awhile, and was now trying to make a comeback in Chicago. I had no understanding of what "making a comeback" entailed, or how he was going to do it. I had barely begun to plumb the depths of the man I had agreed to marry without a moment's hesitation, and I couldn't begin to imagine what life with him would be like. I always thought of myself as being a practical and level-headed girl, but in this case I guess I was something of a risk-taker, too.

We were quietly married in Howes Memorial Chapel on the Northwestern Campus in Evanston on August 26, 1961, just eighteen days after we'd met. "At least folks back home won't be able to say it was a shotgun wedding," mother joked. Later, when a concerned friend said, "But you've married a perfect stranger," I said, "I'm not worried because he *is* perfect as far as I'm concerned."

Only a few family members and friends were in attendance for the wedding and the reception that was held in the small living room of our furnished apartment on Chicago's near north side. We had so little money that I handwrote the invitations. Our gold wedding rings cost just $50, and even with my blue lace wedding dress, bouquet, cake and reception snacks, our simple but memorable wedding cost less than $200. It was a great investment that would yield a lifetime of dividends for both of us.

Ready to Roll!

With both of us working, and only a few hundred dollars between us, there was no time or money for a honeymoon. Harry went into action as soon as we were settled, practically living on the telephone as he began to call every music contractor in Chicago trying to sniff out any work that was coming into town. He reconnected with all the recording studios and radio stations he had worked with in earlier years and tracked down every old music buddy he knew. Before long, everyone in town knew Brabec was back and ready to roll.

I was very impressed with Harry's communication skills, but listening to some of those early phone conversations as he was trying to get work made me nervous. There was a great deal of competition for each job in town and, as he put it, music was a cut-throat business to begin with and it took a lot of moxie to survive in it. In years to come I would often hear him say things that I knew weren't exactly true, but who was I to tell him how to run his business?

By October, many job offers were now coming Harry's way, but with the offers also came frustration because choices had to be made as to which jobs to take. I soon learned how difficult it was for a freelance musician to juggle his job schedule. Often, two jobs were offered that overlapped with one another, making it difficult to choose which one to take. At this particular time, Harry's choice was taking the Lyric Opera work, which would run from October 14 through December 1, or a ten-week tour with the ballet company that would have netted him $350 a week. But neither of us could stand the thought of him being gone for ten weeks so soon after we were married, so he passed on that job.

In a letter to mother, I wrote, "Harry had another $150 recording job last Monday, so it works out that, in two days this month, he has made more than I made working four weeks. Isn't that something? The rehearsals for the Lyric Opera start Friday and everything will be fine for awhile then."

In November, after Harry had been getting to and from work via public transportation, we were both relieved when a musician buddy had a used car for sale that we could buy for only $230. We were really hurting for money in those days, so the opera job was a real blessing. I'll never forget how exciting it was the night Harry came home with a surprise. I was sitting on the couch when he opened the apartment door and came over to kiss me. Then he pulled a wad of bills out of his pocket and began to rain cash on my head. He had cashed his first opera paycheck. I don't recall how much it was for; I only remember that it was a *lot* of money to us then. In fact, I had never seen that much cash at one time before and I was so tickled that we both began to laugh and throw bills up into the air, letting it fall all around us like kids playing in a pile of leaves.

Harry worked hard for that money, and my journal note for October 19, 1961 gives an idea of what the Lyric Opera's rehearsal and performance schedule was like at that time:

Harry has been working his tail off, bringing home some good money, usually rehearsing from four to six hours every day, with performances every night except Sunday. For three days in a row he had to be to work by 10 o'clock, rehearse until 4 o'clock, and then go back for an eight-to-midnight performance. That got him home at one a.m. But he can never go to sleep for at least an hour after he gets home because he's always on such a "music high," and by the time 8:30 a.m. rolls around, he's pretty tired. So am I, because I always get up and sit with him for awhile after he gets home, and then I have to get up and go to work, too.

Harry loved playing operas, but since opera was my least favorite kind of classical entertainment, I was rarely in the audience when he was performing with the Lyric. I did love the first opera I ever saw at the Lyric, however, which was *Madame Butterfly* in 1958. I had a seat in the center aisle thirteen rows from the stage. That ticket cost $8, which was considered expensive in those days. (In 2010, main floor ticket prices had increased to between $83 and $194.)

Feast or Famine

In the months that followed the Lyric work, it was feast or famine, sometimes little or nothing in a month, other times several jobs with conflicting schedules. Harry regretted having to turn down a December 1 show with Marlene Dietrich because he was still tied up with the Opera, but he was delighted to get the Leningrad Kirov Ballet job at the Arie Crown Theatre on December 7–10. Other work that month included a show at the Blackstone Ballroom with Crazy Otto (with whom he had worked before), a show with Morton Gould at McCormick Place, and a concert with the Park Forest Symphony. He also did a 7UP commercial for one of the two biggest recording studios in town and got tremendous compliments about his work. That was when I learned a little more about the jingle recording he had done earlier in his career. (See Chapter 7.)

Some days were longer than others. For example, on one Saturday I documented in my journal, he had an hour's rehearsal from ten till eleven for a concert to be held on Sunday, followed by a rehearsal from noon till five for a show he would play on Monday evening. After a trip home for dinner, he played a dance job from ten to midnight. As he put it, he was "one tired cookie" when he got home that night. There would be many days like this in the future.

When he wasn't out playing, Harry seemed to live on the telephone. It took a lot of detective work to find out which contractor was hiring musicians for this or that job, and he took every job he could get, regardless of the money it paid or where the job was. It was hard work and I was proud of him. But no amount of effort could make up for the fact that, music-wise, Chicago was dead in January and pickin's were slim at a time when we had just $300 between us with twice that amount in bills due that month.

"Maybe I should just give up music and go out and get a regular job," he said. But I simply wouldn't hear of it. I loved him so much for offering to give up *just for me* the only other thing in the world that meant everything to him at this point, but the price of "security" wasn't worth it to me. Music was Harry's life—had been since he was a kid in school—and I knew that if he gave it up, he'd just wither and die inside. A steady income would have been nice, but I knew it could never replace the glorious feeling Harry had in his heart after doing a magnificent job on a concert or even a high-school dance, or the radiant feeling I got just from watching him perform. I meant it when I said I loved the crazy, mixed-up way of life we were living and the financial challenges we faced together. I figured my job and some good luck on Harry's part would get us through.

In January, he played a concert with the Little Symphony of Chicago and a performance of *Rigoletto* with The American Opera Company (which seems to have disappeared over the years). In February and March, Harry played some concerts with the Park Forest Symphony, Milwaukee Symphony, and a couple of Saturday night dance jobs at the Hilton. He served as an adjudicator for the Chicago Public Schools Ensemble Competition Festival (percussion and woodwinds) in March, and shortly afterwards got four weekend performances of *Aida,* presented by the Lithuanian Opera of Chicago. (I enjoyed this opera not only for its pageantry but because I was seated close to where Harry was playing.)

It was also in March that Roy Knapp, Harry's old teacher, told him there might be an opening in the percussion section of the Cleveland Symphony. Things looked good for awhile, but he was later advised that the position had been filled. About the same time, he heard about an opening in the percussion section of the Los Angeles Philharmonic and wrote to the Orchestra's General Director, George Kuyper (1899–1987) about it. Kuyper knew Harry's reputation and was very interested in him, but he said the percussion position could not be settled until August because of a "slight dispute with the union regarding auditions."

Finally, after many months of worry, he got the job he had been pursuing for some time: the 1962 summer season of Melody Top Theatre. At last—a few months of steady income we could count on.

♪ Music Sidenote ♪

George Kuyper got back to Harry again in August about the Los Angeles Philharmonic job, asking if he held membership in L.A.'s local. I don't remember if this is what killed this job or whether Harry simply passed on it because by then he was in the middle of his first season with Melody Top and his opportunities to play in Chicago (where his heart was) were looking up.

CHAPTER 2

Melody Top Summer Theatre

Do you ever get the feeling that we're in the wrong business? —Harry

Harry never wrote about his Melody Top experiences in any of his letters, but he kept a scrapbook of programs and reviews of shows he played. This was a job he really enjoyed, and it was terrific fun for me because I had a front row seat for every great musical that came into the theatre. The lineup of stars was mighty impressive to this small-town girl who never dreamed she would marry a professional musician, let alone one who would not only make sure she had the best seat in the house for every job he played, but would also take her backstage to meet some of the performers.

Melody Top was originally a summer stock theater in Milwaukee, Wisconsin that began in 1950 in a tent, but later was converted to a wooden dome-like structure with tent sidewalls that existed until the early 1990s. I don't know when the second Melody Top tent theater opened in Hillside, Illinois (just outside Chicago), but Harry played its last seasons in 1962, 1963, and 1965. This music-in-the-round theatre was an unusual umbrella-type tent that seated over two thousand people with no seat more than 18 rows from the stage. All rows were in tiers, allowing every spectator an unobstructed view of the stage. The tent was supported by brick and mortar buildings that included rehearsal halls and shops, refreshment stands, and the box office. A newspaper article at that time said the total cost of this complex was $210,000.

Melody Top rehearsals began on May 21, 1962 for the June 5 opening of *Carousel* with Howard Keel. I wanted to see the opening show, but all the tickets were sold out. According to a clipping from

"Kup's Column" (Irv Kupcinet, legendary Chicago columnist, 1912–2003), the show had opened with a $65,000 advance, which apparently amazed Richard Rodgers, co-author of the musical. (Rodgers, who wrote the music for 43 Broadway musicals, would have been 60 years old at this time. He died in 1979.)

The Melody Top pit orchestra was a good one, and, as its drummer, Harry was having fun and making valuable contacts as well. The guys who were booking the McVickers Theatre and the Shubert were in the orchestra, so now Harry had an "in" to get into the Shubert in the fall. There was a rumor that the show would need a percussionist, and if that happened, and Harry did a good job at Melody Top, the job would be his. Clearly, to get ahead in the music business in Chicago, you not only had to play well, but know the right people.

Amusing Reviews for 1962 Shows

In addition to *Carousel,* other shows that season included Phil Ford and Mimi Hines in *Hit the Deck,* Jane Morgan in *Kiss Me Kate,* Phyllis Diller in *Wonderful Town,* Arlene Dahl in *One Touch of Venus,* and Walter Slezak in *Fanny.* Harry's scrapbook yielded some interesting reviews.

Of Ford and Hines, Chicago *Sun-Times* critic Glenna Syse said, "For moxie, for hoofing, for clowning, for that 'let's give the folks their money's worth' drive—they're hard to beat."

A note in "Kup's Column" reported that the backstage Jane Morgan-Earl Wrightson feud during *Kiss me Kate* was more interesting than what was happening on stage. "The two haven't spoken for four years, when each charged the other 'hit too hard' in the same musical. But the topper came the other night when Wrightson slapped La Morgan with such 'feeling' that the table on which he spanks her broke!"

The *Tribune's* music critic Thomas Willis proclaimed that Diller's humor was lost in *Wonderful Town.* "Some place along the line," Willis wrote, "some dear friend of Phyllis Diller's should have taken her quietly aside and said, in her best Rosalind Russell voice, 'Look, dear, *Wonderful Town* just isn't for you.'" He also said the Bernstein score got a good workout from the chorus and "the sometimes over-enthusiastic orchestra," which Harry found amusing. Another reviewer commented that Dobbs Frank, musical director, had "whipped his small pit band into Broadway shape for the Leonard Bernstein music."

Harry was particularly fond of Walter Slezak, whose "talent was as ample as his girth" (critic Glenna Syse), and he also liked this play because it was all about a man's great love for his wife.

A Rip in Time

Hit the Deck was one of Harry's favorite shows because Phil Ford had a great sense of humor, and he and Harry often joked around backstage. Always impish, Harry decided to play a joke on Ford one night during the performance. In one scene, Ford normally stood behind a chair and then threw his leg over the chair to sit down. For the joke, Harry got a piece of an old window shade we had and slit it in several places so it would tear easily. As Ford moved into this scene, Harry sneakily brought out the piece of window shade material. At the exact moment Ford threw his leg over the chair, Harry ripped the shade, slowly and loudly, and throughout the theater it sounded like Ford had just ripped his pants. I regret that I didn't get to see this, but Harry gleefully described it to me when he got home that night.

At first Ford look stunned, he said, and then he laughed, stood up and threw his leg over the chair again as if to test Harry to see if he could catch that one, too. He did, and Ford cracked up as the whole audience howled with laughter. It was a good joke, but I thought Harry was pushing his luck a bit here. I later learned this wasn't the first or last time my risk-taking husband would interact directly with the cast during a show, or do something else on stage that other musicians wouldn't dream of doing.

First Vacation and Other Work

When Melody Top closed for the season, Harry and I took our first vacation to Lake Como, Wisconsin, where he used to live. We visited his old home site and the people there, and it did his soul good to reminisce with them and the neighbors across the street that hadn't seen him since he was five. We knew practically everyone in the area by the time we left a week later. We had saved a lot by going off-season, paying only $6 for our motel room (regularly $10), and enjoyed great privacy. There wasn't another soul in the motel that week or anyone on the lake the first couple of days. It was as if we had bought the town. When we went to dinner, we were the only ones in the restaurant.

When Harry took me fishing, I caught more and bigger fish than he did, which made him very proud of me. He taught me how to play pool in the local tavern where I beat him more than once, which prompted him to dub me "Billiard Barbara" (the first of many nicknames he'd give me in years to come). In all, this was a very quiet and romantic vacation for us that made up for not having a honeymoon. (It would be many years before we'd finally take a "honeymoon trip" to Niagara Falls.)

Harry came back to three jobs on Saturday: a morning rehearsal for a concert on Sunday, another one from noon to five for a show on Monday, and a dance job that evening. The Sunday concert at the Museum of Science and Industry was notable for the fact that it was the only symphonic music being heard in Chicago at the time because the Chicago Symphony was on strike. This particular concert was presented by the 34-piece Chicago Chamber Orchestra directed by Dieter Kober, and this was the third concert in this particular series beside the lagoon in Jackson Park.

On Monday, Harry had another rehearsal and performance of the show Kemper produced for its Golden Anniversary that year, a private event strictly for their employees and friends that reportedly cost $50,000 to produce. Hosted by veteran broadcaster Jim Conway, it starred Peter Lind Hayes and Mary Healy, the Ruth Page Chicago Opera Ballet Company, The Kim Sisters, and The Freedom Singers. Lou Breeze led the 25-man orchestra. Harry played xylophone for the first number, and I vividly remember how stunned I was by his xylophone virtuosity that night. In *the Merry Widow* ballet that followed, he played xylophone, bells, and timpani; after that, nothing, except he had to stay in the orchestra for appearance's sake. The show ended with a big community sing. It was way too long, but I didn't care because I got to hear Harry play as I'd never heard him play before.

He later told me that the xylophone part in the first number simply said "ad lib here" for so many measures. *And boy did he ad lib!* I sat there transfixed as he nimbly moved those two sticks up and down the keyboard, faster and faster, playing what seemed like a million notes as the act and the music climaxed and finished. He simply knocked my socks off, and the minute I saw him after the show I said, "Wow, honey! I didn't know you could play like *that.* "

"Neither did I," he said, rather amazed himself. It was apparently one of those great in-the-moment musical experiences that could never be duplicated.

♪ Historical Sidenote ♪

On December 6, 1962, a Chicago *Sun-Times* headline blasted, "It's Official: Rebels Beat Petrillo." When Bernard Richards, who had never held union office, was elected the new president, this ended the 40-year career of James C. Petrillo as president of Local 10 Chicago Federation of Musicians and one of the oldest and most powerful regimes in American unionism.

The 1963 Melody Top Season

Journal note, April 24, 1963:

> *Harry went into the Civic Theatre the 11th of May, which means he will go directly from the Shubert to the Civic, and directly, without even one day off, into Melody Top. So that shoots any chance of a vacation, let alone a weekend off. He has now worked for a solid year, if you figure starting from Melody Top last summer and making the cycle back to Melody Top again this year. He had had only one week off when he left the Opera to go into the Shubert plus a few days when we went to Wisconsin. He's been very lucky, and we are happy he's working so steadily because, when fall comes, there's always the possibility that things won't be so busy.*

In June before this season opened, there was a Saturday that I complained about to my mother. I couldn't get a thing done that day because Harry had dragged every single piece of drum equipment out of the closets, drawers, and storage area downstairs and had them strung out in the middle of both the living room and bedroom floors until I could barely find my way through the maze. He was putting new heads on two of his drums, packing up instruments for Melody Top, cleaning out his tool chest and making a big mess in general. Ah, for a musician husband who just played a horn, I thought.

That season got off to a slow start with the house not selling well, but it was my favorite season because it featured several of the great musicals I had enjoyed earlier in movie theaters. Included were Gordon and Sheila MacRae in *Guys and Dolls*, Jane Morgan in *The King and I*,

Jaye P. Morgan in *The Unsinkable Molly Brown,* and Forrest Tucker in *The Music Man.*

Sometime in June that year, Harry decided he needed some rest from months of non-stop work, so he asked his old friend, Fred Wickstrom, to sub for him for a few days so we could get away for awhile at the Wagon Wheel Lodge in Rockton, Illinois. Here we played some golf, swam, lazed in the sun, and had some fine meals at the lodge and in nearby restaurants. Then Harry was ready to get back to work again.

He didn't talk much about any of the stars that season, except for Forrest Tucker, who had a wonderful sense of humor. Harry had loved his silly *F Troop* TV show, and he naturally sought him out backstage to get acquainted. Prior to appearing at Melody Top, Tucker had entranced Chicago for 56 weeks in 1959–60 at the Shubert, a performance I was remembering as I saw this show again at Melody Top. Of this appearance, dance critic Ann Barzel said Tucker's performance on the theatre's circular stage was "if anything, a shade more exuberant as he covers the larger territory with a hop and a skip and a jaunty two-step." The best part of this show was its "Seventy-Six Trombones" production number which had Tucker and the whole band marching on stage, down the aisles and along the inner rim of the tent. They marched up and down, around, across, and back again until they simply enveloped the entire audience and brought the house down.

Melody Top's Last Season

In 1965, Melody Top opened the week of June 8 with *South Pacific* starring Giorgio Tozzi, followed by Phil Ford and Mimi Hines in *Bells Are Ringing,* Sally Ann Howes in *My Fair Lady,* Jaye P. Morgan in *Annie Get Your Gun,* Janet Blair in *The Sound of Music,* and Anna Maria Alberghetti in *West Side Story.*

Chicago-born Giorgio Tozzi must have felt right at home in this Melody Top production, and critics loved him even if most found the show itself rather dull. His singing engulfed the theater and his handsome presence reminded me very much of Rossano Brazzi's performance in the 1958 movie version of this musical. I liked the music so much that I did arrangements of several numbers for my marimba performances.

I think Harry enjoyed this season of Melody Top more than any of the others because he had so much fun mingling with cast members. Phil Ford was back again this year and, although there were no onstage jokes this time around, I'm sure Ford never forgot his first surprising encounter with him. I had fun backstage, too, where I met various performers.

Harry was particularly fond of the five young girls in *The Sound of Music*. The night I saw the show, we went backstage and he lined them up in front of him in stair-step order. With them dressed in their perky red and white outfits, and Harry in his white jacket behind them, it made a dear picture.

When I saw *West Side Story*, he introduced me to three of the boys who immediately went into a routine he had asked them to do to give me a laugh. Two of them suddenly grabbed Harry, one clutching him around the neck while a third pretended to stab him with one of his drumsticks. He did a pretend gag, I snapped a picture, and we all had a good laugh.

I doubt that any of the other musicians ever did this kind of horsing around backstage, but Harry had a way of making friends and spreading laughter wherever he went, and people just liked to be in his company.

"The Rain in Spain"

Harry liked some shows a whole lot more than others, but *My Fair Lady* was way down on his list. This music was very boring for a drummer to play, he said, and he didn't like the tunes in it to begin with. But I liked the show so much that, when Harry got some free tickets for a couple of friends, I went along to see it a second time. As it turned out, Harry wasn't the least bit bored by this evening's performance.

This show had opened to rain, and the tent had sprung a few leaks then, with drips so bad in one place that one guy actually opened an umbrella for awhile. It had been raining on this particular evening, too, and a thunder-and-lightning storm was brewing as the performance began. After about an hour of the first act, the lights went down for a scene change. When they came up again, the first words out of the star's mouth were "The rain in Spain—" and, at that same moment, there was a tremendous clap of thunder as the heavens opened up right along with the tent. The production fell apart as stage hands began to throw plastic covers over the props and the actors left the stage. Harry quickly covered his drums with the plastic tablecloth I had loaned him earlier, then he and the other musicians jumped out of the pit because they knew where all the water would soon be flowing.

There was an announcement to the effect that they would try to wait out the storm, but it wasn't getting any better and people were beginning to open umbrellas inside because the tent was now leaking badly in several places. All of a sudden, down the tent's main seam it was as if someone had started to pour buckets of water through the hole, and at least a dozen people really got drenched. I was lucky to be sitting elsewhere at the time, but Harry finally took me around to the back entrance in case the storm took a turn for the worse and we had to get out of there in a hurry.

Meanwhile, the musician's pit *was* filling up with water. It was actually a big pit in front of the stage deep enough so that the musicians weren't a distraction to the audience viewing the stage over their heads. Being the lowest spot in the tent, it was naturally the first place the water gathered.

I found a clipping in one of Harry's scrapbooks about how the Melody Top tent was both fire-proof and storm-proof. Storm-proof, perhaps; leak-proof, no. And I tell you true, being in a big tent in the midst of a severe lightning storm with hard winds makes one feel very insecure. We waited almost an hour before they finally decided to cancel the performance. All ticket holders got a ticket for the next performance, and Harry and the musicians were happy because they got paid for a third of a performance and got home earlier than usual that night.

After this "wet experience" and two or three boilermakers, Harry drew a delightful picture of the conductor and several musicians in the orchestra pit performing as it filled up with water. The trumpeter has a plunger in one hand, the bassoon player is blowing bubbles, and the trombone player is broadcasting a *HELP!* message while a crocodile floats by in the forefront. The conductor's caption reads, "Do you ever get the feeling that we're in the wrong business?" (This piece of artwork can be seen on TheDrummerDrives.com website along with other "Brabec masterpieces." Harry never lost his ability to draw like a child, and I loved it.)

Backstage with Pete Fountain

One of the exciting things about being married to Harry was that he made me a part of his musical life. The wives of most professional musicians either took their husband's work for granted or simply sat in the audience for a concert or show (if they went at all), but Harry always let me tag along with him whenever I wanted—which was most of the time—and I was often backstage with him before and after a performance.

In that last season of Melody Top, on the one night a week when the theater was available for other shows, I had the pleasure of meeting New Orleans jazz clarinetist Pete Fountain. Harry had gone out there the one night that Fountain's group was playing the tent because he wanted to meet Fountain's vibe player, Godfrey Hirsch, whose playing he had always admired. The musicians welcomed us with open arms, not only because Harry was never bashful about introducing himself, but because it is just the nature of professional musicians to want to meet other pros. Harry had a great time talking to Godfrey, and they spent some time on stage before the show checking out his vibes. Pete Fountain was very charming to me, insisting that we have our picture taken with him and Godfrey. After the show began, we stayed to hear a few tunes and then left. As I commented to Harry on the way home, who needed tickets when they were married to him?

This was just one of two special treats I had this day. Harry had decided it was time for me to see my first Cubs ball game, so he bought box seats to make sure we did it in style. Unfortunately, it was 90 degrees that day, and before the game was over we were sunburned and wishing we had bought cheap seats in the shaded grandstand. (I laugh now when I remember that the $7 we paid for those seats seemed like such an extravagance at the time.)

We got quite a show that day. "Cubs Win; Roznovsky Beaned," was the newspaper's headline the next day. Jerome Holtzman wrote in his column, "They hit two home runs, stole three more bases and got a distance-going six-hitter from Larry Jackson in a 7–2 victory over the Houston Astros." Harry and I saw only one more Cubs game after that. We just never seemed to have time for this sort of thing. I was always so grateful that he wasn't a sports nut, but he did love the Chicago Bears and never missed a game on television.

End of an Era

Melody Top closed at the end of the 1965 season, and the closing was particularly memorable for the fact that the last checks to the musicians bounced. We learned that Harry's check didn't clear the second time through when our account was suddenly overdrawn. The Union told him that his money was downtown, and all he had to do was bring in the check (which at this time was in the mail to us from the bank). So we went downtown the next day for the loot, and everyone's name was on the list for reimbursement except you-know-who. From there we went directly over to Melody Top's office on Michigan Avenue, only to be told they didn't have the money either. It took several days, and Harry had a hard time keeping his temper as we were bounced around from one place to another, but we finally ended up with the money and got squared away with all the checks that had bounced because of this fiasco.

♪ Historical Sidenote ♪

In January of the following year, it was reported in a Chicago *Sun-Times* article that Melody Top and other properties related to the operation of the summer theater were auctioned off for $3,025 to satisfy federal tax liens that IRS officials said totaled $46,081.28. The three guys who originally owned Melody Top—Rach, Vaughn, and Mann—split up in late 1965, and Mann took over the Mill Run Playhouse, but it folded shortly after opening with an operating loss of $185,000. Money was reportedly refunded to people who had bought advance tickets, but we wondered if all the musicians got paid.

CHAPTER 3

Divinely Connected by the Marimba

No one could have imagined then that my choice of a musical instrument would eventually link me directly to the man I was destined to marry.
—Barbara

Have you ever considered how some of the decisions you made in your youth dramatically affected your adult life? I've often reflected on the fact that I never would have met Harry if I hadn't fallen in love with the marimba when I was in grade school.

It all started when a band instrument company came to my school and displayed all their instruments in the gymnasium. A salesman demonstrated each one of them and encouraged kids to pick an instrument they'd like to learn how to play. While my girlfriends oohed and aahed over the clarinet, sax, and trumpet, I was simply transfixed by the little two-and-a-half-octave, three-foot long marimba. I had never seen one before, and I rushed home saying, "Oh, mother, I just HAVE to have it." No one could have imagined then that my choice of a musical instrument would eventually link me directly to the man I was destined to marry.

I often think back to those days and remember the financial sacrifice my parents made to give me this instrument, which I think cost about $125. That was a *lot* of money when you consider that my father was a low-income self-employed mechanic and mother was then being paid five dollars a day as a pie maker at the Greyhound Bus Station.

The school's music teacher, a pianist, knew nothing about how to teach marimba, so I quickly adapted what I knew about playing the piano to the marimba and began to develop my own style. In 1949, three months after I got the marimba, I played a solo in the school's Christmas operetta. My home town of Buckley, Illinois is a small farming community, and no one had ever heard of a marimba in that town before I introduced them to it. In fact, I may have been the only marimba player in the whole county, and most people called my instrument a xylophone because that's what it looked like to them. But it sounded completely different and, unlike the xylophone, it lent itself to solo playing—no piano accompaniment needed.

I was soon driving my mother nuts as I pounded the keyboard for hours every night after school, practicing scales and arpeggios and the same measures of a song over and over again. But, God bless her, she never complained; only encouraged me to enter various amateur contests as I gained more skill. I never won anything but applause, but I began to gain stage experience and confidence and was soon a featured soloist and a provider of background music for various functions around Buckley and in nearby towns. I loved making a little extra money and being the center of attention, but I didn't have a clue about where all this performing was leading me. All I knew at that time was that I had been bitten by the entertainment bug and I wanted to do something special with my music talent in Chicago as soon as I graduated from high school.

Better Marimbas and Music Lessons in Chicago

I had always worked in the summer, doing everything from selling Cloverine Brand Salve to dozens of people in town who didn't need the product, to babysitting, house cleaning, detasseling corn, being a car hop for a local drive-in, and a soda jerk at the Greyhound Bus Station. In the summer before my senior year, I decided I wanted to trade in my "baby marimba" for a larger one. My folks couldn't pay for it, so I got a job at the corn canning factory in the nearby town of Milford.

The work was awful, but I was willing to do anything to get a better marimba. For eight and often twelve hours a day (as long as it took for the last truck of corn to get processed), I wielded a hatchet-type blade as I chopped worms off wet ears of corn. Every whack splattered juicy corn kernels all over my rubber apron, hands, and face, to the point where I and other workers had to break every fifteen minutes just to scrape ourselves down and clean our glasses. To make matters even worse, all day long a conveyer line of tin cans waiting to be filled marched overhead like little tin solders, drumming an incessant clatter that nearly drove me mad until I learned how to mentally tune it out by singing to myself. Fortunately, no one could hear me over that din.

Later, because I had fibbed about my age to get this job (saying I was 18 when I was only 17), I qualified to work the clean but dangerous corn-shucking machine that could easily have taken one of my hands or an arm with just one careless movement. This work would prove to be the hardest physical work I would ever have to do, but it certainly was character-building and even fun at times. I rode to work daily with my biology teacher who was also working there that summer. We were pals because he and his wife, the school's music teacher, had accompanied me for one of the amateur contests I had entered. She played piano, he played maracas, and we had a ball.

With the money I earned that summer, plus a small loan from one of my prosperous uncles, I was able to buy a pretty good marimba. In my senior year of high school, I was thrilled when James Dutton, a noted marimba teacher at the American Conservatory of Music, agreed to take me on as a private student. Because I was a straight-A student, I was given permission to leave school at lunch time on Fridays and be excused from that afternoon's study hall so I could catch the Green Diamond train to Chicago and trek over to the Conservatory for an hour's lesson.

I thought I was pretty hot stuff, running around in Chicago at age 17 and traveling to and fro in the elegant Green Diamond streamliner. It was one of Illinois Central's finest trains, departing at 8:55 every morning from St. Louis and arriving at IC's Central Station in Chicago at 1:50 p.m. I caught the train in Gilman and, as I recall, the round-trip ticket cost $2.50 and the trip took about an hour and fifteen minutes. I would quickly walk the mile or so to the Conservatory in the Fine Arts Building on Michigan Avenue, take my lesson, and then walk back in time to catch the 5 o'clock train home. If my lesson was late, or ran long, there were times when I had to run to catch it. On the way home, I always had a cup of tea (all I could afford) in the fancy dining car with its white cloth-covered tables, which made me feel very sophisticated.

After graduation, a couple of girlfriends and I signed up for a three-month airline/railroad communications course at Gale Institute in Minneapolis. I left after only one month since by then I was the fastest teletype tape reader and typist in the class with a good job offer from the Pennsylvania Railroad in Chicago. But after a few months of working the night shift and continuing my weekly marimba lessons, I got a higher-paying clerical job with Kaiser Aluminum and moved into the famous Three Arts Club on the near north side of Chicago. This was a safe, supportive, and economical residence for young women studying the three arts of music, drama, and painting, and the years I spent there were some of the most satisfying of my life. Here I found many friends who shared my musical interests and goals, including another marimbist and student of James Dutton who introduced me to other percussionists.

Shortly after settling into the Club, I traded in the marimba I had bought in high school for a professional instrument, a four-and-a-half octave Musser marimba I'd purchased from Lyon-Healy. (Spoke with Mr. Lyon himself, who assured me that if I was dissatisfied with any of the keys, I could bring them back. I did exchange four of them later.) I continued my music lessons with James Dutton, got involved with his percussion ensemble, and eventually met Gordon Peters and other percussionists that Harry knew. (One of them, Ed Poremba, would eventually become one of Harry's competitors for the best jobs in the city.) The thread linking me to him was drawing tighter all the time.

I was soon appearing in percussion ensembles and solo marimba recitals arranged by Dutton, and gradually gaining more experience and confidence as a performer. A year after coming to Chicago, I was chosen as one of a group of musicians who would tour schools in several states for eight months. I was paired with another marimbist, and we spent countless hours working on our act as the tour sponsors invested a considerable amount of time and money to promote our program to schools. Being so excited about this opportunity to perform, I was quite upset—and the tour sponsors were livid—when this girl suddenly decided to get married and backed out of the tour. This turned out to be a good thing for me, however, since I was then put on the path that would lead me to Harry.

I ceased taking lessons in 1959 when Dutton told me I was finally ready to pursue my dream of playing dinner music in hotels and clubs. I quit my secretarial job, designed a brochure, had some professional pictures taken, and began to try to find places to perform. Word-of-mouth advertising led to one new job after another for women's clubs, private parties, and weddings that needed background music. By then, I had memorized more than four hours of music, all of it my own arrangements (only three of which I ever wrote down, so now they're gone forever).

Included in my repertoire were fourteen medleys of the popular musicals of the day—the same shows I would be hearing Harry play a few years later at the Shubert and Melody Top theatres. (I've always been fascinated by how the threads of my life and Harry's seemed to be tied together so many years before we met.)

♪ Music Sidenote ♪

James Dutton, who was a great influence on me and countless other mallet players and percussionists, died in 1999. In reading his bio on the Web, I was struck by the fact that, prior to beginning his career as a concert marimbist, he had studied marimba and vibes with Clair Omar Musser (marimba virtuoso; 1901–1998) and drums and timpani with Edward Metzenger (1902–1987)—as did Harry and countless other professional percussionists of his era.

"Get an Act, Honey"

By now I was really bugged about the idea of trying to get dinner music engagements in top-flight supper clubs and hotels, but I soon got a rude awakening about the difficulty of breaking into this area of the music business. This seemed like a realistic goal to me because it was common in those days to hear pianists playing background music in dining rooms and cocktail lounges. I figured I ought to be able to do the same thing with my marimba. I auditioned for three agents, one from MCA, the biggest booking agency in the U.S. This guy told me bluntly that if I were to remain a single, he wouldn't be able to place me in enough jobs to warrant the money they would spend to promote me.

Another agent confirmed that unless I had "an act," he couldn't begin to sell anything like a marimba, which half the country had never heard of. "Dinner music on a marimba just isn't in demand, honey," he said. "You go create the demand for it and then come back and see me."

I was excited when, through a referral from a prominent Chicagoan, I got an introduction to Oscar Marienthal, who owned three night clubs on Rush Street (Mister Kelly's, Happy Medium, and the London House). He was very kind, liked my playing, and said that if I could form a trio, I should come back and see him. This wouldn't have been all that difficult because I now knew several musicians in town. But the problem for me was that this would mean I'd have to play in cocktail lounges, most of them so full of smoke that I figured I'd just die—not to mention drunks, perhaps—and the hours would be excruciating. I just didn't want that. I decided that if I couldn't find high-class places to play, I'd just stick to doing women's programs and weddings.

I began to make a lot of phone calls, sent out numerous letters, and finally got the interest of the owner of the Surf & Surrey restaurant and piano bar on Chicago's South Shore. That's when I learned that some jobs required membership in the Chicago Federation of Musicians, Local 10-208. "Get a union card, and then get back to me," the supper club owner told me.

Supper Club Debut and Musician's Union Surprise

I paid the $125 and joined the Musician's Union, which did nothing for me except collect my money and wish me luck. Oh, yeah, joining the Union also meant I couldn't play any more club dates or private parties for less than union scale unless I wanted to sneak and not report any jobs like that, which is what some of my musician friends at The Three Arts Club were doing. (The penalty for breaking this union law was a $500 fine and suspension from the Union for at least a year.) Fortunately my club dates paid enough that I didn't have to worry about this rule. What I hadn't counted on, however, was that I would be breaking Union rules merely by taking the Surf & Surrey job.

The minimum wage then was $22 for the first three hours. Since I was hired to play background music six hours a night on Sunday and Monday, on the off-nights I was supposed to charge a flat rate of $4/hour, or $24, plus another $2 for playing alone. When the owner first called me to confirm the job, we didn't discuss pay at all because I assumed he would be paying Union scale. When we finally got down to talking business, however, he told me he would give me $20 a night— take it or leave it—because he could get plenty of other musicians for that amount. He said that unless I could bring in a bigger crowd than he normally got on those two nights, I would never be worth any more than that to him. So I did some fast thinking and decided to do it because it was either that or never getting a chance to prove that my music would go over well in a supper club setting. To make matters worse, to cover both of our butts I had to sign a contract stating that he was paying me $26 a night even though I was getting only $20, which meant I had to pay income tax on money I never received. I can only wonder now how many other musicians were forced to do the same thing in those days.

This job was everything I hoped it would be, and more. I gained valuable experience, met a high class of people that appreciated my music, and soon earned the nickname of "the girl with the Pepsodent smile." I shared the spotlight with Ben "Rinkytink" White, who played piano the other days of the week. In looking again at the ad I stuck in my scrapbook, I was reminded that they spelled my name wrong; "Schaumburg" became "Schoenberg." Years later in one of my business books, I'd write about the benefits of publicity, saying I didn't care what they said about me so long as they spelled my name right. (You wouldn't believe how many people want to stick a "k" on the end of Brabec. Used to drive Harry nuts.)

I didn't have a car to get to jobs so I had to rely on cabs. My marimba was nearly seven feet long, and it came apart in sections that I packed in five canvas cases I had designed and sewn on my $50 portable Montgomery Ward sewing machine, which came with a lifetime guarantee. (They weren't kidding. When the machine needed a little servicing after fifty years of use, the sewing machine repairman told me that this little machine would be running beautifully long after I was dead. They just don't make sewing machines like this any more. But I digress.)

When I called a cab, I never said that I might "need a little help" getting my marimba cases into the cab. I'd simply haul them downstairs and leave them by the door. Then I'd get all dolled up in my red chiffon dress, rhinestone high heels, foxy white Borgana fur coat with faux leopard collar and cuffs, and look very helpless when the cab arrived. I mean, how was I supposed to lug those things down a flight of concrete steps in my three-inch heels? I suspect today's cabbies would put up quite a fuss about this kind of thing, but in those days all it took was a little charm and a nice tip. And there was always some sweet guy at the club at the end of the evening that would help me pack up my marimba and get it out to a waiting cab. A couple of them even offered to drive me home.

Entertaining Women's Clubs

Prior to meeting Harry, I had auditioned for the Illinois Federation of Women's Clubs, which introduced me to hundreds of program directors who were looking for programs for their club meetings. The ten-minute audition for my "Around the World via Music" program got me 34 jobs paying from $25 to $75 each, which were scheduled between March of '61 and the following May. So there Harry and I were in late August—newly married, without a car, and with Harry trying to figure out what jobs he could take and how he'd get there using public transportation or a cab, while also worrying about me doing programs at the same time and getting my marimba to jobs, which he now wanted to do for me.

He accompanied me on my first job in September and, although I didn't realize it until later, he was very nervous about being in the audience that day. I was also nervous about playing in front of him since he was far more skilled than I, so I didn't let him hear much of my practicing that first two weeks we were married. Part of my program involved speaking and the playing of other percussion instruments: a little set of orchestra bells on a stand over the middle of the keyboard; a Chinese cymbal attached to one end of the marimba for my oriental tunes; a pair of castanets I held in my right hand along with one mallet when I played "Espana Cani"; and a pair of maracas on a pedal I played with one foot while I was doing my South American number.

Yes, I finally had "an act" that was proving profitable. As I told my mother at the time, "I can't tap dance, sing, or look sexy behind the marimba, but at least I can add some novelty to my performance." Of course it was Harry's friend, Maurie Lishon at Franks Drum Shop, who had set me up with these instruments a year earlier.

After my program—which had more than one clam (mistake) in it due to my nervousness about Harry being in the audience—he said I scared him, the way I used four mallets to play, because I did everything wrong, yet it came out right. I ceased performing after my last job the following May, figuring that one professional musician in the family was enough. But I was always grateful to have had a little taste of the music business before I met Harry because it helped me to understand what he was going through as he struggled to make a living as a freelance musician.

Truth be told, I knew I was a good entertainer but only a passable musician whose heart was really in business. By this time I'd had ten years of solid business experience as a secretary and office manager in Chicago's Loop. Since my income was going to be needed for awhile, I knew I needed to focus on what I did best. My interest in playing marimba even for my own enjoyment diminished once I found my true life's work as a professional writer. Today I just play a little piano once in a while.

CHAPTER 4

On Being Czech

"Do you come from a Czech home?" one Bohemian asks another. "No, it was white with blue shutters."—an original Harry joke

arry Joseph Brabec was born in Oak Park, Illinois on August 15, 1927. Raised in Cicero, a community heavily populated with Czechs, he took great pride in his Czech heritage, but he was also quick to make light of it, as the above joke indicates. Bohemians invented the trampoline, he said, which is what led to the first bounced Czech. To him, a Bohemian funeral was "a cancelled Czech."

Bohemia, which no longer exists, is an historical region that became the core of the newly formed state of Czechoslovakia in 1918. For many years, people who came from this part of Czechoslovakia were known as "Bohemians," and that's what Harry always called himself because his ancestors came from this land. (Czechoslovakia peacefully split into two separate countries on January 1, 1993, then becoming Czech Republic and Slovakia.)

Brabec in Czech means "sparrow," so some of Harry's Czech school friends called him Birdie. "Though he had a Czech name, he had a very limited vocabulary in that language," remembers Gordon Peters, a Czech who took lessons from Harry in school. "One of the expressions he often used with me when I gave excuses about something was, 'That doesn't cut any ice with me.' So I translated this phonetically into Czech for him: *Thoh neh zezzeblet* ('that doesn't cut ice'). He used to break up at that."

I never heard Harry use that expression, but it makes perfect sense that he would have used it in the forties because people were then using ice boxes for refrigeration and getting blocks of cut ice delivered to their home. A sign in the window with four big numbers would be turned to indicate the number of pounds of ice the iceman was supposed to deliver that day. Harry picked up one of those signs in the sixties and it hung forever on his tools pegboard like a piece of art.

He may have had only a few words of Czech, but he sure made me and others laugh when he swore because he used most of them in a long string that had no literal meaning but served his purpose. *Pozor* was one of the first Czech words he taught me, and it was always delivered when he figured I was about to open my yap at the wrong time in response to something he had just said (or hadn't said) to someone. It might have been a fib, perhaps, or a curious comment about business voiced for the purpose of getting information of one kind or another. Sometimes he would play dumb—even stupid (often the best way to get know-it-all folks to tell you something you want to know)—and just as I was about to say something that would have loused up his grand plan to get information (or not give it to the person he was speaking to at the time), he'd give me what I later came to think of as his "evil-eye look" and say *POZOR!* in his most authoritative voice.

The person Harry was speaking to at the time never understood the message I'd just been given, and probably didn't notice the special look that accompanied it. Of course it wasn't exactly evil, but to this wife who always tried to let her husband be boss, it was certainly a commanding "Bohemian glare" I respected.

The formal definition of *pozor* is "attention, look out, beware of, on the watch for," but in my case, it simply meant "Zip your lip—*don't say another word!*" Sometimes, too, it meant that Harry thought we were dealing with a liar or unscrupulous person we shouldn't trust. I've always tended to trust and believe everyone, but he had a knack for spotting a phony a mile away.

♪ Personal Sidenote ♪

Harry worked with a lot of Jewish musicians, and he came to love many of their words and phrases, as well as their food. A favorite Jewish word he used throughout his life (probably because he felt it described him) was *chutzpah*, which is "the height of nerve, brass, cheek, or unmitigated gall." A little chutzpah makes life interesting, but sometimes Harry had a little too much of it for his own good.

Actually, Harry had some Jewish blood in his veins from his grandfather, whose name was Birnbaum (with an "i" not an "e"). As he explained to a friend, "My grandfather's family roots go back to the Austro-Hungarian empire, which Bohemia (now Czech Republic) was part of. Bohemia was one of the only countries that had a high regard for the Jewish people, and what with intermarriages being what they were in those days, and with the misspelling of names at Ellis Island or any of the other ports for immigrants, there may be some Jewish blood in my uncle, too."

Czech History and the "Bohemian Sausage Cheer"

In 1991, Harry received a letter from a John Brabec who was researching his own Czech ancestry and thought he and Harry might be related. In this excerpt from Harry's reply, he shared some interesting Czech history and remembered the "Bohemian Sausage Cheer" of his high school basketball team:

My knowledge of Czechoslovakian geography is not very good, so I don't know how close Senomaty or the other towns you mentioned may be to my ancestors' home of Pisek. I have visited Czechoslovakia three times and went to Pisek once. Unfortunately, it was impossible to get into the town's records, even though I had a government official with me. That was in 1976 and 1977. My maternal grandparents (whose names were Melichar and Smutny) came from the Pilsen area, but were married in this country.

While in Prague, I saw a sign advertising a play written by a Brabec, whose first name I've forgotten. I was told that while Brabec is not a very common name in Czechoslovakia, it is also not an obscure one. I did see the Brabec name in Vienna quite a bit, and the principal cellist of the Vienna Opera is a Brabec. I talked with him by phone but we couldn't get together due to conflicting schedules.

The Czechs settled mostly in the western part of Chicago, and as families grew up and married, they kept moving farther and farther westward. For example, I live in a town about forty miles from downtown Chicago where many Czechs are found, and I went to school with quite a few of them. The Czechs at one time were so well organized that they had their own cemetery (Bohemian National) and two daily news-papers, one of which still exists (*Denni Hlasatel*).

As far as Czechs settling in this country, it seems that the craftsmen and machinists went to Chicago or New York, and the farm people settled mostly in Iowa and Nebraska. There are quite a few Czech festivals in western Iowa and Nebraska throughout the year, and later this month Barb and I are going to a two-day Czech Festival in Cedar Rapids, Iowa.

In your letter, you mentioned the names of Slaby and Svoboda. In the Chicago area, these are (or were) very common Czech names. I went to school with quite a few of these people and many businesses also were owned by them. It has been said that, at one time, the Chicago area was the largest populated area of Czechs in the U.S. In the town where I grew up (Cicero), and the town next to it (Berwyn)—both of which adjoin Chicago—speaking both English and Czech was a must. However, many of our parents refused our learning of Czech, saying, "We are Americans and should only speak this native tongue." How I regretted that through the years! When I was in Czechoslovakia, I was really at a disadvantage. I was told by one man, "You should speak Czech; after all, I speak English," and he was right.

We had several "sokols" that had a Bohemian school on Saturday morning. Of course these classes and sokols for the most part have disappeared. We had so many Bohemians in the two towns that many of us picked up a few Czech words and phrases which when said either got us into trouble or made others laugh at us. Morton High had a state championship basketball team that had five of the twelve players related to each other. Of the other seven, six were Bohemians. Occasionally a game would be stopped by the referees because the players would be shouting words to each other in Czech and the officials didn't like that. We even had a cheer which we yelled at our opponents. (Please excuse the spelling, and I hope the words make some sense):

Hu sah sah, Hu sah sah,
Hit him in the head with a Klobasa!

♪ Historical Sidenote ♪

I'm glad Harry was spared the knowledge of the destruction caused by the June 2008 Cedar Rapids flood. It devastated the Czech Village, home to both the city's annual "Houby Days Festival" ("houby" in Czech means mushroom) and the

National Czech & Slovak Museum & Library, of which Harry
was a member. This is the leading United States institution
involved in the collecting, exhibiting, preserving, and inter-
preting Czech and Slovak history and culture. The flood
happened so fast that there was just enough time to move
only a couple of truckloads of things beforehand. Afterward,
there was hope that most of what had to be left could
eventually be salvaged, but the rebuilding and restoration of
the museum and library is going to take years and will cost
some $20 million.

Louis M. Blaha and J. Sterling Morton High School

I knew little about Harry's Czech background when we were married, and
nothing about his school years at J. Sterling Morton High School in
Cicero, Illinois until something happened on one of my program dates in
May, 1962.

Harry had accompanied me to the Edgewater Beach Hotel where I
was performing that day because he knew I was doing a program for a
Bohemian Woman's Club. But he was astonished to find that the program was in honor of Louis M. Blaha, whom I had never heard of so
hadn't mentioned to him. In the middle of lunch before I had a chance to
perform, a woman had a heart attack and died within three feet of me.
That ended the meeting and I never played the job, but when they offered
to pay me anyway, Harry asked me if we could simply donate the money
to the Blaha fund. We needed that money then, but Harry just couldn't
take it, and once he told me what Blaha had meant to him, I understood
completely.

I have since learned much more about Louis Blaha and Harry's
school days. As I was writing this book, his cousin, Arlene Lechich (née
Strejc), sent me copies of the music pages of her 1943 and 1944 Year-
books so I could see pictures of Harry performing as a marimba soloist
and playing in the school's dance orchestra and concert band. Of the
concert band, the 1943 Yearbook stated that the school's bands had made
the name of J. Sterling Morton High School known throughout the
country, and that the secret of its success was none other than Louis M.
Blaha. "It is due to him that the band library contains hundreds of
musical forms of the most famous American and European composers. It
is because of this that today there are former Morton musicians in
various symphony orchestras throughout the United States."

As the head of Morton's music department, Blaha led the marching band, concert band, and orchestra, and Harry played in all of them. Morton's concert band was rated the best in the country at that time, and it was of great service to the community when it played for flag dedications, football games, and various other social events. Concerts always featured the most talented musicians as soloists, and many of them went on to become professionals and carry Morton's name throughout the country. The band maintained a membership of about one hundred and twenty members, and these musicians represented the cream of the crop of the entire school district.

The 1943 Yearbook stated that the dance orchestra that year, which had sixteen experienced players (with Harry on drums, of course), was the first to be conducted by Blaha, and that it had made an excellent appearance at most of the afternoon dances throughout the school year. "Through many practice sessions together, the students arrived at a point near perfection, and in the opinion of the student body, this year's dance orchestra is strictly 'solid.' It is the best we have had for many a year, and gives out with music that is really danceable. Whether it's jive or sweet music you crave, you can find it here."

The next year, the Yearbook stated that the dance orchestra had gone down in history as the finest Morton ever had. When one considers all of the above, it's easy to understand why Harry and so many others at Morton were consummate professionals long before they left high school. No wonder they all moved so easily into the world of professional music. In fact, more than half of the Music Department graduates became professional musicians, conductors, composers, arrangers, soloists, or teachers.

Certainly Blaha inspired his students as he introduced them to the music of the world's great masters and guided them in future pursuits. Gordon Peters confirms that Blaha provided "a disciplined, professional environment for learning. He was a musical father figure to all his students; a great musician (played French horn), totally dedicated, and probably the most important 'musical pivot' for me and Harry and countless others."

"Blaha's Blasting Bohemians"

In 2003, when Harry began to feel particularly nostalgic about his old friends at Morton, he tracked down Ruth Edwards (née Ruth Ann Shuma), a pianist and good friend who often accompanied him when he was playing marimba solos. After 55 years of no contact, they began a wonderful letter exchange with frequent telephone conversations that gave both of them great pleasure. In one of his letters to her, he spoke about Blaha:

> I'm so glad that you, amongst many of our schoolmates, continued with your love of music to become successful in a chosen career. I give a great deal of credit for that to Louie Blaha. One story about him that sticks in my mind so vividly was the time when he called me into his office and asked me what I was going to do when I got out of high school. You might remember that the war was at its height then, so I said I'd probably go into the service, and when I got out I planned to be a professional musician. So he said we needed to sit down and make a double list, putting my musical good points on the left side and, on the right, my weak musical points and what I should work on.
>
> After about half an hour of this, I left his office feeling I might have a chance of making the pros. A few days later in rehearsal I came slamming in with a real fortissimo entrance that wasn't in the score. Blaha stopped, looked up at me and said, "Schlahone," *(this is a slang Czech word I can't spell, which means "hose"—I was tall and skinny in those days),* "you want to be a professional musician? You should be a *shoemaker!"* He went back to conducting and, after a few more bars he stopped, looked up at me and added, "And if you *were* a shoemaker, you'd be a lousy one!" His point was well taken.

Harry closed this particular letter with a comment about all the wonderful days he and Ruth had with "Blaha's Blasting Bohemians." I often heard him tell the above story to others, and he always spoke of Blaha with great respect and fondness. Ruth and I became quite close during Harry's last hospitalization, and in a letter to me, coincidentally dated the day he died, she wrote: "Harry and I shared a time in our young lives when we were lucky enough to begin to bloom in a culture that nourished us and encouraged us to believe we should and could realize and make the most of the talent we were given as God's gift. After so many years with no contact, we were still linked by that, and it was as though we had picked up saying, 'Now, let's see, where were we?'"

♪ Personal Sidenote ♪

In one of my later phone chats with Ruth, she told me that Gordon Peters had reminded her of the time he and Harry had sneaked into her room at the hospital after regular visiting hours, but she was so out of it that she didn't even know they were there. What I found fascinating about this story was that at this same time there was this 13-year-old girl in Buckley, Illinois who was having a ball with her little marimba. Never could she have imagined that her life was directly connected to these three people in the Chicago area, and that, incredibly, she would first date Gordon, who would introduce her to Harry, and then she would be blessed decades later to have both Gordon and Ruth as friends to give her emotional comfort after he was gone.

Aren't the threads of life absolutely amazing? Anyone who doubts that God is at work in our lives needs only to remember this little story, which no one could possibly say was "just a coincidence."

Ruth told me that Harry's job as librarian was one of great responsibility, and one not given lightly by Blaha. Harry was in charge of all the music for both bands and the orchestra, and I realize now that this experience explained his meticulous attention to detail and why he was so careful in the way he filed all his personal and business papers, why he kept such beautiful notebooks and scrapbooks, and why his collections of books, LPs, and CDs had to be arranged "just so."

After school, Ruth had a long career as a professional accompanist and university teacher who presented workshops for piano teachers, teenagers, and adult students around the country. In chatting with her about her Blaha memories, she told me she learned a lot from him, but he also terrified her. "He always seemed very severe, and yet he was very supportive of people who really worked hard and were devoted to the orchestra or bands, and he valued that. I think he did a lot behind the scenes. He was never very overt about his approval of someone, yet he managed to give his support to those who deserved it, and he got what he wanted out of the kids."

Harry's cousin Arlene, who studied harp with Blaha, agrees. "He helped me by letting me take the school harp home with me one summer so I could do more practicing. I often played on the porch to my neighbors' enjoyment. He also let Harry take two timpani home with him one summer, but I don't think the neighbors would have appreciated his practicing them on the porch."

Jetta Vasak, another school chum, said Blaha was a close friend of her parents, and he had told her mother, a cellist, about Harry. "As I recall, his grammar school conductor had asked Mr. Blaha to let Harry come daily to Morton rehearsals before he got to high school because of his obvious talent. Mr. Blaha had happily agreed. My first vivid remembrance of Harry at Morton was when I was a freshman. He looked so young and lanky standing in the back, practicing on the pad during rehearsals. Everyone loved him. When he served as librarian for the band and orchestra, I would hang around with him in the music department because he was such good company. We spent a lot of time together, so we decided to tell everyone we were cousins so they wouldn't get the wrong idea. When I was a sophomore or junior, he had some cards made up in Morton's printing department that said, 'Jetta Vasak, Master Faker of French Horn & Piano.' (I didn't know he had figured me out.)

"In 1962 or 1963, I was ecstatic to learn that the Chicago Symphony was playing at Ravinia. After the concert I went backstage and saw Harry and Gordon Peters and a couple of others. I have never forgotten that wonderful day. We were a real family at Morton, and I relish every memory."

A note from Evelyn Kapicka, also Harry's chum in school, brought more insight on his early years as a musician. "I got to know Harry out at Lake Como because his parent's home was next to my grandfather's home," she said. "Harry and I spent many summers enjoying Lake Como, and it was then he decided he would call me his cousin and I agreed. I can remember hours of his practicing the drums. At the beginning, his mother just set up a chair with a pad so he could practice. I used to see him in the halls of Morton, and we would exchange hellos, but it was always as cousins. It was many years later that we took our children to a 4th of July program at Ravinia, and we got to see Harry before the performance and were delighted to know he was playing. My children were thrilled and never forgot seeing Harry play. In later years, my husband was transferred to Chicago and worked with a woman whose husband was in the Symphony, so we kept up with Harry indirectly until my husband retired. Then Harry's real cousin, Russell Brabec, began his great family research project and brought Harry back into my life. It's amazing the twists and turns life can take, but somehow, old friends and memories seem somehow to surface."

♪ Music Sidenote ♪

Ravinia Festival is the oldest outdoor music festival in North America and is lauded for presenting world-class music. The Festival attracts about 600,000 listeners to some 120 to 150 events that span all genres from classical music to jazz to music theatre over each three-month summer season. In 1936, Ravinia became the summer residence of the Chicago Symphony Orchestra, which remains the centerpiece of the music festival today.

Courting Girls in the Forties

Hmmm . . . did you notice that both Jetta and Evelyn said Harry had dubbed them cousins? I'm wondering now if he just had so many girls interested in him that he was trying to avoid girlfriend problems by calling some of them cousins. In time, as I tracked down one old school chum of Harry's after another, I eventually learned that Nancy Geiger (née Steiner), was one of his girlfriends in school. I couldn't resist calling her, and we had a delightful chat.

"Harry always told me he couldn't date girls in high school because he never had any money," I told her. "So tell me . . . what did you guys do on a date?"

She laughed. "Well, he'd ride over to my house on his bike . . . and then we'd take long walks." From Nancy, I learned that Harry had also dated Ruth Edwards, so now I had to ask *her* what her dates with Harry were like. And she *really* laughed.

"Harry always took me to the school dances," she said, "and then I'd sit at a table all night and listen to him play. And there were usually several other girls around the table whose boyfriends were also in the band."

No wonder Harry didn't hesitate about asking me for a date with only 22 cents in his pocket. I guess he figured that if I couldn't find a way for him to cash his Symphony paycheck we could always just go for a long walk down Michigan Avenue.

As I was putting the finishing touches on this book, Loren Binford (see Chapter 7) kindly took the time to do a little research at the library, where he turned up copies of several newspaper articles from the forties that mentioned Harry's name. One of them from March 29, 1946 gave me quite a chuckle.

Maryon Zylstra was then writing a column for the *Chicago Daily Tribune* called "the Inquiring Camera Girl" that paid $5 for the most interesting questions submitted to her by readers. The question under discussion in this day's column was "Do men do the courting or do they only think they do?" To get the answer, she visited the Blackhawk Restaurant where Chuck Foster and his Orchestra were performing with Harry on drums. She queried Foster, Harry, vocalist Betty Clarke, bass player John Kalish, saxophonist James Hefti, and Herman Belli, alto sax.

Betty Clark's response was especially interesting—she was thinking then the way many women think today, basically that a woman can always wrap a man around her little finger if she uses the right technique *and* also lets the man think he's chasing her.

Here's how Harry, just nineteen at the time, answered the columnist's question:

"At first, I believe, the fellow courts the girl. He picks her out and tries his best to get acquainted with her. Then after he knows her quite well they both do the planning. Some girls are very difficult to get to know, though, and demand a lot of courting."

Harry had certainly refined his "getting acquainted" skills by the time we met, and clearly I wasn't one of those girls who demanded a lot of courting. (See TheDrummerDrives.com website for the complete column.)

♪ Historical Sidenote ♪

In speaking with Harry's school chum, Bob Robertson, I was saddened to learn what happened to Morton's once-great music department. Bob, a clarinetist, was in Harry's living room the day he got his first drum. He and Harry played in both the Cicero grade school and high school bands. In 2005, curious about his alma mater, Bob visited Morton High School and was devastated to learn that the music department no longer existed. "A woman was teaching guitar lessons and that was the end of it. 'Where's all the music?' I asked. 'We were national champions in classical music!' She told me that when Western Electric, one of the town's biggest tax payers, moved out of town, the schools ran out of money for teachers, and one of the first things they cut out was the band and orchestra."

Since then, Bob has been on a mission to bring music back into the Morton grade and high schools. "In one of the school pictures I have from 1947 of the orchestra, there were 125 kids in it," he told me. "I decided that one way to get music back into the schools was to contact the parents, so we developed the Morton Music Makers program to get the kids involved. In 2009 we started music again in the Cicero grade school, and now 150 kids are engaged in beginning band training at Unity Jr. High School. The money we're now collecting from parents and school alumni is being used to pay music teachers who give private lessons."

One of the alumni members who lives next door to Barry Manilow in Palm Springs solicited his help in providing musical instruments for both the Cicero grade schools and Morton East High School, and he gave them a generous gift. For more information about this program, see MortonMusicMakers.com.

Trekking to Berwyn for Goodies

When Harry was growing up in Cicero, the community was heavily populated with Czechs and many meat markets and bakeries that, sadly, either no longer exist or have changed dramatically as the culture of the community has changed through the years. As Harry put it in one of his letters, "The neighborhood has changed so much that when you ask for Bohemian sausages, you have to ask with a Spanish accent."

One of the first things I learned as Harry's wife was how to fix his favorite Bohemian meals, which included quite a few mushrooms and dishes involving sauerkraut and dumplings. This wasn't difficult to do because all of Harry's aunts, cousins, and friends shared recipes for dishes they knew he would love. He weighed only 140 pounds when we married, but my good cooking soon put some meat on his bones—as well as on his belly and my hips.

Regular treks to Cicero and Berwyn to stock up on his favorite sausages, lunch meats, breads, and pastries were always an important part of our life, even when we lived in Florida and Missouri. Harry could go only so long without his favorite Bohemian bread and "delicacies," and then we'd have to take a few days off from our business to trek north. We'd always have lunch in one of his favorite Czech restaurants and then hit his favorite shops, beginning at Vesecky's Bakery in Berwyn.

Here, Harry would stand in front of the display cases pointing and saying, "I'll take six of those, twelve of those, and you'd better throw in a couple of those, too." There were countless breads and sweets to choose from, but we had our own standard shopping list of things we liked. Everything froze beautifully and we had a big freezer, so we'd always buy at least a dozen loaves of seeded rye bread, half a dozen of the plain square loaves, a dozen poppy seed rolls, a dozen salty horns, and half a dozen "mutts" (hot dogs stuffed in salty horns), plus a dozen sweet rolls and at least two dozen kolacky with cheese, prune, pineapple, and apricot toppings. The only thing we didn't buy there was Houska, because that was one of the first things I learned to make after we were married, and mine was perfect, Harry said.

Then we'd head over to Shotola's meat market (in Cicero; now gone) to stock up on fresh Bohemian sausages (such as Jaternice and cream sausage), smoked butt, veal loaf, head cheese and assorted cold cuts, pickled delicacies, and anything else Harry's little heart desired that couldn't be found wherever we were living at the time. In both these shops he was like an impish little boy, gleefully pointing here and there to order, but always checking with me to confirm the quantity we should buy since I was the one who had to package or prepare all of it. By the time we finished shopping, the trunk and sometimes part of the back seat was overflowing with pastry boxes and food sacks stuffed to the rim. The smell of all the fresh-baked goods and sausages wafting through the car literally had us and our dog Ginger drooling by the time we got home.

"Food, Glorious Food!"

There's a song in the musical show *Oliver* titled with the above words, which could well have been Harry's personal theme song since he ate not only for sustenance, but for pure enjoyment. "I have a weight problem," he said. "When it comes to eating, I can hardly wait."

You never met a man who loved his food more than Harry, and he considered himself very lucky to have married a woman who loved to cook as much as he loved to eat. I'm not exaggerating when I say that Harry *lived* to eat. He loved everything—except marshmallows. When he got up in the morning, he wanted to know what was for lunch so he could savor the thought all morning. At lunchtime, he wanted to know what I was planning for dinner so he could "work up his taste buds" for that meal. (I didn't *dare* change the menu because that would have messed up his taste buds.)

"How about some beef and tomato gravy with bread dumplings?" I might suggest. No matter what I offered, he was happy with it, and might smack his lips and say, "Sounds good . . . but could you throw in some chocolate pudding for dessert?"

> Harry: "I'm hungry, what've we got to eat?"
> Me: "Well . . . there's some chili . . ."
> Harry: "That's the *last* thing I want to eat. *First* I'd like . . ."

> Me: "Eat just enough to whet your appetite, dear."
> Harry: "I don't want to wet it, I want to *drown* it!"

> Me: "How would you like your eggs this morning, dear?"
> Harry: "Multiplied!"

> Me: "Would you like hominy for dinner tonight?"
> Harry: "How many of *what*?"

Hagar the Horrible was one of Harry's favorite cartoon strips. He especially liked the jokes about eating. One of his favorite strips was the one where Hagar's wife is questioning him about all the food he's putting away. "What about your diet?" she asks. Hagar replies, "It's too late for me—save yourself!"

Harry had a prayer he said on days when he ate too much that went like this:

> *Now I lay me down to sleep,*
> *I pray the Lord my soul to keep.*
> *If I should die before I wake,*
> *I know it'll be from a bellyache.*

I always loved cooking for Harry because he was such an appreciative eater. One year for Valentine's Day, I surprised him with one of my woodcarvings of a sitting Indian chief holding a big bowl on his lap and a large spoon and fork in his hands. My homemade card asked if "Chief Hole-in-the-Belly" would be the valentine of "Squaw Cook-um-all-the-time." If so, I promised to keep his big pot full.

CHAPTER 5

The Shubert Theatre Days

The memories of the Shubert gang will stick to me like a Bohemian love for mushrooms.—Harry

arry didn't reminisce in his letters about the shows he played at the Shubert Theatre, except to say once that "the memories of the Shubert gang will stick to me like a Bohemian love for mushrooms." Fortunately, I captured several amusing stories in my journals, and Harry's scrapbooks yielded other interesting details.

The Shubert Theatre originally opened in 1906 as the Majestic Theatre after its namesake encompassing building, The Majestic, which is now the Hampton Inn Majestic. The Majestic Theatre didn't survive the Great Depression of 1932, and it remained dark until 1945 when it was purchased by the Shubert Organization, remodeled, and reopened as the Sam Shubert Theatre. But it was sold twice after that, and since 2000 it has been owned and operated by Broadway in Chicago, with the marquee now reading Bank of America Theatre.

Harry was fortunate to have played this theatre in its Chicago heyday when great musicals were being produced one after another. After playing the 1962 Lyric Opera season, he had just one week off before going into the Shubert for seventeen weeks to play *Carnival* (the stage adaptation of the 1953 movie musical titled *Lili*). It starred Anna Maria Alberghetti, who had won Broadway's 1962 Tony Award as Best Actress for this role, and Jerry Orbach (1935–2004), who was making his Broadway debut as the puppeteer who would later become especially well known for his starring role as Detective Lennie Briscoe in the *Law & Order* television series. The real stars of this show, however, were the puppets, and Horrible Henry in particular. *Tribune* critic Claudia Cassidy described him as "a walrus of enormous presence, with tusks, a green nose, and an indelible personality of purest salt. He stole the show until in sheer self-preservation people buried him in a basket." Of the show itself, however, she said it was "for the sticks, mistakenly routed to Chicago." Kup said "Carnival reminded the drama critics of Kukla, Fran and Ollie—and they wished it were as good."

Harry needed timpani for this show, but because he and the other drummer who had played the Lyric together before this show opened had an argument of some kind, he no longer had access to this guy's timpani. It cost $10 a week to rent a set and, although we were hard pressed for cash, we scared up the necessary $300 for this purchase and hoped the show would run long enough to cover this cost. Fortunately it ran for 17 weeks.

One night after a show, after I had gone to bed, and after Harry had a few beers too many, he found my colored ink pens and drew a very funny picture of him playing his new timps. I found it on the table the next morning. He was always dead to the world when I went to work in the morning, and he soon got in the habit of leaving little "breakfast notes" or one of his drawings to surprise me.

Shortly after *Carnival* opened in January 1963, the Chicago area was hit with a week of sub-zero temperatures that dipped to 22 below, according to the weather reading at the Palmolive Building where I was then working as an office manager for a small investment company. Because our old car wouldn't even turn over in weather like that, both Harry and I had a very cold walk every day to catch public transportation to get to our jobs. My bus stop was only a couple of blocks away, but Harry had a six-block walk to the train that took him downtown to the Shubert. He wore long underwear to the job, a sweatshirt under his white shirt nightly, and two pairs of pants because his only black suit was quite thin. By the time he walked six blocks in sub-zero temperature, often wading through snowdrifts to get home, he was literally chilled to the bone, stiff as a board, and so constricted by his frozen clothing that I sometimes had to pull his underwear down because he couldn't bend over. Of course we found this funny.

After *Carnival* closed in late April, Harry played percussion on two shows that he enjoyed very much: a week-long show with Danny Kaye at the Opera House, and then *The Threepenny Opera,* which had a good run at the Civic Theatre in May. Harry really dug that music, but I didn't care much for it. But the Danny Kaye show . . . that was something else.

It was always a special treat to be in the audience when Harry was in the pit playing a show. The Kaye show included the tap-dancing Dunhills, the Marquis Family, and Senor Wences. Kaye didn't come on stage until after intermission, and the audience was hungry for him by that time. As *Sun-Times* critic Glenna Syse described it, "Kaye can wrap nearly 4,000 people around his left digit as if it were a campfire circle, a parlor game."

"Kaye . . . can turn into a triple-tongued, silk-stringed puppet before your eyes," wrote the *Tribune's* critic, Claudia Cassidy. "He can sound like anything or anybody, and look like it. He is one of the funniest men in the world, and one of the most endearing. But he can't work, and he shouldn't, with second-rate material." She described the Johnny Mann orchestra as being "ear-splitting," and it did get loud at times, but it was a wonderful night out for me, and Harry loved being able to work with Kaye.

By August of this year, while still working Melody Top, Harry was giving thought to what he would do in the fall when this season ended. The following letter to my mother gives additional insight into the life of a jobbing musician in those days:

> *Right now, Harry has so many irons in the fire he doesn't know what to do. Every job he could take seems to overlap with something else. He couldn't play the last two weeks of "Bye Bye Birdie" because "Stop the World" is coming into the Shubert during the second week of that show, and you either play all or nothin' at all. "Stop the World" could run for two weeks only, or could run for four weeks. If it runs four weeks, it will overlap with the start of the Ballet, which comes into town the 18th of September for three or four days, and Harry really loves to play the Ballet. He also got an invite to tour with the Wayne King Orchestra for four weeks, but that job would begin the same time the Opera starts its rehearsals on September 25, and that runs through December first. Meanwhile, back at the Shubert, the new show he has been hired for starts November 10th, which means an overlap there again. He's really in a panic right now, trying to figure out how to work part of all of them. The average person doesn't have a clue about what a freelance musician's life is like.*

Harry had given considerable thought to playing with Wayne King again, inasmuch as he had toured with the band for two years in 1949–

1951. It appealed to him that they were going to spend several days in Lake Tahoe and in San Francisco and Los Angeles as well. He had toyed with the idea of looking for work in California as well as Vegas (which I really did not like), and now he was thinking that this would be the best and least expensive way for him to look around and "get the lay of the land," as he called it. But the thought of being apart for a month was upsetting to both of us because we still felt as though we were on our honeymoon. He ended up playing *Stop the World* in September 1963, which ran for about eight weeks and was followed in November by *How to Succeed in Business without Really Trying*.

In between these shows, Harry and I once again slipped away to the Wagon Wheel for a few days. This lodge, which was finely decorated with antiques, was a short drive from Chicago and offered everything Harry needed in the way of peace, quiet, and good food. We were also celebrating the fact that we were at last making some financial headway, and when we got home, Harry treated himself to a new suit and, later, we bought a better used car—a 1960 Ford that cost $1095.

How to Succeed in Business without Really Trying

How to Succeed was a great musical that starred Dick Kallman as J. Pierrepont Finch, Willard Waterman as the company president, and Dyan Cannon as the romantic interest. She was dating Cary Grant at the time, who Harry encountered backstage with her more than once. (You may recall that they eloped in July 1965 and were divorced soon afterwards).

Also in the show was Maureen Arthur, a loveable gal that Harry often kidded with backstage. She played the part of the huge-breasted, dumb redheaded secretary named Hedy LaRue, and she had one classic line in this show that no one who saw the show would ever forget. In the scene where J. Pierrepont Finch asks her about her secretarial and typing skills, wanting to know how fast she can type, she proudly exclaims in her dumb-redhead voice (with extra emphasis on the last word): "I type like a *jackrabbit!*"

Harry loved the way she delivered that line, and years later it would become one he would often repeat when he became something of a typist himself. For many years, he was both a musician and the only office help I ever had for the publishing business I started in 1981. It eventually became a full-time job for both of us, and Harry found many new uses for his musical hands along the way. He was no secretary, but he typed pretty good. He learned the hunt-and-peck method when I yelled for help one day, and before long I was calling him my "three-finger-two-thumb wonder" because he typed with one left finger, two right fingers, and both thumbs. I had never seen anything like it, and he rarely made a typo. One day I commented that I was 45 years old before I realized that I could type my name with only the fingers of my left hand. "That's nothing," he said. "I can type it with one left finger."

For years afterward if anyone happened to comment on his typing for any reason, he'd proudly say in dumb-Bohemian mode, "I type like a *jackrabbit*," and we'd both laugh as we remembered all the fun of that particular show. This show was memorable for another reason as well.

"I Hope You Boys Don't Play Too Loud"

Before *How to Succeed* opened, the theatre had to undergo a little construction work. This show required so many percussion instruments that there wasn't enough room in the pit for all of them. For the first time ever, several front-row seats off the right side of the theater had to be removed to make way for the timps, bells, xylophone, chimes, cymbals, and various stands to hold all of them.

Harry came home with a great story after this particular show opened. He was seated behind the xylophone just in front of a woman in the first row. Being so close to him, she leaned over to him and said, "I hope you boys don't play too loud." Of course Harry smiled his most charming smile and said something comforting to her. But this particular show happened to open with a huge cymbal crash, and the imp that always resided on Harry's shoulder prompted him to keep the cymbals hidden from the audience's view until the lights dimmed. Of course, no one was prepared for that opening crash, which almost knocked those first-row patrons out of their seats.

Harry broke the monotony of that show and amused himself night after night by gleefully repeating this little scene for every performance and then watching to see how different people reacted to it.

I believe this show ran until late April of '64, which may be why he never played the 1964 season of Melody Top. The schedules probably conflicted. After we took a much needed vacation and moved to a better apartment, he played a variety of jobs, including a commercial Chevy show at McCormick place, some work with Grant Park, and a few other concerts here and there until the next show came into the Shubert.

♪ Personal Sidenote ♪

In March of 1964, Harry learned that the Honolulu Symphony had an opening for a percussionist. The last thing I wanted to do was move to Hawaii, so I was truly grateful when the reply Harry received indicated that the position had already been filled. In April, Harry contacted Eric Leinsdorf at the Boston Symphony Orchestra in regard to their current opening for a percussionist, but he learned a week later that his letter had arrived two days after the auditions were held. "Just my kind of luck," he said. He had now tried to get into four symphony orchestras—Los Angeles, Cleveland, Boston, and Honolulu—and this would not be the last time another orchestra door would close for him.

Harry's Meat Baster Stunt in *Oliver*

Oliver was scheduled to come into the Shubert in late December 1964. Harry was glad to get this work, but unhappy to learn that the show was going to play in Cleveland for three nights first. He had turned down several jobs the first few years we were married because they would have required him to be on the road for days or weeks, and neither one of us wanted to be apart for any length of time. Just a few weeks earlier, he had turned down a four-week tour with a percussion orchestra that would have paid $225/week and expenses. We joked then that we'd rather starve together than eat well separately, but this time he simply had to go. To make matters worse, those three days were just the start of a really hard week. In a letter, I told my mother about it:

> *Harry is taking a 2 o'clock plane out to Cleveland today, and he sure hates to go. He called me three times in the last hour to say he would miss me, in between telling me other things he thought of at the last minute. He has a terrible week coming up. He'll play the show in Cleveland on Thursday, Friday, and Saturday, and then catch a night flight to Chicago, arriving around 2 a.m. Sunday morning. After catching a few hours sleep, he has to trek downtown with all his drums to rehearse the show from noon to five, then transport and set them up at the Shubert. He'll get home about 8 o'clock Sunday night. On*

Monday, there's a rehearsal from noon to five and a show that night. On Tuesday he has a special concert at 10:00 a.m. at the school where he's now teaching a weekly percussion class. Then there's a matinee on Wednesday and a show that night. With any luck at all, he'll finally be able to rest on Thursday. By then, I figure he'll either be as grouchy as an old bear or so tired that I can do anything I want with him.

I loved seeing *Oliver,* but regretted that I once again missed seeing Harry pull another one of his stunts. The setup for this show called for a ramp over the edge of the pit, and guess where the drummer got stuck? It was bad enough that he had to endure all that thumping overhead as actors came onstage via the ramp, but the water scene proved to be too much. At the front of the stage right near where Harry was sitting there was this scene where one of the characters had to throw a cup of water in someone's face, and he was in the direct line of fire. Every night for the first few nights of the show, he was splashed with the residue of the water and it really began to aggravate him.

He complained to the show's director, and in his scrapbook I found the note that was left on his music stand in response. "She's really trying VERY hard not to splash you. She's cut down the amount of water, not throwing it so hard, etc. It's just that the scene is played too close to the foot of the stage. Sorry."

But the problem persisted, and one night Harry came home and asked me if I had a meat baster, and could he borrow it.

"What for?" I asked.

"I'm going to fill it with water, and the next time I get splashed, I'm going to shoot some back."

And the next night he did just that. When he told one of his pit buddies what he was planning to do, an unsigned note from one of them appeared on his music stand: "I disapprove of water pistols. Have you considered real bullets?"

Now, with the baster resting in a glass of water ready to be filled and "shot," Harry waited for the splash that was sure to come. As soon as he got hit, he stood up and shot the baster-full of water as far as it would go. This not only broke up the actress, but brought laughter from the guys in the pit and some members in the audience that were close enough to see what had just happened.

Can you think of another drummer anywhere who could have thought up such a stunt, and then had the nerve to pull it during a live performance? Funny thing—after that, the actors rearranged themselves on stage so as not to splash the drummer, and Harry was both dry and happy for the run of the show.

Funny Girl

Harry was happy to be back at the Shubert again in November 1965 when *Funny Girl* opened. He was also teaching classes for the second year at Maine Township North and South schools, and his daytime schedule here, combined with six shows a week at the Shubert was wearing him out. I saved his first week's rehearsal schedule in my scrapbook, and it's easy to see why I didn't see much of him during that period:

> Monday, leaves 8:00, home at 5:30; leaves at 7, home by midnight
> Tuesday, leaves 12:30, home at 3:00;   "   "   "
> Wednesday, leaves 11:00, home 5:30; "   "   "
> Thursday, leaves 9:00, home 4:45;   "   "   "
> Friday, leaves 12:15, home 3:00;   "   "   "
> Saturday, leaves noon, home 5:30;   "   "   "
> Sunday: OFF!

After rehearsals were over and he had his day hours free again, Harry had a chance to see a Bear's game with a friend who had an extra ticket. It was his first pro-football game, and he was *so* excited . . . until he got there and found that their $5 seats were behind a pole. (It might have been along about then that Harry began to moan the words from that old hillbilly tune, "If it weren't for bad luck, I'd have no luck at all.")

At least Harry was having good luck in getting new shows as they came into the Shubert. There were always two drummers in the pit. If the show didn't travel with a drummer, a local drummer would be hired. Harry was very happy to play percussion for the shows, especially when several instruments were called for because that meant doubles, which meant more money. Basically, a percussionist would have one "home instrument," such as xylophone, and each instrument after that was called a "double." So if Harry were playing xylophone, bells, and chimes, or perhaps timpani, each additional instrument meant another double. In those days at the Shubert, one double paid $40, so when he would tell me that a job had two or three doubles, I knew the paycheck would be substantially larger as a result.

Funny Girl opened in November and ran until January 8, 1966, and a clipping in Harry's scrapbook noted that it opened with ticket sales of more than $300,000. Marilyn Michaels played the role originated by Barbara Streisand, which was certainly a tough act to follow. As critic Glenna Syse noted, "Anyone who even takes on the job of following Miss Streisand has to be brave, or foolish, or both." But she did a terrific job with the role and got good reviews as the "poised and neat comedienne who triggers practically all the laughter of the evening" (critic William Leonard).

Good reviews were given to Lillian Roth, who played Fanny Brice's mother. Older readers might remember that Roth became known as a "tragic songstress" when her book, *I'll Cry Tomorrow,* was published in 1954. It told about her fight against alcoholism and mental illness and how she made an incredible personal comeback after sixteen years in what she called "a nightmare world." Millions wept in 1956 when her extraordinary story was sketched on the TV program, "This is Your Life." She was 55 at the time she played this role in Chicago.

In 2006, when I was going through Harry's huge book collection and trying to decide which ones to keep and which ones to sell on Amazon, I came across Roth's book, which was personally inscribed to *"Bob & Harry–Good 2morrows."* For the life of me, I couldn't remember how Harry had acquired that book or where he had met her. (Funny how we forget so many little details of our life as the years pass.) Only when I began to go through his scrapbooks for material for this book did I find the newspaper review of *Funny Girl* that mentioned Roth's name. Aha! The light bulb came on and I suddenly connected the dots. Of course I'm assuming now that Harry made it a point to talk to Roth backstage because he could relate to her struggle, given his own life circumstances. Considering the poor condition of this book's jacket, I figure he must have searched local used bookstores and finally turned up a copy and asked her to inscribe it to "Barb & Harry." But she obviously thought he said "Bob" instead of "Barb," and now I find myself wondering if she was then wondering who the heck "Bob" was, and why this sweet drummer wanted Bob's name in the book.

In December, a few weeks into the run of the show, "Kup's Column" included a memo to the Shubert Theatre orchestra saying it was coming in too loud and clear, and that many patrons were complaining that they couldn't hear the lyrics in *Funny Girl*. The next column reported that a number of Shubert musicians (and I'll bet Harry was one of them) called to report that if the music was too loud, the Shubert Theatre conductor, Jack Lee, was responsible, not the men in the pit.

Hello, Dolly!

Harry learned early in December that he would be playing *Hello, Dolly!* right after *Funny Girl* closed in January 1966, and that it was expected to have a long run. Shortly after the show had been announced, some 35,000 pieces of mail poured into the Shubert requesting tickets, and it opened with an advance of a million dollars. (My journal noted that the best seats were going for $9, which was considered a high ticket price in those days.) *Dolly* would turn out to be one of the longest-running shows at the Shubert, playing to full houses for a year.

One of the interesting things about this particular musical is that "Hello, Dolly" is its only memorable song. As one critic noted, Carol Channing "sang, growled, and meowed" her way through a few other tunes, but no one remembered them. There were many memorable dance numbers, however, all choreographed by Gower Champion, who also directed this production.

As always, Harry was concerned about his part, especially after the other drummer coming in with the show from Oklahoma City told him the percussion part was "pretty tough." For each show he was going to play, he would listen to a recording of the music to familiarize himself with it before the first rehearsal. But he needn't have worried because, as always, he played the show masterfully, and Carol Channing herself told Harry backstage one night that he and the guys were doing a wonderful job in the pit.

Life is certainly curious. Twenty-four years later I had a chance to speak to Carol Channing and I took it. It was in 1989 when I found myself in Hollywood as the featured guest on ABC-TV's "Home" show doing a week-long segment built around my popular *Homemade Money* book. The show's co-host, Robb Weller (a very nice guy, by the way) wangled a dinner reservation at Spago for me and two of the other gals who were sharing the spotlight with me on the show. This *very exclusive* restaurant in Beverly Hills caters to the stars and is one that few "civilians" can get into. But we had one of the best tables in the house and it was fun to see several stars we recognized.

When Carol Channing and three women friends came in and were seated next to us, I simply couldn't resist going over and telling her how much I had loved seeing her in Chicago when she played *Dolly*, and that my husband was the percussionist in that show. I kept it very brief, and she was very gracious and said she certainly remembered him, and thanked me for saying hello. My girlfriends were very impressed by this. Of course, I realize that she may not have remembered Harry at all, and was just being nice. Either way, it remains a memorable musical moment. This trip was also memorable to me because one day when I was in makeup for the TV show, I sat next to great television personality Steve Allen (1921-2000), and we had a very nice chat in between being creamed and powder-puffed profusely. I found him to be a very charming and unpretentious fellow.

Getting back to Carol Channing and the Shubert, critic Glenna Syse gave *Hello, Dolly!* a wonderful review, calling Channing a "dilly of a dolly" and raving about her acting. But she didn't even mention the *music,* let alone how great the pit orchestra was. (I think few critics understand how important a good pit orchestra is to any musical production.)

Music critic Lawrence Lee wrote a touching column about the show's closing, saying, "As the orchestra played the title tune for the last time, Miss Channing blew kisses but then broke into a sob and turned her back to the house. In an instant she whirled around and continued downstage as the red curtain swept shut. The last thing the audience saw was her high-wattage smile and a long white glove, waving good-by." (Guess they spelled "goodbye" differently in those days.)

Harry left the show in June 1966 to take the full-time job of assistant stage librarian for the Chicago Symphony (see Chapter 9). At that time, "Professor Brabec" also started percussion classes and private teaching at Northwestern University, and he was still teaching a class at North Park College, too. On the day I wrote this journal entry, I also noted that the day before he had worked at a Jewish temple five minutes from home and had a good time. Said it felt good to be playing something other than "Hello-you-know-who."

With the money rolling in that year, we had a wonderful Christmas and gave each other many gifts we couldn't afford in earlier years. My favorite gift, however, included a wonderfully nostalgic music present that cost Harry only five bucks. Early in our marriage, I told him that before I began to play the marimba I had tried my hand at the clarinet. I was envious of a girlfriend's more expensive beautiful wood clarinet, but all my folks could afford was the rental on a *metal* instrument. I told Harry that I always believed I was a lousy clarinet player because I didn't have one made of wood. So that Christmas he found an old wood clarinet in a hock shop, complete with a battered case, and he wrapped it up in a newspaper with a humorous gift tag that read: "Them That Waits, Gets."

A Very Personal Shubert Theatre Story

FLASH FORWARD: In September 1992, on the day my sisters and I buried our mother, Marcella, a number of remarkable "coincidences" turned her funeral from a day of mourning to a celebration of her life, and the Shubert Theatre played an important role that day.

Since a memorial service had been held in California, we decided to have only graveside services at the family's cemetery in Milford, Illinois. My sisters and I had debated at length over whether we wanted to hire a minister for the occasion. There was no minister in that area who knew mother, and rather than have a stranger speak words at her funeral, we thought it might be preferable for each of us to speak and say prayers. But at the last moment we relented, thinking mother might not feel at rest without this religious element in her funeral. So we told the funeral home to hire a Methodist minister—anyone who was available that day. Thus, his name was literally picked out of a hat.

You can imagine then how incredibly joyous we were to learn that this minister was no stranger at all. In fact, after a few minutes of conversation, my sister Mollie looked at him and said, "You look very familiar to me," and it was then that everything connected. Some 25 years earlier, she and this man, Bryce, had dated in college, and he was one of the *only* fellows Mollie had ever brought home for dinner. Our "strange" minister not only knew Mollie, but had some special memories of mother as well, and he spoke of her with great warmth at the ceremony. The miracle of this happening was that Mollie and Bryce had not communicated in all these years, yet he was there for us when we needed him.

Later, when we were back at our aunt's house to celebrate our mother's life with food and conversation, we were speaking with Bryce when he commented that his wife was doing a musical show that evening in the nearby country theater. Cousin Sonnie then exclaimed that this was a strange coincidence, because her son was playing one of the lead roles. It was one more example of what a small world it is. Suddenly, we all felt that we should attend the musical show that night, not realizing that two more strange things were about to happen as a direct result.

It was a "dinner theater" to the extent that our $8 ticket bought dessert, and we watched the show from one of perhaps fifty tables. We were amazed when the couple that joined our table turned out to be from our home town of Buckley. Not only that, the woman was someone my sister Mary had gone to school with. And only the day before, she told me, she had been talking to *her* sister, who worked in Cooperative Extension Service, about the book I'd written. Again, small world.

Harry had been unable to attend the funeral because of illness, so the next day I called him to relate all the special occurrences of the day. I had no sooner hung up the phone when he called back to comment on the musical play we'd seen. "Do you remember the time, about 25 or 30 years ago, when your mother came for a visit and I took her to the Shubert Theatre in Chicago where I was playing at the time? And do you remember the *show* your mother saw that night?"

Suddenly, knowing what was coming, I said no, it couldn't be . . . but it was. The show we'd gone to see on the same day we had buried our mother—*How to Succeed in Business without Really Trying*—was the *only* show mother had ever heard Harry play. He had bought her a front row seat right next to where he was playing, and before the show he had taken her into the orchestra pit, introduced her around backstage, and in general gave her a night she said she'd remember forever.

When mother was young, she wanted to be both a writer and a pianist for the silent movies, so I know she would have loved knowing that my sisters and I, without really trying, succeeded in giving her a sendoff we'd never forget, and that this story about her would end up in my book about Harry.

For those of you who are still trying to deny that God is always at work in our daily lives, think again. The odds of any one of the above "coincidences" happening on this particular day are simply astronomical, but all of them? *No way.*

Harry's 1966 Percussion Recital

I don't know what prompted this creativity on Harry's part, but each year that he played the Shubert he worked up a zany invitation to a New Year's Eve program I had to type for distribution to his buddies in the Shubert orchestra. Some whose names I recall were Bill Corti, Andy Lumbrazo, Ed "Poggy" Poggensee, and Doc Schwartz. They got such a kick out of this nonsense that Harry made it an annual event.

**YOU ARE CORDIALLY INVITED TO ATTEND
THE PERCUSSION RECITAL OF
HARRY J. BRABEC**

December 31, 1966
11:59 p.m.
SOLDIER FIELD

~ Program Notes ~

Mr. Harry J. Brabec through the years has given many exciting recitals at *Soldier Field*. His most memorable one was last year's performance of "Concerto for Two Conductors and Bass Drum" with conductors Bernstein & Leinsdorf. Herewith are excerpts from his many rave reviews:

"Superb!"— Hopalong Cassidy, Buckley News, Illinois

"Without a doubt, Mr. Brabec's recital last night was really something!" — Quicksand Marsh, Penwiper, Kansas

"At Mr. Brabec's recital, I have never seen such audience response as this." — Roberta Dettmering, Left Overshoe, Idaho

"Even though Mr. Brabec is of Italian extraction, we must give him credit for his attempt at trying to improve the music of our country." — John Svovoda, VP, Talman Savings, directed to Franta Kroll, Editor of *Denni Hlasatel*

CREDITS

All percussion equipment used in this recital courtesy of Chicago City Dump, plus tin cans left by neighbors, and remnants that nobody else dared pick up at the old Melody Top Theatre.

Air conditioning by Free Wind Enterprises
Insect Repellent by I-Gotum-Scratch, Inc.

***** PROGRAM *****

Szpactto & Fug ....R. R. Daley
    9 Gourds & One Tuned Cowbell

Symphony #7-1/8...Brabec
    Molto – Nothing
    Andante – Something
    Shirtzo – Noble
    Finale – *Thank God!*

~ Beer Brake ~

Concerto Fore 18 Bass Drums & Trombone ....E. Poggy
    Trombone Soloist, Vladimar Jaroslav Cohen

Nocturne #67647...F. Reiner
    Unaccompanied
    Gong, Sleigh Bells & Rat Poison!!

Slit Slatt Shutt...A. Lumbrazo
    Slap Stick – Italian Gong – Square Triangle
    3 Tubens (C – F – & O) and 2-Iron if necessary
    + Window shades (slightly used)

Pizza Parlor Blues...B. Corti
    2 Sausage – 1 Cheese
    3 Tuned Cymbals – 1 Woodblock
    6 Decks of Cards–- 3 Cigars
    8 Black Mushrooms
    1 Vomit Bucket
    Psychiatrist

Encores at the Public's Request
(No more than six)

Ladies will please remove hats.

After receiving Harry's "prestigious invitation," Doc Swartz sent this acknowledgment:

> *I have read and heard noised around about the concert that you intend to give shortly out in the Stock Yards. How nice of you. Wonderful. Grand. Be sure to put plenty of rosin on your pedals. Be careful, don't get any on your you-know-what.*
>
> *I have sat in front of drummers all the way from Kristefek to Joe Russek and Joe Sukumsky, and I think that the end result will make Verdi's Anvil Chorus sound like a Children's Lullaby. – Respectfully yours, Jake the Plumber*

Bill Corti sent a New Year's card that included this note and six S&H Green Stamps:

> *Dear Harry, Enclosed find stamps to cover admission for your fabulous concert New Year's Eve as my many friends around Taylor and Halsted Streets are dying to attend. May I add that my head swells with pride to be part of this most auspicious musical extravaganza of this or any other season!*

So You Want to Leave Show Biz?

The Shubert job was hard work. I never understood how musicians could do the same show night after night, week after week, month after month, without being bored to tears. I never objected to Harry stopping off for a drink with one of his buddies after a show because I knew how hard it was for him to unwind after any kind of performance. But something happened one night that kinda upset him and made him feel old—so much so, in fact, that I wrote a little poem about it to cheer him up:

> So . . . you think you want to leave Show Biz?
> Well, I can understand why that is.
> Long rehearsals and crazy hours;
> a drummer's life is no bed of flowers.
>
> Twenty-two men in a pit build for ten . . .
> where does the drummer go? Cast out again—
> into the audience, or under a ramp
> that mashes his crew cut and drowns out his vamp.

There're the autograph hounds who bar your way,
when you just want to go home for the day.
But what *really* hurts is they're not after you,
but some "star" in the show—they just want to get through.

Then you and your buddy stop off for a beer,
'cause after a bad night you need a little cheer.
And some jerk in the bar tops the day with this one:
"Say, fellas, you two look just like father and son."
And you ask yourself, "Has Show Biz done this to me?
I'm just thirty-seven and my friend's thirty-three."

So . . . you think you want to leave Show Biz?
Well, I can understand why that is.
But whether you do, or whether you don't,
your decision can wait but my verses won't.

CHAPTER 6

Flashback to the Forties & Harry's Big Band Days

The "hot" bands played big band jazz, but oh, those one-nighters! I'm sure I could build the inside of a bus blindfolded.—Harry

anish philosopher Soren Kierkegaard said that "Life can only be understood backwards, but it must be lived forwards." Before I continue with Harry's story, I want to take you back to the forties and fifties before I knew him.

Reconstructing this part of his life was an exciting challenge for me as a writer. I had documented much of his musical history after we met in 1961, but for the first three decades of his life all I really had to go on were my fuzzy memories of stories he had told me about his past and comments in his letters about musicians he had known and worked with over the years.

Halfway through the writing of this book, I began to feel like a detective who was trying to put a huge "Harry Brabec Puzzle" together. Completing the borders of his life and all the brightly colored center sections (our life together) was fairly easy, but big holes soon began to emerge in the middle because I knew so few details about his life before we were married. With the help of a couple of his old friends and one of his students, I began to track down and talk to more of his school chums and musicians of that era who knew or had worked with him. Bit by bit I found answers to many of the questions I had about this part of Harry's life.

Meeting so many new people that he knew or had worked with, but that I'd never known or communicated with before, was a real joy to me, especially since everyone had only good things to say about him. As one of my friends put it, "What a beautiful gift Harry left you. Every time you find a new acquaintance, friend, or musician who knew him, it must be like opening a beautifully wrapped package with a surprise inside."

That it was. Some of those surprises were delightfully amusing while others were simply astonishing. I couldn't believe how much about Harry's life I didn't know even after nearly 44 years with him.

Frank Kaderabek is a virtuoso trumpeter who went to school with Harry. My long conversations with him revealed many surprising pieces of information about Harry's musical life, beginning with his days at Morton High. "I was three years behind Harry in school," Frank told me. "We met when I was in the Cicero grade school band and Harry had just gone into high school and into the famous Morton High School band. We got along and became friends and went on to play many jobs together while we were in high school."

Now that information was certainly news to me as Harry had never told me that he was jobbing all through high school. I knew he made a little money playing somewhere once in a while and that he gave his folks almost everything he earned, which he said was why he never had any money to take girls out on dates. Mostly what he talked about regarding his school days was his wonderful music teacher and all the fun he had playing in the school bands and entering drum and marimba contests where he won dozens of medals.

Jobbing in High School

"There were a lot of jobbing opportunities in high school," Frank continued. "Harry and I were only in school together one year before he graduated, but we played many dance band jobs, party events at the Lions and Kiwanis clubs or the Fraternal Order of Eagles, and weddings. GIs were coming home on leave to get married, and then they'd go off again. School dances were usually held in the cafeteria on a Friday afternoon, and Harry and I would usually play for two or three hours."

I naturally wondered how much these jobs paid. Frank laughed and said, "Usually a dollar an hour. We weren't in the union, so if we got a job that paid $10 for the evening, that was a biggie. Mostly, we'd play four hours somewhere and get four bucks. A dance in the cafeteria might pay only two or three dollars."

I knew Harry had been rejected by the Army for flat feet, but now I wondered why the Army couldn't have used him in a band. "The Army had some pretty stringent physical requirements in those days," Frank told me. "Even as a musician you had to march and play parades, and guys with flat feet were rejected for that reason."

During the Korean War, Frank was in the West Point Band. When he came out of there he went with the Dallas Symphony, which had a short season. "Most of the smaller symphonies like Dallas and the National Symphony that Harry joined in 1946 had a season of maybe 24 to 28 weeks. That left summers free for other work."

Up to this point, I had been trying to create an accurate time line of Harry's life as a professional musician before I met him. I couldn't figure out how he had worked so many different jobs when he was always telling people that he was with the Civic Orchestra from 1944–1945, the Chuck Foster Orchestra from 1945–1946, the National Symphony from 1946–1949, Wayne King from 1949–1951, and NBC from 1959–1960. But now I suddenly saw that all these orchestras had seasons that ran for less or little more than half a year, so there were always weeks—often months—in between when Harry and every other musician of his day was scrambling for work wherever it could be found. Like Frank, Harry worked Grant Park in the summer, picked up dance jobs, night club work, recording sessions, a concert here, an opera there, and any other job he could find. Frank's experience offers more insight here.

"I was with the Dallas Symphony for five seasons," he said, "and there was no sick leave, no pension, no nothing. You played the twenty weeks and they thought they were giving you a passport to heaven. So I'd play Grant Park for eight weeks, and in between I might be on the road with the Ringling Brothers Circus, or playing the Ice Capades, doing a tour with Wayne King, and so on. Everybody was always scrambling for work."

In one of Harry's letters, he confirmed his work in the summer of 1949 with a mention of Eric Leinsdorf's superb conducting of "Madame Butterfly" at Grant Park that year. In talking to Harry's high school girlfriend, Nancy Geiger, I got an answer to another question I had. I knew his mother had died sometime that year, but I wasn't sure of just when until Nancy confirmed that both she and Harry were working Grant Park that summer. "I went with Harry and his dad one night when they went to the hospital to visit his mom, and she died shortly after that."

Nancy also remembered that she had bummed a ride with Harry one night in the mid-sixties when they were both working the Lyric Opera. Of course he didn't mention that he had just worked with someone he went to school with, and now I know why. It was just something he took for granted. Morton produced so many professional musicians who ended up working in the Chicago area that Harry was always working a job with one old school chum or another. Lane High School also produced a lot of fine musicians and many of them became friends with Morton kids because they participated in the music contests always being held in those days.

Two Years with Wayne King

Wayne King (1901–1985) was sometimes referred to as "The Waltz King" because much of his popular music involved waltzes. His orchestra (one of the "sweet bands") was heard continuously on radio and in ballrooms across the country from 1927 to the mid-sixties. Between 1949 and 1951 when Wayne King was a bigger name than Lawrence Welk, Standard Oil of Indiana sponsored the *Wayne King TV Show*, and WNBQ (the predecessor call-letters of today's WMAQ-TV) fed it to eleven Midwestern NBC affiliates. Frank Kaderabek said he didn't see much of Harry after he left school, but when he was playing with Wayne King in Chicago, he often watched the TV show just to see him playing drums.

After one of Harry's correspondents, a Mason, sent him a tape of a Wayne King recording, he replied:

> The Wayne King tape was just what I wanted. Especially appreciated was the one tune where Burke Bivens sang. I was on the band with him, and he was the *true* writer of "Josephine," even though Wayne received credit for co-composer.
>
> I was with Wayne King from 1949 to 1951. This was the band that had the large chorus, and we did a weekly television show. Of the thirty people in the group, we had five Masons—all belonging to different lodges. We knew King was a member but he never recognized that any of the men were his brothers. We used to joke that we had enough Masons on the band to open a lodge, but we wouldn't let King through the door. After I left him, I went with the Chicago Symphony where there were about fifteen of us. When I left, there were only two.

Of course Harry's LP collection included many of King's albums, and he was sorely tempted to again tour with the band when he got an invite in 1961 to join the orchestra for four weeks, but we were newly married at the time and neither of us could bear the thought of being apart then. I don't know how much Harry made when he was with King in the forties, but this job offer was for $350 a week, which was good money in those days.

In a reminiscent letter in 1999, Harry wrote that a friend of his in a recording studio had sent him copies of the LP recordings he did with King on November 12, 1950 at the Edgewater Beach Hotel in Chicago:

> Time has taken its toll in scratches and hiss, but for the most part they're pretty good. The guys in the band were really some of Chicago's best. Although King was a taskmaster at times, we had a lot of fun, and those of us that are still living keep in touch. A couple of years ago when I was going through the personnel of the band in my mind, I realized that, of the Wayne King band, there were only five players, including me, still left.
>
> One of the girl singers (Gloria Van) sang with Hal McIntyre and Gene Krupa, and her husband (James "Lynn" Allison), was one of the singers with Glenn Miller's Crew Chiefs (Air Force Orchestra). He was originally a saxophonist with several of the big bands. After I sent Gloria a copy of these recordings, she told me she hadn't remembered that we did those songs of hers, and remarked how good everybody sounded.

Touring and Recording with Chuck Foster

Harry was a long-time subscriber to *Joslin's Jazz Journal,* which was published by Gene Joslin and dedicated to the glory of record collecting. (I believe it ceased publication around 2006.) Each issue featured collector and dealer wants, classified ads, feature articles and columns on recording artists, plus other news and information for record collectors. After Gene published a photo of the Chuck Foster Orchestra in the November 1997 issue and misidentified some of the band personnel, Harry sent a note to correct those errors.

After Gene responded with a request for more detailed info about the band, Harry sent a letter that was published in the *Journal.* That brought him some reader mail which he answered with even more information relative to each individual's questions. He was surprised to be contacted by half a dozen people who were interested in the Foster band because he didn't think the band was that well known. To avoid duplication of information from these various letters, I've pulled the informative content of all of them together here to create a good history of the Chuck Foster orchestra and its personnel, along with some juicy "inside stuff" I'm sure you won't find anywhere else. Harry writes:

> At the time the album photo was taken (see the website), the band was playing at the Hotel New Yorker during the late summer and fall of 1945. The piano player is Lonnie Anderson and the singer is Marilyn Paul. That skinny kid behind the drums is me, who has since put on some poundage and years. We were working the New Yorker at night and doing recordings, transcriptions, V-disks and soundies during the day. We were kept busy, but it was a good band with many good players.
>
> I joined the band February 19, 1945 as Chuck was leaving the Blackhawk Restaurant in Chicago. In fact, at that time, Chuck was revamping his band from three saxes to four, and that's when six sidemen joined, along with two vocalists. We went out on a bunch of one-nighters, sort of a shake-down cruise, playing such locations as St. Louis and New Orleans. In July of that year, we went to the New Yorker. Of course, from the time I joined the band until I left, there were many personnel changes.
>
> It was a good, tight band with a lot of good musicians, and we always worked with no layoffs. I remember that a guitar player was let go the day before I and four others joined the band. Foster did away with the guitar chair so he would have more money to hire some better players. I remember I was making $90 a week, which was pretty good money compared to what the sidemen in the swingin' bands were making.

Foster and Band Personnel Stories

Harry continues:

> Chuck had a couple of personal quirks, but for the most part he was a pretty nice guy to work for. Every once in a while he'd go off on a tangent. His favorite drink was Scotch and milk. He said it helped relieve the ulcer pain. I never tried it, but I had visions of it tasting like iodine.

He was married to Delores, who I believe was his second wife. He came from the Pittsburgh area, and when I joined the band, there were about four fellows that he knew from back there. Chuck's sister, Gloria, sang with the band for awhile, and I knew her, but she left the night before I joined the band and joined Carmen Cavallero, whom she later married. Last I heard, and this is many years ago, she gave up singing and stayed married to Cavallero until his death a few years ago.

The lead alto man was Jimmy Hefti, Neal's brother. Jimmy went with the sweet bands and Neal went the other way. At no time did Jimmy try to latch onto his brother's connections. The singer on the album cover is Marilyn Paul. Dick Roberts, the male singer, died a little while after he left the band. Lonnie Anderson, the piano man, married a woman about twice his age (he was about thirty at the time) and she set him up in his own cocktail lounge in L.A.

The girl singers were involved in a unique story. Shirley Richards joined us in St. Louis just before we went to the New Yorker the first time. This was some break for a kid who never had any big band experience to go to New York on her first job. She was a real sweet girl and all the guys in the band looked after her like a sister. Well, after about three months on the band, she decided to go out on her own, and the first job she had was at the Ambassador East Hotel in Chicago, home of the famous Pump Room. A few years later, I ran across her at the RCA Victor Studios in Chicago where she was doing office work.

But the strangest story of them all is about Marilyn Paul. When Shirley Richards left, Foster must have auditioned at least twenty girls. Some had great voices, but just didn't fit into the band's sound. All of a sudden, without any tryout, here comes Marilyn on the band permanently. Now, prior to this girl-singer situation, we were one tight-knit group. Everybody got along with one another and especially with Foster. We had every kind of personality on that band you might find on the outside in "civilian life." There were drinkers, lovers, readers, health advocates, painters, and others, which made for a happy group.

Well, after awhile, this gal got her claws into the old man and, little by little, everything changed. Cliques formed, Foster started getting nasty, and everybody was against everybody. It came to a head in Chicago at the Blackhawk when this gal pulled some stunt that really infuriated the whole band. I forget now what it was, but for once, the whole band was together again. Anyway, en masse, we went to Foster and told him that we were all handing in our two-week notice and leaving if that girl didn't go. Nothing was said for that two-week period, and when the fifteenth day came around, we all came to work and started out right on the bandstand.

Now Marilyn had a bad habit of coming onto the bandstand during the middle of our first set, and sure enough, here she comes prancing across the dance floor, making her grand entrance. We finished the tune we were playing, and to a man, we all got up and started packing. Foster darn near had a fit and immediately called a meeting of the band. Almost with tears in his eyes, he promised us that this girl would be gone by the next night. After all, where was he going to get fourteen new musicians to cut his book and preserve his reputation?

Well, the next night, right on time, a new girl vocalist joined the band, name of Betty Clark, who left a few years later to join Blue Barron. Unfortunately, the damage was already done and things never returned to what they were, and in a matter of about six months, Foster had almost an entirely new band.

I finally left the band in May of 1946 to join the National Symphony in Washington, D.C. Later, Chuck came into Chicago and was at the Martinique Night Club and was stuck for a drummer. So I came in and lasted only a week. The style of the band had changed and my playing style also changed, so it was like oil and water—we didn't mix.

I made one album with Foster that included performances from August 13, September 27, and October 18, 1945. If I remember correctly, they were all done at the Hotel New Yorker in New York. I remember August 13th in particular because that was when the cease-fire was ordered in the Pacific and finally the war was over. I may be on the 1945 broadcast from the Blackhawk, too. I joined the band when they left the "Hawk" in February, and we returned in December.

Harry didn't have the Chuck Foster records in his collection until sometime in the nineties when a friend from his past found copies of two Foster albums and sent them to him. He was pleased to have them, but I was just thrilled because there was a picture of the orchestra on one album showing the whole band, with a great shot of Harry on the drums. The curious thing about these records, however, is that Harry wasn't playing on the album that had his picture on it, but on the other album with a different band picture. Harry said it was common in those days for record producers to just slap any picture on an album that they had handy. The one he is playing on is simply titled *Chuck Foster and His Orchestra, 1945–1946*, and Harry is listed on it as part of the personnel. In checking the recording dates, however, I found what appeared to be a discrepancy. The August 13 recording date wasn't mentioned here, and other dates Harry hadn't mentioned in his letter included February 19–20 and October 11, 1946.

The August 13 recording date was finally confirmed about three years after Harry died, when Charlie St. George, a big band friend of mine on the Web, sent me a CD of two remote broadcasts of the Chuck Foster band, one from the Terrace Room of the Hotel New Yorker dated August 13, 1945, the other from the Terrace Room on September 8, 1945. This suggests that whoever was writing the liner notes for the Chuck Foster albums may have been as careless with the details as with the cover picture.

One of the musicians who wrote to Harry after the article was published in *Joslyn's Jazz Journal* asked about the Bob Chester band, to which Harry replied, "Tony Calamello, one of the tenor sax players from that band joined Foster's band and told tales of Chester being kind of a stinker to work for. While we were in New York, Chester heard of the band and wanted me to join him, but I figured I had enough problems, I didn't need any more with a leader who had a temper problem. I do know that he was backed by Tommy Dorsey and that's about all the information I have about him."

Chuck Foster, born in 1912, died in 2001.

♪ Music Sidenote ♪

Charlie St. George, "OlSarge," broadcasts a weekly "Big Bandstand Sunday" on KNCT FM Radio (Killeen/Copperas Cove, TX) which can be heard on the Web at KNCT.org.

Recordings, Transcriptions, V-Disks, and Soundies

While Harry was with the Chuck Foster Orchestra, the band worked the New Yorker at night and did recordings, transcriptions, V-disks, and soundies during the day. The album he made with Chuck Foster specifically states that it is the original "for Radio only" recordings. (Transcriptions were recordings that were going to be broadcast over radio at some later time; private recordings to be used only by the radio station.)

V-Discs ("V" for Victory) were a morale-boosting initiative involving the production of several series of recordings during the World War II era. By special arrangement between the U. S. government and various private record companies, these 12-inch 78 rpm gramophone recordings were created for both the Army and the Navy between October 1943 and May 1949. They featured many popular singers, big bands, and orchestras of the era. These twelve-inch discs held only six-and-a-half minutes of music, but they must have been a delight to those who heard them.

Soundies were displayed on a coin-operated film jukebox machine called a Panoram that was usually found in night clubs, bars, restaurants, factory lounges, and amusement centers. The forerunners of the music video, their era ended in 1947. These three-minute musical films were produced in New York, Chicago, and Hollywood, and covered all genres of music and featured leading bands, orchestras, singers, and movie stars of the day. More than 1800 of the soundies' mini-musicals were eventually released to home video. (Several can be seen on YouTube today.)

I still remember how excited and thrilled I was the day Harry opened a package from one of his musician friends from his Chuck Foster days and found a videotape of two of the three-minute soundies he had made with the Orchestra. On playing it, we saw that it was the exact scene from the album photo, right down to the vocalist on stage. (She was a stitch, but the male vocalist's cowboy costume and presentation was so amusing that we couldn't listen to his sweet voice without laughing. Some singers should have stuck to radio.)

The only problem with the soundie recording was that it was filmed in reverse, thus Harry appeared to be playing left-handed instead of right-handed. We had to view the film in a mirror to see the recording the right way. As he explained to me, it took two cameras to get the finished product onto the jukebox-like machine, which meant it went from a normal picture to a reversed print, then back to a normal picture on screen. Although Harry tried, we couldn't find anyone at the time to re-record this tape for us in reverse. However, a year after he died, John Melcher, one of his former drum students from his days at Disney (see Chapter 10), connected with me on the Web and he then had the technology to do this. I was delighted when he converted the VHS tape to a DVD for me and said he might be able to get these soundies refor-matted for viewing on TheDrummerDrives.com website.

Musicians in Glenn Miller's Band

One day after Harry had returned from a trip to Borders to buy a new CD, he said to me, "Know how to tell when you're getting old? It's when you walk into a record store to buy the new Glenn Miller CD and the clerk asks what kind of music that is."

Harry never played with Glenn Miller, but he knew many of the musicians who did. Among his regular correspondents was John Featherstone, with whom he enjoyed sharing musical memories and trading music tapes and CDs. John was a retired Major who hosted a military music radio program in London. In 1995 when he asked Harry about the musicians in the Miller Band, Harry replied:

> I knew some of the boys in the band. I didn't know Mel Powell, but from what I heard, he was well liked by Goodman, even if at times he was given a hard time. I think he is now (or was) teaching at a California University, but is in bad shape physically. I knew Ray McKinley quite well and was saddened by his death a few weeks ago. The band sure is getting smaller. I also knew Bobby Nichols, trumpet player, whose behavior at times was questionable. Also Hank Free-man, who played lead alto. Nice guy, good player, but he never received the credit he was due. Frank Ippolito was the second drummer on the band. When called upon, he played all the toys (xylophone, bells, tympani, etc.). I also knew Manny Wishnow, a viola player, through his brother Jack, who was a French horn player I worked with. It's hard to believe that it was just after the war that I knew these fellows and that was almost fifty years ago.

This suggests to me that Harry probably met these musicians during his days at NBC or when he was doing recordings at Universal and RCA.

His LP collection included many Miller albums on the RCA label, so it's only logical to assume that the "ghost band" led by Ray McKinley in the mid fifties probably also cut albums on the RCA label and appeared on television shows airing on the NBC or CBS radio or television stations.

Miller died (went missing) in 1944. After the war ended, many of the Miller musicians went on to studio careers in Hollywood and New York while others became a part of the ghost band that was authorized by the Miller estate in 1946. This band, first led by Tex Beneke, played to very large audiences all across the U.S. until 1950 when he and the Miller estate parted ways. In 1956, after the success of the movie, *The Glenn Miller Story*, the Miller estate asked Ray McKinley to lead a new ghost band, which he did until 1966. This band was the original version of the current ghost band that still tours today.

In a letter to his Browsers pal Phil Holdman in 2000 (see "Browsers," page 152), Harry commented on an article Phil had sent him about Jack Leonard, one of the top male vocalists of the 1930s who sang with Tommy Dorsey's band:

> I particularly liked the article on Jack Leonard. I don't know if you're familiar with the story or not, but Johnny Desmond began feeling his oats a little bit while with the Glenn Miller Army Air Force Band. More concerned about his fame as a singer, he began to neglect some of his other duties, such as helping set up and tear down the band. Miller got him off in the corner one day and said, "Listen, you'd better share the load. Remember that Jack Leonard is stationed down the road, and it wouldn't be too difficult to get him transferred into this unit." I guess Desmond came to realize he had a pretty good deal going with Miller, and thereafter behaved himself accordingly.

Johnny Desmond died in 1985. I figure Harry probably heard that story from Ray McKinley. In a March 1995 letter to John Featherstone in London, he wrote about a new Glenn Miller album he was trying to find at that time:

> This is music never before released. It was reportedly found just recently, hidden in some dark corner of the BBC or the RAF, I forget which. About a month ago, there was an announcement of this discovery on our news with a release date being the following Monday. I, like many others, waited

and tried to purchase the CD on that date. Well, it didn't come out when it was supposed to, and after waiting and checking all my contacts, I was given two answers for why it was not available then: (1) It is not to be released in this country for some time, but only in England (which sounds plausible); (2) but this sounds a little far fetched: I was told that our government wouldn't allow the album to be released because it contained propaganda material. Well, for God's sake, there must be at least ten records or CDs that have messages sent to the Germans from Miller broadcasts. My own thinking is that somehow our government is trying to get control of the release of this CD so they can get the royalties. It's absurd. There is a U.S. Air Force Band Museum where they sell records of the Miller Band, and those include propaganda messages.

John sent a copy of the CD to Harry, but soon afterward it did become available here.

The "Sweet Bands"

The "sweet bands" were active during the 1930s and 1940s, and included such bands as Guy Lombardo, Les Brown, Russ Morgan, Eddie Duchin, Xavier Cugat, Claude Thornhill, Henry Busse, Sammy Kaye, Freddy Martin, Hal Kemp, Wayne King, and Chuck Foster.

When Tom Lee, one of Harry's regular big band correspondents, asked him how the musicians on the sweet bands felt about playing that type of music, Harry sent this very interesting letter, which mentioned a couple of other groups he had played with:

They played with mixed emotions. I also played with Boyd Raeburn, Jerry Wald, and the Dorsey Brothers, so I can give both sides of the story. The "hot" bands played big band jazz, but oh, those one-nighters! I'm sure I could build the inside of a bus blindfolded. And remember, this was the in the days before there was a restroom on the bus and interstate highways. But still you played your heart out and had fun.

The sweet bands, of course, were less strenuous and one-nighters were usually of a short duration. I did three and a half weeks with Foster through the Carolinas and that was no picnic. But at least the sweet band players could have their wives with them, and some even had their pre-school children along. It would be funny to see a band truck being unpacked and finding cribs and strollers coming out. Of course it was hard on the wives because they would have to get from one major city to another by train or bus, sometimes making two or three transfers. But they managed.

The musicianship on these bands was excellent because of the precision that was required to play that type of music. It was really evident when the band was required to play a show. These bands played hotels or night clubs that usually had a three- or four-act show and maybe a line of girls. This is when these "sweet musicians" put on a different hat and played some heavy stuff. Many a name act was surprised by the high quality of music that came out of these bands.

In answer to another question Tom posed about Ernie Rudy taking over the Kaye band, Harry wrote:

Some time in the early fifties, Rudy (Rudisell) and several other band members quit *en masse* and he went on to form a band of his own. He had been with Kaye for a long time (may have been an original member), but he was not second in command. It may be noted that, throughout the industry, Kaye did have the reputation of not being the nicest guy to work for. A musical phony, some called him, but I learned a long time ago never to knock success. One rumor had it that he had about ten toupees, all with slightly different lengths of hair. He would wear number one through ten, and then revert back to number one so as to give the impression that he had gotten a haircut.

Harry's comments about his one-nighters brought to mind a story he told me about one night when the Foster band was on the road between locations. They had stopped for dinner and, on the way out, some of the guys picked up some booze for the bus. Later when Harry was partaking from his bottle, he suddenly became sick and told the driver he had to get off the bus *right now*. It was pitch dark out there in the country, so someone handed him a flashlight. After heaving his guts out in the grass, he flashed the light on the results and almost got sick all over again when he saw it was glowing in the dark. The guys were none too happy to learn they had all bought some really bad hootch.

CHAPTER 7

Chicago's Radio/TV Orchestras & Recording Studios

If a musician or singer made a noticeable mistake or if the announcer ran long or short on his copy, another complete take was required. If you couldn't deliver consistently perfect takes, you didn't last long in the studios, no matter how good you sounded.
—Loren Binford, jingle business researcher

rying to document Harry's years at NBC, and the times when he was doing jingles and recording sessions, proved to be the most difficult part of his musical life to reconstruct. But thanks to contacts provided by Loren Binford (see page 82), I was able to track down a number of musicians who either knew or worked with Harry in the mid-fifties.

The NBC Studio Orchestra

Harry often spoke to me about his years at NBC, but it was always in the form of anecdotes or references to guys he worked with. I knew he was a part-time staff percussionist at NBC during his years with Wayne King (1949–1951) and was on staff full-time from 1959 until the studio orchestra folded sometime in 1960. His letters reveal that his old friend Joe Sperry, who was in the Chicago Civic Orchestra with him, was a TV floor manager at NBC when he was doing the *Wayne King Show* on television, and this is surely when Harry bought Sperry's drum set that he used for the rest of his life (see Chapter 14).

I know he worked alongside, and took a few lessons from, Jose Bethancourt when they were both at NBC. (Bethancourt was Guatemala's foremost marimba teacher—a world-class artist commonly thought to be the man responsible for introducing the marimba to America. As one of James Dutton's students in the fifties, I was privileged to meet him one evening when he spoke to our ensemble group and gave us a "group lesson.")

Harry's music friend Maurie Lishon may well have been his entree to NBC because he was a bit older than Harry and very active in all the radio and television stations during the forties and fifties. His book, *Franks for the Memories* (Rebeats 1993) describes this period of time while offering clues about what Harry's life was probably like when he was at NBC:

> *"WGN, ABC (which was WENR in those days) and NBC all got their TV channels at approximately the same time. Their staff radio schedules were full up, so they needed outside men on some of the stuff and I was the first call on drums on all of them. I came out of the army in hock up to my neck, and I was hungry. I didn't turn anything down. Between swings at the theaters, television shows, recordings and club dates, I was doing two and three dates a day. I was [. . .] working at WGN for Bob Trendler, working for Joe Galichio and NBC, working for Rex Maupin at ABC, Caesar Petrillo at WBBM-CBS; all on a substitute basis."*

♪ Music Sidenote ♪

I'm wondering if Maurie misspelled a name here because there are several pages on the Web that indicate that Joseph Gallicio's (not Galichio) orchestra aired on the NBC network radio station WMAQ and later on the CBS radio station WBBM. Lishon's book mentions all the people that Harry knew and worked with over the years, from his old teacher Roy Knapp (then staff drummer at WGN) to Bobby Christian (NBC), Frank Rullo (WENR), and Hubert (Hugh) Anderson (NBC-TV).

For more information about this period of time in Chicago's music history, Lishon's book offers colorful background information and photographs showing how the studio orchestras worked, how and when they did transcriptions and commercials, stars of that era that appeared on the shows, and what it was like to work live on television.

In one of his letters, Harry wrote, "While the NBC Studio Orchestra in Chicago was intact, I was the staff drummer and worked with the bands of Woody Herman, the Dorsey Brothers, Wayne King, and the Dixieland groups of George Brunis and Art Hodes."

The NBC orchestra also aired on WBBM, and one of Harry's letters confirms that he knew Mal Bellairs from his days of "doing radio transcriptions at WBBM in the fifties, where Bellairs was a well-known broadcaster." In a letter to his Browsers pal, Phil Holdman, Harry also said he had a lot of memories of the guys with the Art Van Damme Quintet: "Occasionally up at NBC, they would add an extra drummer for the Latin tunes, and it was such a pleasure to work with them."

(An article on the Web reports that "On January 24, 1955 WNBQ announced it was pairing Murphy and Westfall with resident *Creative Cookery* star Eddie Doucette and expanding the show to an hour and fifteen minutes long. Also joining *The Bob & Kay Show's* house band, The Art Van Damme Quintet, was Joseph Gallicio's 16-piece orchestra.")

I know Harry also worked with such personalities as Bob Hope, Tony Bennett, Danny Thomas, and many others because he mentioned these names in one letter or another. It seems pretty clear to me now that he could have met and worked with any or all of these entertainers either while at NBC or at any time during the forties and fifties when he was doing phonograph recordings in his off-season periods with whatever orchestra he was then working with.

"We're having a recording session get-together of all the Chicago radio staff musicians in December," Harry wrote in a letter to his drummer pal Doug MacLeod in October 1985. "That should be fun, but the ranks are going to be a little thin in some areas. We figured that out of fifteen staff drummers, only three of us are left."

After playing a job somewhere in 1990, Harry mentioned NBC in another letter to Doug, saying "It was a good concert tonight with a big studio-type band playing all the good music of the thirties and forties. I enjoy playing that music, and we had a lot of the old gang from NBC there, so it was nice talking about the good times at the station."

Chicago's Jingle Business

Loren Binford, a retired trombone player and singer in Arlington
Heights, Illinois, has been in the jingles industry all his life. In the fall of
2005, he decided someone ought to try to remember how the jingle
business began in Chicago, how it grew, and how it worked. He began
then, and continues today, to interview singers, instrumental musicians,
studio engineers, advertising executives, composers, and orchestrators
who worked in Chicago creating and performing the music for radio and
TV commercials during the late 1940s and 1950s. He has gathered a
wealth of material, but says he has a long way to go yet to document a
complete history of the jingles industry, especially in the 1930s.

"I have neither the energy nor the competence to write a book about
this time in Chicago's music history because I have eye problems and no
computer to do research," he told me. "I merely want to collect as many
memories as possible from the oldest survivors before they are all gone
so we will have an archive of first-hand information. A great many of the
people who did jingle work before 1960 have passed away. Most of the
survivors are now in their late seventies, eighties, or even nineties. Few of
these old-timers have, to my knowledge, written much about their own
studio careers, and so far no one has expressed an interest in writing a
comprehensive history of Chicago's jingle business. I hope the younger
folks who began after 1960 will write their own stories. Eventually
someone will put it all together."

Regarding Harry's jingle work, Loren says all the old-timers agree
that the earlier jingle sessions seldom used many musicians beyond
piano (or guitar), bass, and drums. "While trap drummers worked most
sessions from the beginning, extra percussionists probably weren't
needed before the mid-to-late 1950s. Frank Rullo and Bobby Christian
surely did most of that before the city got really busy. It probably was in
the 1960s that Harry played his jingle sessions. There were a lot more
producers then and more occasions for multiple sessions to go on at the
same time, which required more performers."

It's true that Harry did some jingles in the sixties and beyond, but
my research and conversations with others suggests that he first began to
do jingles in the late fifties after he left the Chicago Symphony. According
to Binford's research, at that time instrumental musicians holding the
best-paying steady jobs (the radio staffs, the Symphony, and a few other
positions) were "frozen" by the Union, which meant they couldn't play

jingle sessions or most other freelance engagements, but only phono-graph sessions.

"Sometime after 1956," Binford explains, "the freeze was also enforced for musicians playing five-night steady engagements at night clubs, hotels, and other situations. Off-night musicians were not frozen. At that time, many who were doing jingles gave up their steady jobs or moved to off-nights. Some theatres, such as the Shubert, were not frozen because their orchestras worked only for the run of a show, so employ-ment was irregular. The freeze wasn't lifted until April, 1968."

Since Harry wasn't working full-time as a musician between 1957 and 1961 (before we met), he could have been doing jingles at any time during this period, as well as when he wasn't touring with Wayne King between 1949 and 1951. Because of stories he told me, I know for sure he was doing a lot of *recordings* in these years. According to my Web research, the NBC orchestra was still doing a lot of phonograph recordings and jingles at Universal during the late fifties, and vibist Duane Thamm confirmed that Universal was indeed a very busy recording studio at that time, often making five or six radio commercials a day.

I remember one story Harry told me about a commercial he was doing for some kind of hair product. He was given a line about the use of this product that he had to say while also playing brushes on the snare drum. But this man who could easily play two instruments at one time told me he had a devil of a time trying to *talk* and play at the same time. Thanks to Loren Binford's research on the history of the jingles industry in Chicago, I think I know now that this product was probably Halo Shampoo, because another musician Binford interviewed said he made this commercial at a time when Harry would have been at NBC.

Making Recordings and Commercials

Sam Denov, Harry's friend and fellow CSO percussionist now retired from the Symphony, confirmed that the Chicago Symphony season was only 34 weeks long during the fifties (when scale wages were $145/week), so when the season ended, all the musicians scrambled for whatever extra work they could find in the city, whether it was doing recordings or other jobs around town.

In 1956 when David Carroll made *Percussion in Hi-Fi*—the first of two classic percussion albums on the Mercury label (see Appendix)—

Harry was one of the six percussionists working alongside Sam, Bobby Christian, Frank Rullo, Dale Anderson, and Hugh Anderson.

Hugh was a percussionist friend from Harry's high school days when they were both participating in drum contests. Hugh (and his brother, Dale) attended Lane High School and, like Harry, had studied with Roy Knapp. Harry and Hugh had also worked in the same arena at CBS and NBC in the fifties. A letter in Harry's scrapbook from Hugh, shortly before he died suddenly in October 1975, indicated that he was playing *Odyssey,* then in its fifth week of an eleven-week run.

"June was a good month for me with about six good studio calls," he wrote, "including one at Disney's, which is the first time I've been there for a long time. I'm glad to hear that you're working at Grant Park and haven't lost any of your ability. It's good to know that one can still play. Don't know what it would feel like to stop playing."

When the second percussion album, *Re-percussion in Hi-Fi,* was made later in 1956, several additional percussionists were hired, including Dick Schory. An extra percussionist in the Chicago Symphony when Harry was there in the fifties, Dick moved easily from the Symphony into recording studios and conducting, and went on to become a major influence on both classical and popular percussion music. Through the production of more than a dozen albums for RCA, he popularized percussion music in the late fifties and early sixties and paved the way for an entire movement in pop music that lasted through 1969. Through the years, he has worked closely with music educators to broaden acceptance and understanding of percussion instruments and compositions. In 1960 he wrote, "If it can be struck and can be classified as a percussion instrument, someone somewhere has scored for it."

I called Dick to see if he might be able to fill in some other holes in Harry's recording life, but all he could do was confirm the vast number of recordings that were being made in the fifties and sixties at Universal and other Chicago studios. "There were so many opportunities to play in those days," he said, "and we did a lot of commercials for both radio and television, as well as recordings for commercial release on the Mercury label. Often David Carroll would contract an orchestra for performers who were cutting albums."

I laughed when Dick told me that when he was hired to do a recording at Universal, he and Bobby Christian would get to the studio early and then pick the parts they wanted to play and do a little wood-shedding before the rest of the musicians came in. I don't know whether

Harry ever did this or not on any of his recording dates, but I'm sure he never would have practiced a part in front of other pros on a job.

Some of Binford's research relating to the musicians and contractors involved in this industry in the fifties answered some questions I had about when Harry might have made some of the jingles and recordings he told me about. Several musicians Harry considered friends were also doing jingles in the fifties, including Bill Corti and "Toots" Tootelian, whom Harry would later play with in both the Shubert and Melody Top theatres. Bill is gone now, but Toots confirmed that since Bobby Christian and Frank Rullo did most of the percussion for recordings at Universal, Harry probably played timpani when he did recordings there.

Rudy Macciocchi, another school chum who played French horn, confirmed that he and Harry worked together quite a bit doing jingles and recordings at Universal, but he couldn't recall what instruments Harry might have played. (I was saddened to learn that Rudy died a few weeks after we talked because he was another one of Harry's friends I knew personally and cared about.)

Booking Agencies, Contractors, and Recording Studios

My journal notes after we married often mentioned that "Harry had another recording session," or "he did a commercial this week," or "Harry played a hotel job tonight," but it never occurred to me to document details of these jobs. It was just part of his regular work at the time and I guess I quickly came to take it for granted, just as he did.

Henry Brandon and Bill Walker were also mentioned in Binford's research, and these were contractors Harry worked with. (In fact, you may recall my saying earlier that the first job Harry got just days before our wedding was one from Bill Walker for a recording at Universal that paid $150.) During his career, Bill Walker wrote the music and produced the soundtracks for thousands of radio and television commercials.

Harry often mentioned the name of Henry Brandon, a leading agency for booking bands into Chicago. Brandon had his fingers in a lot of "music pies," one of which was hiring musicians to make up a band when a band leader would come into town with his book. Loren Binford connected me to Anita Smith, Henry Brandon's secretary in the 1960s, and we had a delightful chat. She still had the address book she used to book musicians for Brandon, and Harry's phone number was in it. She confirmed that Brandon had probably hired him for a number of hotel jobs, Saturday night dance jobs, recordings, and even some jingles both before and after 1960.

It was in talking to her and reading Loren's research information that the name of Joe Light came up as the man who ran the payroll service for Music Corporation of America (MCA). In checking old tax returns, I was reminded that Harry had income from MCA in 1959 and other years after we were married. He also had income in the early sixties from CBS and Talent & Residuals, the latter from some earlier jingle recording, I presume.

Anita said that after Brandon died, she began to type tax returns for Joe Light in 1963, and only then did I remember that the name of our first accountant was "Joe" (who never put his name on our tax return—only his address). When I learned Harry hadn't paid his taxes for the two years before we met, he said he knew someone who could help him, and that man was Joe Light, who did returns for many Chicago musicians. Obviously Harry knew him from working with Brandon, but what I found really fascinating here was that I had just met by phone the person who had typed the Brabec's 1963 tax return.

Talk about *six degrees of separation.* Also called "the human Web," six degrees of separation refers to the idea that if a person is one step away from each person they know, and two steps away from each person who is known by one of the people they know, then everyone is at most six steps away from any other person on Earth.

One of the most interesting conversations I had was with Everett Zlatoff-Mirsky, another musician I connected with through Loren Binford. Everett is a violinist and viola player who knew Harry in the fifties. "I started working over at Universal in 1956, and did recordings there until I retired in 2003," he said. "As a youngster in the business, I was advised by Harold Kupper, a Chicago Symphony musician, that the best way to make it in this business was to 'just go and do the job, don't socialize, don't try to make friends; just do the job and get out.' Over the years, however, you start to know people, and Harry was occasionally on the same recording sessions I played. I played Lyric Opera's first season and I probably worked with Harry every year after that when he was playing the Lyric. I never knew him as a friend, but I heard only good things about him as a player and a good guy."

I knew Harry had done some recording in the RCA Victor Studios in Chicago because one of his letters mentioned running into a woman there that had been in the Chuck Foster Orchestra. But that was the extent of my knowledge about the recordings he might have done there until Everett gave me the following insight into what the Universal and RCA recording sessions were like for him and perhaps Harry, as well.

He confirmed that Frank Rullo and Bobby Christian were the leading percussionists for the studios and always the first ones to be called, but since Harry got jobs through both Bill Walker and Henry Brandon, Harry was probably on the list to be called whenever an extra percussionist was needed.

"I don't doubt that Harry was doing recordings and jingles right and left in those days because this was such a thriving business in the fifties," Everett says. "Universal had three recording studios going day and night, and RCA, which produced many vinyl records, was also doing jingle work when things were really humming. It was common for them to have seven to ten sessions going on at once. Some weeks I'd have as many as 35 recording sessions at RCA and Universal."

Hotel Jobs, Night Clubs, and Chicago Gangsters

Remembering what Harry had told me about moving his drum set around on jobs, I asked Everett then about all the hotel jobs Harry told me he had played in those days. He said he often had to move his drums from one hotel room or recording studio to another, and to make this job easier, he rigged the bass drum with special hardware that connected it to all other parts of his drum set—the snare drum, tom-tom, cymbals and other toys—so he could easily pick up the whole set at once and quickly move it from one place to another (which probably explains why his back was shot by the age of forty).

Everett said that made perfect sense because he often found himself moving from one recording studio to another at Universal, and he often played hotel jobs as well. "We'd have different gigs in different hotels, and sometimes two in the same place. There might be a wedding in one room in the afternoon, and then a banquet with dancing after dinner in another room."

Everett mentioned that Brandon also booked bands into many of the Chicago night clubs like the London House and Chez Paree (which closed in 1960) where acts came in for engagements. Didn't they come in with their own drummers, I wondered?

"No," he said. "They knew they could get top quality people in Chicago, so this might explain how Harry came to work with some of the leading entertainers he said he had worked with."

This might also explain how Harry ended up playing in some of Chicago's night clubs and ran into some of Chicago's gangsters. He probably gave me the details at the time I heard the following story, but you know how it is when you get older and memory fades.

Everyone has seen movies about how Chicago gangsters were everywhere in the 1920s, but there were still some thugs around in Harry's day, and he told me he played more than one night club job in the forties and fifties that got a little uncomfortable at times. I remember him telling about one night in particular when this guy came in late after most everyone else had left the place and the band was getting ready to quit for the night. He laid his gun on the table, smiled, and asked the boys to keep playing. And they did just that for a long time while he sat there and drank until he was ready to leave. I don't know the name of the place, but there were a number of night clubs in Chicago then that Harry might have played in. The Green Mill, perhaps? This legendary jazz club on North Broadway in Chicago has been offering nightly entertainment since 1927 and was once a known hangout for gangsters.

Harry's high school friend, Frank Kaderabek, confirmed Harry's gangster story, saying he had also played some jobs where hoods would come in and plunk down some money on the table and request a song. "Actually, they were very appreciative of the musicians," he said. "I remember one time where a guy came in and requested the band to play a particular tune, and then told them to keep playing it until he told them to stop. Those in the club couldn't figure out why the band kept playing the same tune over and over again, ignoring their own requests, but that gun in the guy's pocket explained it clearly enough to the band members themselves."

Harry's cousin Arlene said her dad used to play in night clubs attended by gangsters. He told her they were usually very generous with their tips, and it wasn't uncommon for them to plunk down a hundred-dollar bill to have the band play one of their favorite songs.

In chatting with Loren Binford, he said Harry might well have been playing at the Villa Venice, a gin mill where gangsters hung out in the fifties. "Actually, there were several places like this in those days. I remember one story I heard that suggested the gangsters liked the musicians, and didn't want to hurt them. The drummer always left his drum set on the stage and other musicians might have left their instruments, too, so one night when a gangster said, 'Why don't you guys take your instruments home tonight, there might be a fire,' they didn't question it. And there *was* a fire that night."

When Harry told people he had played all kinds of places, he wasn't kidding. As he put it in one of his letters, "Through the years I have played every type of music imaginable, from burlesque to ballet, from circus to symphony." He also played a strip joint in his youth, when anything for a buck seemed to be his motto. He told me about this experience, saying it was the most boring work he'd ever done, and when he didn't have to watch the girls to catch their bumps and grinds, he was looking at his watch to see how soon he could get the hell out of there.

A Tale of Two Drum Shops

Since this chapter opened with a brief quote from Maurie Lishon's book, *Franks for the Memories,* it seems appropriate to end it with the "rest of the Franks Drum Shop story."

Every percussionist in Chicago knew Maurie Lishon and relied on Franks Drum Shop for the equipment and repair services they needed. But things changed in 1963 when Maurie suddenly found himself with a competitor. Five years earlier, Bill Crowden had gone to work for Maurie with the understanding that, after five years, he would be given a 25 percent ownership in the shop. But when the fifth year ended and he reminded Maurie of his promise, Maurie said he had changed his mind and was going to bring his son into the business instead.

Bill quit immediately, and within a few months opened a competitive shop next door called Drums Unlimited. And it was then that Maurie began to show an unpleasant side of himself that few in the business had ever seen, and one that cost him a lot of customers. William F. Ludwig II has documented this story in his autobiography, *The Making of a Drum Company* (Rebeats Press, 2001).

For my purposes here, suffice it to say that Harry was just one of the many drummers in town who thought Bill had gotten a raw deal and began to give him their business. Remembering how Harry and Bill used to kid around, I tracked him down to see if he had any "Harry tales" I hadn't heard, and he didn't disappoint me.

Without a moment's hesitation he said, "I still remember the time Harry called and told me he needed two timpani delivered to the Drake

Hotel for a job he was playing. Of course I knew the drums had been delivered to the right room in the hotel long before they were actually needed. So you can imagine how I felt when Harry called me two hours before the job, saying he was at the Palmer House, ready to go, but where the hell were the timpani?

"I panicked because I knew there was no way on earth that I could get those timpani to the job in time. You'd have to understand the layout of both hotels to understand this, but basically you had to drag the drums through the kitchen of the Drake in order to get to the dining room where they were needed. So reversing this process, and then trying to get across the street (where parking was impossible), and then through the Palmer House's tricky door setup would have taken way more than two hours' time. It simply couldn't be done."

I had never heard this story, but the punch line didn't surprise me a bit as Bill concluded, "As I envisioned what this kind of mistake could do to my business reputation and was about to have a heart attack, Harry laughed and said he was just putting me on. He was at the Drake and the drums were there. I should have known better. He was just being his usual mischievous self."

♪ Historical Sidenote ♪

Franks Drum Shop went bankrupt in 1984, at which time Bill Crowden bought the business name. His business thrived until Chicago's changing music scene prompted him to close up shop in 1991.

CHAPTER 8

The Chicago Symphony Years

There are only two men in the world I hate, and
Fritz Reiner is both of them.—Harry

There's an old joke about how to get to Carnegie Hall, with the punch line being "practice." In addition to years of practice, Harry worked his way up to the Chicago Symphony Orchestra (CSO) gradually and steadily, first by being an exceptional music student and contest winner as a child in grade school, then by excelling on the snare drum and marimba while in Morton's high school bands and orchestra and winning one rudimental drum and marimba contest after another.

Nurtured and encouraged by the best teachers in a school that was regularly producing outstanding musicians, Harry was recommended fresh out of high school in 1944 for acceptance into the Civic Orchestra, the CSO's training orchestra. After one season there, he joined the Chuck Foster Orchestra for about a year and a half before joining the National Symphony Orchestra in Washington, D.C. for three years (1946–1949).

As I understand it, one got a job like this because someone recommended him. Word would go out that there was an opening in this or that section, and someone in a position of power would recommend a musician, and the way through the door was paved.

The National Symphony Orchestra

The National Symphony Orchestra, founded in 1931, performs at the John F. Kennedy Center for the Performing Arts in Washington, D.C. For the first period of its history, however, the orchestra performed in

Constitution Hall. Symphony historian Norman Schweikert confirmed Harry's tenure with the National Symphony and included interesting information that wasn't in his files.

While there, Harry worked with conductor Hans Kindler. During Kindler's tenure, the musicians received a salary of $40 a week for three rehearsals and one concert. The regular season ran five months from October to April, but there was also a summer season called "Watergate" that began in June and ran for about five weeks. Conductors for the Watergate season while Harry was in the Orchestra included Richard Bales (noted composer and conductor of the National Gallery Orchestra in D.C.) and Howard Mitchell (cellist and conductor of the Orchestra between 1950 and 1969).

Harry and I didn't talk much about his time in Washington, except that he said those years were happy ones and that he made a lot of friends there, but he was so wrapped up in music then that he spent very little time seeing the city's historic sights. We finally got to see the city together years later on one of our trips east.

In December 1995, Harry wrote to his old friends, Les and Betty Tichnor: "Can you believe that it will be fifty years this summer that we walked up that gangplank of the Watergate barge and developed a friendship that has lasted this long? Ah . . . memories of Henderson Castle. Well, I won't become too nostalgic, but those were some happy days, even if we didn't realize it at the time."

Four years later he wrote to Betty, newly widowed: "You two gave me so many wonderful memories. Your befriending of that tall skinny kid fresh from the Big Band to the National Symphony was certainly a high point in my musical life. Here were these two wonderful people—from New York, no less—that were the epitome of sophistication, allowing me into their circle of life and giving me a feeling of friendship and security."

It was in Washington that Harry also met percussionists Charles Owen, Boyd Conway, and Ollie Zinsmeister, all of whom had a long career in the United States Marine Band. They would introduce him to music that he would listen to and love throughout his life. I know little about Harry's friendship with Conway and Owen, except that I often heard him speak their names with fondness, and I know he played with both of them, and Ollie, too, in the Windjammers Circus Band after they had all retired.

In one of Harry's letters to Ollie at that time, he wrote, "Charlie and I were the two snare drummers who played the circus, and after finishing it Charlie turned to me and said, 'Boy that's a lotta work!' I thought that was funny, coming from an old pro like him. We did have a good time that day."

I knew Ollie personally, having met him once when Harry and I heard him play a solo with the Naperville Municipal Band. He was a great xylophonist who retired from the Marine Band ("The President's Own") in 1955, and he and Harry had a spirited correspondence exchange in their later years (see Chapter 14).

Rafael Kubelik and Harry

Rafael Kubelík (1914–1996) was one of Harry's favorite conductors. He made his American debut with the Chicago Symphony Orchestra in November 1949 as the Orchestra's fifth music director. Harry joined the orchestra in 1951. He greatly admired Kubelik and felt a kinship with him because they were both Czech, and also because Kubelik appointed him Principal Percussionist a year after he joined the Orchestra.

In Harry's LP collection, I found Kubelik's warmly written inscription on the record Harry had of him as conductor of Smetana's *Ma Vlast* with the Vienna Philharmonic. It was given in January 1969 when Harry was Stage Manager of the Orchestra. Kubelik had returned to the Chicago Symphony as guest conductor to once again conduct *Ma Vlast*, which he had recorded with the Symphony in 1952 when Harry was his principal percussionist. (Harry was never able to acquire the original album on the Naxos label, but he did have a Mercury reissue of the original CSO recording in which he played snare drum.) You can imagine, then, the great pleasure Harry had in once again being able to see one of his favorite conductors after so many years, and share backstage nostalgic remembrances and perhaps a chuckle or two.

I know Kubelik had a sense of humor because, in one of Harry's letters to a Czech friend, he said how much he regretted that he had never learned to speak Czech, adding that Kubelik would often say things to him in Czech knowing full well he didn't understand him, "but it was all done in good humor."

I remember one tambourine story Harry used to tell, but I forget the conductor involved and the piece he was playing at the time. I *think* the music may have been Dvorak's *Carnival Overture* because this piece has a big tambourine part in it, with lots of loud jingling and thumping going on. And I think the conductor had to be Kubelik because even Harry wouldn't have pulled this stunt if Reiner had the baton for he was a man with no sense of humor at all.

Harry said he was playing his part beautifully, holding the tambourine high with his left hand so the audience could see it being played, and hitting it with his clenched right fist. *Bam, bam BAM!* And that's when his hand broke through the head and came out past the rim. He told me he just froze in that position for an instant—and then smiled, opened his fist, and waggled his fingers at the conductor before quickly putting the broken instrument down and grabbing the spare that was always kept handy, just in case. Sam Denov told me this wasn't the first time a percussionist had blasted through a tambourine head in this particular number, but you can be sure that Harry was the first and only one nervy enough to waggle his fingers at the conductor when it happened.

Legendary Brabec-Reiner Stories

Harry's years with the Chicago Symphony during the fifties were the highlight of his symphonic musical life, but unlike most of his friends who went into the Symphony and stayed there for thirty or forty years, his career was short-lived, thanks to Fritz Reiner.

He was very unhappy when Kubelik left in 1953 and Reiner took his place, but he had no idea of all the misery this man was going to bring to his life. For some reason, Reiner decided he didn't like Harry. He picked on everyone, of course, but I think Harry was one of the few men in the orchestra who gave tit for tat in confrontations with him, and Reiner had such a huge ego he couldn't stand being bested by anyone. Harry might have been with the CSO all his life if he had been content to just fade into the background and not make waves, but that just wasn't his nature. One thing led to another and, after five years of being an outstanding symphony performer, Harry's contract wasn't renewed simply because Fritz Reiner had personal reasons for wanting him gone.

In his book, *Symphonic Paradox: The Misadventures of a Wayward Musician* (1st Books Library), Sam Denov notes that Harry was the lone survivor of the pre-Reiner Kubelik era in the orchestra's percussion section, and that the percussionist chosen to replace him didn't last long. "It was Reiner's cavalier methods of hiring and firing musicians, among other matters, that led up to the problems that surfaced a few years later and forever changed the profession of symphony musicians in America."

The Harry-Reiner stories are still remembered today among classical musicians and percussionists of that era, and Sam included two of my favorite stories in his book that he gave me permission to reprint. His book opens with the story of how he came to be in the Chicago Symphony under the baton of Fritz Reiner, and then talks about how Reiner "would descend on any musician without warning, just to have some personal demonic fun, and in the process, keep all the others on their toes. One never knew when it was going to be his 'turn in the barrel' as it came to be called, because it was like being a duck that was in a barrel; an easy target, so to speak."

From here, Sam leads into the first of his Harry-Reiner stories:

Reiner was always able to respond to any situation because of his enormous intellect and limitless memory. On very rare occasions, however, he could be fooled. He had an almost infallible ability to recall just about everything he had ever been exposed to. To attempt to put one over on this man was to risk your career. But my friend and section leader, Harry Brabec, actually tried it and for a time, got away with it.

Every Wednesday evening during the winter season, there was a television show that was broadcast by the Chicago Tribune's *TV outlet, WGN, Channel 9. It was called* Great Music from Chicago *and was syndicated throughout the nation. It featured a reduced Chicago Symphony Orchestra with Reiner or other guest conductors. These shows required the CSO musicians who actually played the show to travel up Michigan Avenue from Orchestra Hall to the WGN studios. The larger instruments were transported by truck, including a trunk full of the percussion equipment needed for the particular show.*

On this occasion, the program included Tchaikovsky's Nut- cracker Suite. *A single player, for the most part, could perform all the percussion parts. The rehearsal, which was scheduled immediately before the broadcast, started with the Suite's "Overture Miniature." The only percussion part called for a triangle.*

As soon as Brabec started to play the triangle part, Reiner stopped the music and inquired, "Where did you get that garden variety triangle? Don't you have something bigger?"

The con began when Brabec answered, "Of course, Dr. Reiner!" He then called offstage to me to go to the trunk and get the larger triangle. That order to me was just loud enough for Reiner to hear it. I immediately went to the hallway outside of the studio and rummaged through the trunk looking for a larger triangle. I panicked when I couldn't find one.

I called in to Brabec from just offstage and reported in a stage whisper that I couldn't find a larger triangle. He nodded to me and whispered, "I know!" I couldn't imagine what was going to happen next.

The next passage in the music that called for the triangle found Brabec holding up the same instrument he had used before. The difference this time was that he held it up very high so Reiner could clearly see it, as if to say that "Here is the triangle you wanted." Reiner looked at Brabec and threw him a salute for having complied with his request. And it worked. A salute from Reiner was about as good a compliment as any musician ever received.

This story illustrates why I dubbed Harry a "daring improviser." He was never at a loss for what to do next, but sometimes he acted without thinking about the possible consequences of his actions. Sometimes he was lucky; sometimes he wasn't.

Of course I heard this story many times, but Harry always told it a bit differently. He took delight in imitating Reiner, and a fellow musician actually caught one of these little performances on tape when the Symphony was playing a concert as part of the unveiling ceremonies for the *Picasso Sculpture* in Chicago in 1967. Harry would always lower his glasses on his nose, bend his head to look over them, and then give an "evil eye" look as he said in his best thick-accented Reiner voice, *"Brahbetz, vhat is dat tinkle, tinkle noise you're making?"* And then he would tell this story pretty much the same way Sam told it in his book.

Duane Thamm, a well-known Chicago jazz vibist, shared this interesting Reiner story, which Harry may well have been remembering when he pulled his triangle bluff. (Like Harry, Duane studied timpani with Edward Metzenger.)

"Metzenger told me about the time Reiner was picking on him about the timpani mallets he was using for a particular number. Reiner didn't like the sound he was getting, so he asked him to try another pair. During the rehearsal, Metzenger kept changing mallets, with Reiner liking none of them. Finally, he just picked up the original pair again and was amazed when Reiner said that was exactly the sound he was looking for."

This is just one more example of how Reiner often picked on different orchestra members, depending on his mood that particular day.

Following is another Fritz Reiner story from Sam Denov's book that I heard Harry tell many times.

A Shotgun Confrontation

From time to time, Reiner began picking on Brabec for what most would consider insignificant problems. Brabec got a strong hint that his days were numbered when, on one occasion, he came into Reiner's backstage dressing room with an unloaded shotgun slung over his arm.

As Brabec entered, he asked, "Dr. Reiner, would you like us to use these shotguns for the cannon shots in the 1812 Overture?" That had been the traditional method in Chicago of simulating the cannon shots required by Tchaikovsky's score. Blank cartridges were fired backstage into an empty large steel oil drum.

Reiner, who was sitting in an overstuffed armchair, looked up at Brabec and the gun over his half-moon glasses, and replied, "No I don't think so. The Overture is noisy enough without the guns. Besides, I don't trust you!"

When Harry told this story he always did his best Reiner imitation at the end—first lowering his glasses on his nose, bending his head to look over them—and then inserting a dramatic story-teller's pause just before saying, "Besides . . . *I don't trust you.*"

In his book, Sam said that Harry was stunned by that remark, and that it signaled to him that the handwriting was on the wall. I take exception to that. Sam told me he wasn't actually in the room with Harry during this exchange with Reiner, but that Harry had come out and immediately told this story to him and several others in his usual humorous fashion, making light of it. Given Harry's sense of humor, he certainly would have found this encounter amusing. Of course he knew Reiner had him in his sights, but given his years of outstanding performance, he never expected to be let go over a personality clash with this man.

The Story Behind the Story

It was only when I began to interview many of Harry's old school chums and fellow musicians and connected with trumpeter Frank Kaderabek that I learned the *real* reason Harry lost his job with the Symphony. Frank joined the Chicago Symphony in 1958 and he was there through the end of the 1966 season. As he and I were talking about Harry, he startled me when he asked if I knew the real reason Harry had lost this job. I said I thought it was simply because Reiner didn't like him for some reason, and that Harry thought this, too. But Frank said there was much more to it than that.

"When I first came into the orchestra and was talking to the orchestra's principal trumpet player, I said, 'Is that the guy that replaced Harry? For chrissakes, he couldn't shine Harry's shoes in a month.' And that's when I learned that Harry's replacement was a buddy of Reiner's— someone who had played in a couple of orchestras with him before—and someone he wanted to get into the percussion section. The only way to do that, of course, was get rid of someone, and Harry was his target. He already didn't like him because Harry wasn't afraid to stand up to him, but he needed a good excuse to fire him. So one day he set Harry up when they were rehearsing the 'Arabian Dance' from the *Nutcracker Suite*. Harry was playing tambourine and Reiner told him he wasn't playing it right, that he wanted it played in a certain way, using his thumb, holding the tambourine up, and making the thumb go down the tambourine.

"But Harry knew this was an outlandish idea," Frank continued, "and said this part couldn't be played like that. Even a trumpet player like me knew that percussionists usually laid the tambourine on a table for this part and tapped it with their hands. But Reiner had come up with this ridiculous idea so he could complain that Harry wouldn't do what he told him to do. Several others in the orchestra confirmed this story, so I know it's true. In those days, everyone in the orchestra was petrified of Reiner because they never knew who he was going to pick on next, and no one would stand up to him because they didn't want to lose their jobs. Because Harry wouldn't play the tambourine part the way Reiner wanted it, he now had an excuse to fire him. 'He didn't play to my satisfaction,' he said.

"It was a great loss to the orchestra that Harry was no longer there," Frank concluded. "He was a top-notch professional and very attentive to the job. He told me how much he loved being in the orchestra, even with an idiot like Reiner. To be pushed out so unfairly was devastating to Harry, and this was obvious to everybody, but they were too scared to speak up."

Since Harry never told me this story, I don't think he ever knew that his replacement was a buddy of Reiner's. As you will soon learn, he was too disheartened to even talk to his friends in the orchestra after his contract wasn't renewed. In checking the tenure of the percussionist that replaced Harry, I found that his starting and ending date was 1957. I remain convinced that Harry always believed he lost this job simply because Reiner hated him. But for a conductor to ace a fine musician like Harry out of his job just to bring in a friend of his was beyond the pale. When I heard this story I didn't know whether to cry or thank God Harry got fired, because if he had stayed in the orchestra I never would have known him.

A Mentor to Many

An astonishing thing I didn't know about Harry until after he was gone was that he had always done in his profession exactly what I've always tried to do in mine, which is to help others. The difference, however, is that I have always received wonderful feedback from readers who have told me how much my books and teaching has helped them, whereas few (if any) of Harry's musician friends ever told him just how much they appreciated all he had done for them, or how much his friendship had meant to them through the years.

I guess it's just not in a man's nature to express such feelings to a fellow musician, and I never would have known about these things if I hadn't put up memorial pages for Harry on my personal domain that attracted some of his old school chums and drummer friends who hadn't been in touch with him for decades. Several sent me wonderful e-mails and letters, sharing stories about Harry and telling me how much he had helped them up the musical ladder of success.

In writing this book, I made a concerted effort to track down others who knew and worked with him, many of whom confirmed that, without Harry's encouragement in school and/or recommendations for jobs after he'd achieved a position of power in the music industry, they might never have become professional musicians or made the kind of contacts they needed for success.

"Harry's reputation as a drummer in high school was legend," wrote Gordon Peters in an article in *The Intermezzo*. "He set high precedents for me, and he was the ideal role model. He suggested what teacher to go to and when: Roy Knapp, Otto Kristufek, Jose Bethancourt, Clair Omar Musser. He studied with them and, of course, I followed his path and advice. By introducing me to Franks Drum Shop, which was like 'Percussion Central,' and to the percussion instrument companies (Deagan, Ludwig, Slingerland), he helped connect me to 'the profession,' and I followed him right into the Chicago Symphony Orchestra. As one who partook in a slice of Harry's life of generosity, caring, patience, dedication, and mentoring, I wonder where my life's trail would have led me without him. I am most indebted and grateful for his faith and friendship. I owe him as do many others."

Adds Sam Denov, "Harry was a very important person in the lives of many musicians, particularly mine. He was responsible for my career in the Chicago Symphony Orchestra."

Harry's great friend, Fred Wickstrom, now retired as founder and chairman of the Percussion Program at the University of Miami, still maintains a freelance performing career in symphonic, pop, and ethnic music. I asked him to tell me how he and Harry ever got together in the first place.

"Harry, my mentor, transformed me from a dance band/show band musician to a percussionist. In the early to mid-fifties I kept running into Harry at Franks Drum Shop, the mecca at that time of drummers in Chicago. Each time I met him I asked the same question, 'Can I study with you?' Each time I got the same answer, 'I don't teach.' Finally one time he asked me what I wanted to learn. My reply was 'triangle, tambourine, castanets,' the toys. I think he must have been so tired of people wanting to learn xylophone, snare drum, and timpani, and they didn't realize (as he did) that playing the small instruments was one's first entry into a symphonic percussion section.

"Our 'lessons' took place in the basement of Orchestra Hall after the Friday matinee. His payment . . . I bought the beer. When I needed to learn something about cymbals he bowed out and turned me over to Sam Denov. Eventually we did work on mallets and snare drum, and I received training on timpani in a more structured setting with Ed Metzenger in Civic Orchestra sectionals. But it was Harry's wonderful mentoring that changed the direction of my life and gave me skills I could use in a lifetime of performance, plus insights that I was then able to pass on to my own students.

"I have often told this story to my students. It was about when Harry coached me on the tam-tam part of *Pictures at an Exhibition*. Without a cue from a different conductor at one performance, I froze at one entrance. I can still hear that voice in the background quietly calling, "Hit it . . . *hit it* . . . *HIT THE GODDAMN THING!*'"

Fred concluded his remembrances by saying, "I once heard Harry play timpani in the pit at Ravinia for ballet. Most timpanists tend to bend over, tap the drum and listen closely when making a pitch change. Harry never did that; he just continued to play, never looked down and always was *perfectly* in tune. He taught at North Park College for a while and told me that one of his students came up with the saying that percussion was the 'icing on the cake.' Not a bad way to look at it."

Rich Sherrill was one of Harry's students in 1972 after he'd left Disney but was still in the Orlando area. His story is typical of how Harry helped young percussionists advance in their profession.

"I was a senior at Oklahoma University in 1972 lacking only a few hours to graduate when I got into Disney's All American College Band," he told me. "This was to be just a summer job for me that year, but it proved to be far more important than that. When I learned that a former Chicago Symphony percussionist had been in the band and was still in the area, I tracked him down and asked if I could study with him. My goal was to get into a symphony orchestra. In fact, I had previously, and very naively, sent my resume to about fifty symphony orchestras across the country basically telling them 'here I am, ready to play in your symphony as soon as I graduate.' I didn't understand the audition system, so of course I didn't get a single response to any of those letters.

"So I start studying with Harry, and those lessons were literally life-changing for me. All of my earlier teachers were kind of mechanical in their teaching methods, and their instruction never went outside what the lesson was supposed to be about. But with Harry, the actual mechanics of the lesson might take only half the hour, and the rest of the lesson would be about life and the realities of the music business. Basically, he not only taught me the rudiments of percussion, but the rudiments of life as a musician. He made me see that you could be the world's greatest percussionist, but if you didn't understand how the music business worked and what you had to do and who you had to get to know to get ahead in it, you were nowhere."

Rich went on to say that this was only part of what Harry had done for him, that he got into the Florida Symphony simply because he knew Harry. "I didn't have to audition or anything. Unbeknownst to me, one day he called the personnel manager of the Florida Symphony, Victor Ligotti, and recommended me for the orchestra. I was told to come to this man's home for an interview, and I went there thinking I was going to have an audition at that time. But we just talked, and he said I was okay because Harry *said* I was okay. That was HUGE to me. I can't tell you how big it was to me to get into that orchestra at that time. I ended

up as principal percussionist and Harry just *gave that to me*. I don't
think he ever realized the great impact he had on other people's lives. All
my practicing and the letter I had sent to the Florida Symphony couldn't
get me that job, but Harry just put that gift on a platter and handed it to
me. How can you ever repay someone for that?"

Of course Harry never expected more than a simple thank you for
his help, and even then, he would just shrug it off as being nothing; he
was just happy to do it. We never talked about this, but I see now that he
was a great believer in "passing it on." Many people had helped him
advance in his career, and I'm sure he felt it was only right to repay that
debt by helping other musicians whenever he could. One didn't have to
be a percussionist, of course. Since Harry made new friends wherever he
went, he knew people in all areas of the music and entertainment business. If he couldn't personally help someone, he usually knew someone
else who could, and he would go out of his way to connect them.

More Stories from Fellow Musicians

It was heartwarming to learn that Harry had given younger drummers
lessons in high school, encouraged them to think seriously about music
as a profession, and was a torch-bearer they all admired and followed. If
he had talked as much about himself as I talked about myself during our
married life, I might have learned these things while he was still alive.
But Harry never bragged about his achievements, even to me. I've joked
in my home business books about how hard he had to work to help me
keep my ego in check as I became known as an author and "personality"
in my field. Whenever I began to pat myself on the back too much, Harry
would just tsk-tsk me and say with a look of husbandly reprimand in his
eyes, "SPS, Barbara . . . SPS," which was his abbreviation for "self praise
stinks." He not only believed that; he lived it.

I remember one night when he got home from a concert in Milwaukee and I asked him how it went. "Pretty good," he said. "The
conductor liked my work and I had fun playing." Years later I got the full
story from Joel Cohen, one of Harry's closest music buddies and a
percussionist who sometimes performed with him.

"Up in Milwaukee, the orchestra was rehearsing *Alexander Nevsky*.
As usual, Harry was at the bass drum. There's a lot of percussion in
Nevsky, as well as six percussionists. At some point in a rehearsal, the
conductor, James Paul, stopped to call out, 'The gentleman at the bass
drum . . . that is the finest bass drumming I've ever heard.' What made

this comment really special was that none of the regular members of the section had been complimented during the rehearsal and, as I remember, none of us had been complimented all season (at least up to that point), so for an 'extra' to get recognized at the expense of the regulars was quite unique."

Joel also shared this story about Harry's snare drum playing: "The year Harry and I did the Bensenville Band concerts (probably 1977 or 1978) was the first time I got to hear him play snare drum. Previous to this, whenever we worked together, he was almost always on bass drum or triangle. At one of the band concerts, Harry was playing on the drum set and there was some piece, probably Shostakovich, where he had some simple snare drum part. But there was one note that he played, a four-stroke ruff that made me sit up and pay attention. There was more excitement in that one figure than I had ever heard out of a snare drum. I still can hear it today. "

I was touched by Joel's other comment about Harry at that time: "He was the only person I could talk to about all the ridiculous things that seemed to land on me in this wacky music business world who would understand and keep the info confidential."

Duane Thamm was in school at the same time as Harry, though not at Morton. "We met at one of the drum contests we were participating in and formed a friendship," he recalls. "After we had both graduated, Harry came to see me when I was playing vibes and drums in a nightclub, and he talked me into studying more then and joining the Civic Orchestra. Years later when he was playing the Shubert he called and asked if I wanted to sub for him. Of course that meant just stepping into the chair without a rehearsal. As I sat there and watched him play chimes and bells with one hand while he was playing something else with the other hand, I told him I just couldn't do that. He was really a great talent."

"I was a student of Gordon Peters in the late 50s and early 60s," wrote Jim Gordon, who said he hadn't seen Harry since he left Chicago in 1966 to move to Detroit. "When I first started playing extra with the CSO, Harry was also doing quite a bit of extra work with the orchestra. He was very kind to me, making me feel at home in a world where I was sure I didn't belong. We often played next to each other and his experience and performance tips were a part of the reason that I was on the top of the CSO extra list for more than thirty years. I remember some of his stories fondly, and also his 'lumberjack' shirts, which he often wore to rehearsals."

Frank Kaderabek, who was three years behind Harry at Morton High and one of those who received encouragement from him, said he idolized Harry and looked to him as a big brother. Frank played only one job with Harry, and it was one he got because Harry recommended him for it. "It was a state fair in Pueblo, Colorado, and they took a band out from Chicago. I had just finished at Grant Park and they needed a substitute, so I got hired. Harry and I roomed together and we had a good time. He was always the best damn drummer anywhere and you indeed can be very proud of him. For those of us that worked with him and knew him, he will always leave a mark. He was an outstanding musician and, above all, a fine gentleman with great professional traits. Reiner was an absolute idiot to pick on him. I played in the Chicago Symphony for eight years, four with Reiner, and I was glad to leave. I didn't like it there. It always seemed the nice people got the raw end of the deal in that place."

Recordings Made with Fritz Reiner

Harry made several recordings while he was with the Chicago Symphony, plus a couple of classic percussion albums and other recordings for several other bands. One day I asked him to make a list for me of the instruments he was playing in each of the symphony and percussion albums so I could always listen for his playing when he was gone. (See Appendix for a list of all known recordings he made.). What follows are Harry's stories about three of the CSO recordings, all done on the RCA Victor label:

• **Bartok Concerto for Orchestra.** This recording of Fritz Reiner conducting the Chicago Symphony has been reissued a few times since its original release in the mid-fifties. Harry was about 25 at the time he made this recording with Reiner, and he said this piece was one of the hardest things for a snare drummer to play, at least sensitively.

Picture this: they have already done the movement a couple of times now because other musicians have screwed up. Then, on the next run-through, Harry misses one of the last notes at the end.

Reiner stops, glares at Harry, and roars, "Now we have to do it all over again because of YOU!"

"By now," Harry said, "the whole orchestra is on pins and needles and I'm scared shit."

But he played it perfectly that time and, as he told me this story, I could almost hear the intense sigh of relief he and the rest of the orchestra must have heaved at that point. Later, Harry said, the guys in the orchestra dubbed him "The Iron Man." So, if you ever listen to this album, you'll need quiet to appreciate the beauty of his playing. And when you get to the end, try to imagine how he must have felt as he played this piece "under Reiner's gun."

Maybe this is what Harry was remembering when he stuck this quotation by Omar Bradley on his bulletin board: "Bravery is the capacity to perform properly even when scared half to death."

• **The Benny Goodman "Chicago" Recording.** In one of Harry's letters to Doug MacLeod, I found a mention of this particular recording which, according to the LP album notes, was recorded June 18, 1966 in Orchestra Hall. "We did this one for some special Symphony celebration," Harry wrote. "That's me thumping on the snare drum—what you can hear of it."

During the writing of this book, I learned that Morton Gould had made another recording with Benny Goodman around this time where Goodman performed a classical piece for clarinet. The drummer who made that recording reported to music buddies that Benny Goodman—the "King of Swing"—couldn't keep a beat or follow Gould's lead in this recording. "Both the conductor and the orchestra eventually had to give up and follow Goodman's lead," he said.

• **Concerto for Jazz Band and Symphony Orchestra.** This album was recorded in 1954. In one of Harry's letters, he wrote, "That's me playing all the 'legit' snare drum. The drum solo was played by 'Mousie' Alexander, a good jazz drummer originally from Chicago. He got his nickname because he was such a short guy. During the rehearsals he would call Fritz Reiner 'Doc,' which really broke us up. We had a lot of fun doing this album."

As for all the Harry-Reiner stories in this chapter, I can almost hear Harry saying, "No, no, you've got it all wrong. Here's how it actually happened." But even badly told, I think the tales about Harry and Fritz Reiner are worth documenting for posterity and, as Harry often added, "for ma's terity, too." I have vague recollections of other Harry-Reiner stories, but memory fades. I wish so much that I had taped Harry telling some of these stories, but after awhile I just took them for granted, never thinking ahead to him being gone some day and me wanting to hear the stories again first-hand. And of course I certainly never thought then that I'd ever write a book about my legendary drummer husband.

What was it about Harry that made him a legend in his own time? Certainly he wasn't famous the way the leading big band and jazz musicians were. He was no head-bobbing, arms-waving drummer like Buddy Rich or Gene Krupa. He kept his drumsticks close, hated to play a solo, and did everything possible to avoid drawing attention to himself when he was playing. Offstage, however, he was a powerful presence no one could ignore, and not everyone could easily tolerate. When Fritz Reiner dismissed Harry from the Orchestra, his name and his run-ins with this conductor became legend, not only among symphony musicians, but younger percussionists as well.

When Harry was invited to participate in the 35th annual Peninsula Music Festival in Door County, Wisconsin in July of 1987, he had an interesting experience after the concert when the other percussionists and the timpani player had gathered like boys around a campfire to tell music tales. Harry was surprisingly quiet because he was still coming back from the open heart surgery he'd had in May and was feeling rather like "the old man" of the bunch. But he soon perked up when one of the guys told a story about this percussionist with the Chicago Symphony who once pulled a fast one on Fritz Reiner where a triangle was concerned. Harry chuckled and quietly said, "I was that drummer." For the next hour, everyone listened with rapt attention as this legendary drummer regaled them with one story after another.

When I heard from Tommy Wetzel, associate principal timpanist with the Milwaukee Symphony who had worked with Harry, I asked if he had any Harry stories to share with me. He said no, but added, "When I think of Harry, it's the stories *he* would tell that makes me remember him as the wonderful character he was. I will always remember him as a great guy, a fun person to work with, and a pleasure to know."

Other Fritz Reiner Stories

Gordon Peters came into the orchestra after Harry left, and he remembers this Reiner story: "In a Gershwin piece they were playing (possibly *Porgy and Bess*), Reiner suddenly stopped the orchestra and said that he wanted to hear a 'sheep's bell' at that point. No one knew what he was talking about, but when Reiner said to go find one, Harry started searching for a 'sheep's bell' by going to Franks Drum Shop and digging around in the 'bell bin.' Every drummer had cowbells, of course, but sheep's bells? Finally someone, probably Maurie Lishon, suggested that with Reiner's thick accent, perhaps what he wanted here was a *ship's* bell. Of course! From there, it was easy to meet the maestro's demands.

I picked up a couple of interesting Reiner stories while talking to Everett Zlatoff-Mirsky, who explained how the audition process worked for symphony musicians in the fifties when Reiner was there.

"John Weicher was with the Symphony from 1923 to 1969 first as Personnel Manager and Concertmaster and, later, Principal Second. As Personnel Manager, his job was to scout for new musicians. He'd go around to all the studios and pit orchestras in the Chicago Theatre, the Shubert, and other places to watch musicians play. Then he'd pick out those he liked and hire them on a trial basis. If they passed Reiner's audition, they were in.

"One audition story I heard was about Harry Sturm (cello, 1956–1962). Reiner wanted him and asked Weicher to hire him. At that time, musicians weren't given a list of music in advance like they are today. They just put stuff down in front of you and you were expected to be able to sight-read it. When Sturm auditioned for Reiner, he played one piece after another perfectly, to the point where Reiner got mad because he couldn't shake this guy. So he asked the librarian to pull out the most obscure piece of handwritten manuscript in their collection and put this piece of music in front of Sturm after he'd already been playing for two hours. It was discolored with age and almost in tatters. Sturm took one look at it, got up, and walked off the stage saying, 'No one, Dr. Reiner, makes a fool of me.'

"And Reiner said, 'Stop! You're hired.' Reiner never again bothered Sturm. He wanted a great player who would never crack under the most extreme conditions.

"Reiner was a truly unpleasant person," Everett adds, remembering all the stories he heard about him through the years. "In fact, he drove one musician insane, a principal flautist who left the orchestra in 1958 after years of being ridden mercilessly by Reiner (name withheld for privacy). He ended up in a mental institution."

Rich Sherrill shared this story he heard about a cello opening in the CSO. (Whether it's connected to the above cello opening or not is anyone's guess.) An orchestra member introduced a prospective cellist to Reiner saying, "Mr. Reiner, he's a really nice guy." To which Reiner replied, "I don't care if he's nice or not, just get me an SOB that can play the cello."

Another story Rich remembers hearing was when the CSO was on tour one time and traveling by train. An anonymous musician yelled "Stop the train! Reiner's grave is just over there and I want to get out and piss on it."

That sounds like something Harry would have said, but these words could have come from the mouth of any one of a dozen other musicians who hated Reiner with a vengeance for the way he had picked on them.

"There are only two men in the world I hate," Harry often said, "and Fritz Reiner is both of them." I know . . . it doesn't make literal sense, but it illustrates Harry's intense feelings for the man who so dramatically changed his life at the peak of his career. Given Harry's hatred for Reiner, I found it curious that he bought the book, *Fritz Reiner* by Philip Hart (Northwestern Univ. Press, 1994). Perhaps he was still trying to figure out all those years later why this man disliked him so much.

The Painful Aftermath

This chapter has included several humorous and legendary stories about Fritz Reiner and Harry, but now it's time to tell you "the rest of this story." And the first part of it is not at all funny.

One day when I was searching the Web for mentions of Harry, I turned up a musician's post about the tribute I had done for him on my website at BarbaraBrabec.com. The writer, identified only as Vaneyes, called my tribute to Harry a "four-part story of love, humor and (especially) adaptation," adding, "Harry was a percussionist for the Chicago Symphony Orchestra. He didn't get along with Fritz. Not an uncommon story."

Later, I turned up a reader's response to the above post that read: "I have not had a chance to read it all yet but it's a wonderful tribute to him, and I thank you for drawing attention to it. He sounds as if he was what is known in the trade as a survivor."

That reader didn't know the half of it. Harry was not only a survivor, but a man who was pushed to the brink on more than one occasion and managed to bounce back each time.

Three Punches to the Gut

After more than a decade of success in his chosen career, you can imagine how emotionally devastated Harry was when Fritz Reiner cast him out of the orchestra—so discouraged, in fact, that he just laid down his sticks for a couple of years and did a variety of odd jobs just to make a buck. He never spoke much about how he felt during those two years of his life except to say he was miserable, and I am only now putting things together here. Because we were so happy together, he didn't want to talk about his first marriage to Doris and this distressing period of his life. I didn't push him for details then, although now I wish I had because this is a big hole in his life that I know little about.

I do recall some of the stories he told me about his ditch-digging days and working on a road construction crew, being a plumber's helper, and doing a stint as a salesman for Proctor & Gamble, where he found himself selling soap out in the boonies. Not surprisingly, he quickly became one of the company's top salesmen. But of course he couldn't make himself do this kind of work for long. Music kept calling to him and, sometime in 1959, he was hired as staff percussionist for the NBC Studio Orchestra in Chicago. It was too little too late to save his marriage, however.

After being in and out of work for so long, the problems that had been developing for some time came to a head, and Doris decided this was a good time to dump him. She filed for divorce that year and took their six-year old daughter Bonnie Jo with her. Losing the Symphony job, and then seeing his marriage end after eight years was a hard enough one-two punch to Harry's gut, but the knockout punch came while the divorce was being finalized in late 1959. He had taken a music job out of town, and when he returned home to pick up his personal possessions, he found the house completely empty. Doris was apparently so angry with him at that point that she sold some of his possessions and put everything else he owned out for garbage pickup. I never could understand how she could have done something like that.

Suddenly, everything was gone. His job, his career, his wife, his daughter, and every material thing he owned, except for what he had taken out of town with him. All the instruments and drum equipment he had left behind, all his music, books, records, scrapbooks, photo albums, school medals, tools, clothes . . . *every material possession he had acquired over a period of 32 years*—gone.

Kaput.

Totally beaten at that point, his spirit crushed, Harry simply gave up.

CHAPTER 9

Taking another Chance on Love and Music

Hope for the best, expect the worst.
Life is a play. We're unrehearsed.
—Mel Brooks, comedian, producer, director

In the summer of 1961, while I was busy working a part-time secretarial job at the Harding Restaurant Company and pursuing my little part-time music career, Harry once again found himself performing with the Chicago Symphony as an extra man working alongside Gordon Peters, his old school chum from Morton, then the orchestra's principal percussionist and, coincidentally, the man I had been dating that summer.

Gordon always went to Maine in August to study conducting with Pierre Monteux, but before he left this time, he suggested that Harry call me, saying I looked enough like him to be his sister. Curious, Harry picked up the phone and asked me to dinner. In truth, Gordon thought he and I were getting a bit too serious and he figured Harry would be a good distraction for me. Yep, I was distracted all right. When Gordon returned from Maine, he learned what a good matchmaker he was.

Harry brought to our marriage little more than what he had taken with him on that job during his divorce, plus a few things he had picked up while living out of a suitcase for two years. Basically, his possessions included a little drum equipment, his jobbing clothes and a few other garments, his mother's Bible, and a pair of channel locks, which he apparently considered an essential drummer's tool. He also brought to the marriage debts that totaled several thousand dollars from unpaid hospital bills, child support, and more.

Bit by bit, I began to learn more about Harry's life before I knew him. By 1960, he was once again back in music full time, but he was still an emotional wreck, still trying to come to terms with the loss of his wife, daughter, and symphony career. He was playing again, but his heart yearned to be back in the Chicago Symphony where he once thought he would have a career for life. After we were married, he told me he really didn't give a damn about anything after his divorce other than playing. He was eating poorly, drinking too much, smoking too much, and eventually ended up in the hospital with ulcers. I remember the stories he told me about that period of his life when he was making money hand over fist doing recordings and transcriptions at NBC, and just throwing the checks in a drawer because he didn't have time to cash them. When he did cash them, he didn't pay his bills, make his child support payments, or file tax returns for 1959 and 1960—something I prompted him to take care of as soon as I learned about this.

Rather than declare bankruptcy, we agreed that he needed to pay all his debts so we could start our life together on a clean slate. I knew a very important thing about Harry then that even he didn't realize until I told him. He had been running away from everybody and everything for the past four years and had not faced up to the fact that he had responsibilities to other people. Had I encouraged him to declare bankruptcy at that time, it would have been just one more retreat from responsibility. In making the effort to right a wrong, one always profits immeasurably, and Harry benefitted much from facing his creditors. In fact, it made a new man of him. It took us the first two years of our marriage with both of us working to pay all of his debts and begin to start saving money for our first home, but we never regretted those early years of financial struggle. By the grace of God, I believe, our paths came together and I was suddenly there to give Harry exactly what he needed to get his life back on track and make both a personal and a musical comeback at the age of 34.

♪ Personal Sidenote ♪

I'd just like to add a note here for the benefit of readers who may be thinking about declaring bankruptcy. I had a good credit record before I married Harry, but we also needed to build a credit record as a couple. After all of his debts had been paid, we asked our bank to run a credit check on both of us.

We talked to one of the bank officers who expressed interest in helping us reestablish our credit, and he said he would run the application through as if we were actually applying for a loan and then tell us what he found. He turned up a clean slate for us and said that if we ever needed a loan to come back and see him. He also told us that it was very fortunate for us that we did not declare bankruptcy, because most reputable banks and many high-end merchants will not give loans or credit to such people. He said that regardless of how bad a record one might have had at one time, once a good credit record was piled on top of it that would "outshine" the bad. And he told us that he would have much more confidence in us, in attempting to clear everything up, than many other people who came in daily for loans. We were thrilled to get a Sears credit card at that point, and the Brabec credit record remained spotless from that point forward.

In December of that year we bought our first new car—a 1965 Chevy that cost only $2,250 with our trade-in. (I'll bet some younger readers didn't know that one could buy a new car back in the sixties for less than $3,000. This is a good example of what inflation has done to us over the years.)

Bad Habits Broken

Like so many other musicians, Harry smoked too much and drank quite a bit for the first few years of our marriage. Never before a job—he was too much a professional to do that—but only afterwards when he was trying to unwind. He never looked or sounded drunk, and I doubt any of his music buddies had any idea just how much he was drinking in those days because he handled his liquor so well. (His being six-foot-four helped, I'm sure.) After work, he would usually stop off for a boilermaker or two in a local bar where he had made some friends and then bring a six-pack and a half pint of whiskey home with him. Even though I had a job to get to in the morning, I always got up when he came home because I knew he needed this kind of companionship from me. I would fix him something to eat and we'd talk for awhile as he smoked and had one beer after another with his whiskey chasers. He'd often stay up long after I went back to bed because he was still so revved up from playing, and the next morning I'd hear him puking his guts out in the bathroom. Naturally I harped about this because it was both upsetting and frightening to me, and I worried that he was destroying his health.

I never knew if his drinking was out of habit from his years on the road with the big bands, whether it was due to the stress of his work, or simply his way of dealing with his insecurities and worry about how he was going to take care of us as a freelance musician. His bad habits finally caught up with him in August 1967 when he began to feel very ill and was hospitalized for a series of tests. When his doctor told him he had diabetes and wouldn't live another five years if he didn't quit this kind of lifestyle, he looked at me, then at the doctor, and said, "Okay, I'll do it for my wife because we've got a pretty good thing going." I cried and thanked God for his decision.

I was astonished when Harry quit smoking and drinking overnight with none of the crutches most people seem to need, and there was no moaning or complaining about how hard this was to do. Once he made up his mind to do something (or *not* do something), that was it—period. He never took another drink, except for one bottle of authentic German beer that he decided to try when we were in Munich. It had been nine years then since his last drink, and I always wondered what would happen if he ever took that first drink of beer again. But after a few sips, he said it was highly overrated, and I finished it for him.

His hatred for cigarette smoking eventually became so strong that when my mother visited she had to go out in the garage in zero weather to have her cigarette fix. He didn't mind that I continued to have a cocktail or even a beer when I wanted one, or that I had a glass of wine with dinner every night, but the smell of coffee always bothered him because his usual breakfast when he was drinking was a fast cup of coffee and a cigarette. After he quit smoking he never had another cup of coffee, but grew to love tea instead. In fact, as the years went on Harry drank tea like most folks drink coffee, and he never played a job or traveled anywhere without carrying a thermos of hot or cold tea with him. I used to joke that without his tea, he was like Popeye without his spinach.

In one of his many scrapbooks for this period of time, I found a cartoon that showed an overweight fellow on an examination table with this caption: *"Diet and exercise? I want to get well—not hungry and skinny."* For his birthday that year, I made him a "Jello cake" and gave him a hollow spoon. He appreciated the humor.

♪ Personal Sidenote ♪

Interestingly, after being treated for diabetes for two years and reaching the point where the doctor said Harry had to start controlling the disease with insulin rather than just pills, he rebelled by switching doctors, going to the one who was then treating baseball players in Chicago. *After a series of tests, the new doctor told him he didn't seem to have diabetes after all.* He said Harry should eat whatever he wanted for two weeks and come back again.

Harry jumped for joy because we were then getting ready for a vacation to Gatlinburg, Tennessee. There, we found a marvelous dining room that gave diners a choice of whatever and how much of anything and everything they wanted to eat for a set price. Harry went on an eating binge the likes of which I had never seen before, often having not one but two rich desserts at the end of each meal. He felt fine, and on revisiting the doctor was declared free of diabetes. Since there is no cure for diabetes, we always figured an inept doctor had either misdiagnosed him or he had a miraculous remission.

Either way, this experience emphasizes the importance of always getting a second opinion when we don't like the first one we've received. Diabetes finally caught up with Harry when he was in his seventies, but it was very mild and he never needed more than an occasional pill to keep him in balance as he continued to eat everything he wanted. Of course I learned how to make wonderful desserts without sugar to keep my guy as healthy as possible.

Touring with the Symphony

During the years when Harry was drumming his heart out in the Shubert and Melody Top theatres and playing a wide assortment of other jobs, he continued to work with the Chicago Symphony from time to time when an extra percussionist was needed. In March of 1965, when Harry was playing *Oliver* at the Shubert, the Symphony was making preparations for its upcoming 26-day western tour in May, and Harry was vying for its extra percussionist work.

It was around that time that we saw the play, *Barefoot in the Park*. Harry squirmed in his seat throughout the performance, saying afterwards that it felt very strange to be sitting in the audience instead of being up on stage. Given his height, it was also uncomfortable because there was never enough room for his long legs in any theater or airplane.

He did get the Symphony tour and was uncomfortable on the plane when it left on May 2 for the first stop in Salt Lake City. Several of the wives went on this trip, and I joined Harry in L.A. on May 5. After we checked into the Hollywood Roosevelt Hotel, we visited Grauman's Chinese Theatre and Tussaud's Wax Museum before having dinner at Jim Diamond's. Understand that this was a *very* exciting trip for me. It was my first flight, and I remember how thrilled I was to be served a beautiful meal and then see an in-flight movie. We were based in L.A. for five days with some bus trips to do concerts in other nearby cities. I loved seeing Harry on stage, so handsome in his white tie and tails.

In between rehearsals and concerts that week, we saw all the usual tourist sights and sampled the food in a variety of restaurants. It was here that Harry reconnected with Hugh Anderson, his old percussionist friend from Morton High days, and I got to meet Hugh and his wife Kathe for dinner at their home one evening. Earlier that day it was like old home week for Harry and Hugh as he drove us around to see the Civic Center, downtown Los Angeles, and a couple of the local drum shops.

In one of them, we met TV personality Pat Carroll, who was quite pregnant at the time and fun to chat with. It was also in one of those shops that I first heard Harry play "Nola" on the xylophone, as only he could play it. He picked up a couple of sticks and began to play the craziest version of this old tune that anyone had ever heard, so deliberately out of key and loaded with clams that the whole drum shop was in stitches. On finishing, he walked away bowing and saying "No autographs, please."

The orchestra played two concerts on Sunday in Whittier and Anaheim before leaving on May 10 for a series of concerts in San Diego, Santa Barbara, and Sacramento. Here, we had time to see the magnificent San Diego Zoo and enjoy a couple of swims in Santa Barbara (where the pool was 80 degrees but the temperature was only 50). Harry didn't have to play the Sacramento concert on May 13, so he took this opportunity to stuff himself at a Hof Brau restaurant before going to hear the concert. After the concert, a bus took us to San Francisco, where we spent the next four days.

This city literally stole our hearts (Harry called it "one hill of a town") and gave us a song that we would come to call ours. (It was, of course, "I Left My Heart in San Francisco.") Here, Harry was delighted to be able to spend some quality time with Johnny Morgando, another drummer friend who I believe was then touring regularly with pianist Roger Williams. (I found info on the Web that indicated John was an extra percussionist on a Mendelssohn/Brahms/Stravinsky recording Harry made with the Chicago Symphony with Kubelik in 1952, so their friendship obviously went back a long way.) Johnny treated us to dinner in his home in the Valley, and gave us a magnificent view of the glittering city at night from Mulholland Drive.

It was on this trip that I first began to realize just how many people Harry knew from his years of working so many different jobs all over the country. Everywhere we went, it seemed, he was running into someone he knew. One afternoon when we were browsing shops on Fisherman's Wharf and stopped for lunch at the Hof Brau, he ran into three old musician buddies he had worked with in years past. I forget who they were, but what I remember distinctly about this meeting was how Harry had greeted the guys.

He not only remembered their names after twenty years, but reminded one of them exactly where they had last met, including the city, the year, and what they'd both had for dinner that night. His friend was simply stunned to think that Harry could remember little details like this, but as I soon came to learn, he had a steel-trap memory for detail. He remembered exactly when we had ever visited a particular city, tourist sight, restaurant, or friend's home. He remembered the meals we had ordered in various restaurants, and always knew when I had last served him one of his favorite dinners (and often brought this to my attention when I failed to make it again soon enough to please him). He remembered all the shops or stores where I had bought something and wanted to go back to, but couldn't remember the name. When I'd step into his office to say I liked the tune being played at the moment and asked him the name of it, he always knew it. He may have been the only drummer who not only remembered the names of thousands of songs, but often knew the key in which many of them had been written. Don't ask me how he did this. All I can say is that when he died, I felt as though he'd taken half my memory with him. If I hadn't documented so much of our lives in writing at the time things happened, I never could have written this book.

Ring Dem Bells!

San Francisco was memorable for another musical reason. Harry *loved* the trolley cars, and it didn't take long for him to realize that each of the trolley motormen was ringing his bell in a specific rhythmic pattern, and that every motorman had his own unique ring. And you guessed it— Harry just *had* to ring one of those bells. So there we were in a loaded trolley car when he decides the time to do this is *now*.

He walks up front to have a little chat with the motorman. I can hear only part of what he is saying, but I get the gist of it. He says he's a percussionist in town with the Symphony, and then he butters the guy up by complimenting him on his bell ringing before asking boyishly, "Do you think maybe I could ring the bell?" (Who could have resisted that request?) At the next crossing where the bell needed to be rung, my drummer boy begins clanging it in a rhythmic pattern all his own. I'm sitting there with a big smile on my face and several women around me are looking at me and smiling, too, as if to say, "What a cute husband you have." Sure enough.

Harry had a similar but much bigger bell-ringing experience in 1976 when we were in Florence, Italy on business for the work he was then doing as producer of the International Exposition of Craftsmen in Virginia (see Chapter 12).

Imagine this: it is 10 o'clock in the morning. To kill time before our meeting, we go up to the rooftop terrace for a view of the city. While there, Harry notices there are three very old bells from when the building used to be a church. He is told that they are still rung every day at noon, and now he's looking forward to hearing them chime. It is almost noon when our meeting ends and Harry asks if perhaps we might *observe* the bell ringing as well?

Better yet . . . could he possibly *ring* the bell? He is both surprised and delighted when they say *yes!* Our business friend and I are amused by his little-boy excitement, and I snap a picture as we watch him confidently grab the bell cord to give it a yank. But pulling the cord for that heavy bell is harder than he thought it would be. Now a worried look comes across his face as he frantically tugs harder at the cord to get the huge bell to ring. *Finally* the rope is down . . . and then suddenly the weight of the big bell pulls it up sharply, lifting his feet from the floor as he hangs on for dear life. Down again comes the cord, and now he's got the hang of it.

After ringing the bell a couple more times, Harry's exciting once-in-a-lifetime experience ends with our being told that he is most certainly the *first and only American ever to ring a church bell in the city of Florence.*

See what I mean about life with Harry being one adventure after another?

Onward to Alaska

My glorious trip with Harry and the Chicago Symphony Orchestra came to an end on May 18. As I was flying home that morning, the Symphony was traveling on to play concerts in Eugene, Portland, Seattle, Anchorage (where everyone saw the devastating effects of its recent earthquake, and where no one had earthquake insurance), and then to Fairbanks. When I got home, I reported to my mother that I had seen and done more exciting things on this trip than I ever imagined possible; had been in seven cities, rode on or in three taxies, sixteen buses, two trains and five planes. Even though the Symphony traveled in style with the finest accommodations and meals, it was very tiring, and I felt as though I'd been on the road for weeks.

Now imagine how the musicians felt. In addition to all this travel and often less sleep than usual, they also had to play rehearsals and performances. This was Harry's first tour with the orchestra, and he couldn't help comparing it to his traveling days with the big bands. "It was *never* this good in the old days," he said.

But he was clearly wiped out when he was writing a letter to me on the plane to Anchorage because the letter opened with "What day is it? Everybody is real beat and the brain cells just aren't working the way they should. Lots of griping and some temper flares. I'm just counting the days till I'll be back with you."

While in Anchorage, Harry shared these interesting statistics about the area: "One out of every 29 people in Alaska owns their own plane and one out of every three has a pilot's license. You can't get to the outlying areas unless you fly. It's 40° below zero in the winter with an average of 72 inches of snow, but I was told they never have more than three feet of snow on the ground at one time. Light dusk still at 9:15 p.m., which remains so until about 3 a.m. when the sun comes up again."

After playing a concert in Fairbanks—which had never had a symphony concert there before—the orchestra flew back to Anchorage, changed planes to fly to Seattle, then changed planes once again to fly to

Vancouver (no concert that night). The next day they flew to Winnipeg with a stopover at Calgary, where it was very warm—suit jackets off, ties loosened. By the time they landed in Winnipeg, however, it was snowing and the temperature had dropped to 31°. Sam Denov told me that part of the trip was particularly memorable not only because of the quick weather change, but because the instrument truck didn't get there on time, and the concert scheduled for eight didn't begin until after ten. "But many folks hung around until we could play," he said.

Clippings in Harry's scrapbook provided details. The bulk of the orchestra property—everything except the smaller instruments—went in a cargo plane by way of Seattle. When it landed for refueling at Bismarck, North Dakota, it was found to have engine trouble and was delayed for nearly two-and-a-half hours. Meanwhile, 104 symphony players milled around backstage snoozing, playing cards, or fiddling with their instruments while Silas Edman, the orchestra's general manager, worried. An hour after the plane landed, the instrument truck was on its way to the hall with a special city police motorcycle escort. One article described the scene this way:

> Mr. Edman was everywhere at once as the truck emptied and chests of music and clothes, players' stools and music stands, a harp case and a dozen double basses, and all the paraphernalia of the percussion section filled up the lobby and cramped backstage area. "We don't need that, it's tails?" queried one player as a box was manhandled up to the stage. "Tails, my foot, it's a xylophone," was Mr. Edman's retort. (Only Harry said "foot" was not the word he used.)

Few of the players bothered to change into their dress clothes for the concert, and the article noted that "there was perhaps never a more oddly dressed orchestra playing a full symphony concert on a Winnipeg stage." The concert finally began at 10:55 for an audience that had dwindled from an estimated 1800 to little more than a thousand. It was shortened a bit and everyone was on their way home a little after midnight.

On May 28, after a grueling 26-day tour, the orchestra headed for home. "Nobody bitched about catching *this* plane," Harry said.

Back with the Symphony Full Time

Fortunately, losing his full-time position with the Chicago Symphony in 1956 did not put an end to Harry's involvement with the CSO, which continued off and on for the next fifteen years. Reiner may have disliked him, but as a musician who was greatly admired by his peers and appreciated for his exceptional playing ability, Harry was often hired as an extra man whenever an additional percussionist was needed for a concert. He eventually returned to the Orchestra full time in June 1966 as both an extra percussionist and assistant stage librarian.

It was during this period that I got to see how the musicians spent their time downstairs while "tuning up" before going on stage; how and where instruments and music scores were stored, and other things that went on backstage before the curtain went up. One of my sweetest backstage memories of Harry's days with the Symphony was when Ella Fitzgerald was appearing with the Orchestra at Ravinia in the summer of 1966. He said she was a sweetheart to work with, and he wanted me to meet her. At the rehearsal break, he took me backstage so I could say hello and get her autograph.

It was hot, and she looked tired and sweaty. She had her feet up on a chair and didn't move a muscle when Harry brought me into the room. She was just as down-home as you could get. Of course by now Harry had charmed her sox off, along with her shoes.

"Hi, honey, how are ya?" she said when Harry introduced me. I don't remember what I said to her, but she gave me her autograph, and I'm sure I must have said what an honor it was to meet her, and then Harry ushered me out of the room after a few minutes so she could rest. But I could see that she liked Harry by the way she smiled when she spoke to him. He did have a way with people.

Harry had endless patience with anyone he liked, but he had no use for prima donnas, a category that included some of the conductors he worked with. One time when the Symphony was playing in Milwaukee, I was backstage watching Harry get things set up for the concert as he wondered aloud where the hell the conductor was (whose name it seems prudent not to mention). He finally arrived just minutes before downbeat, which had Harry sweating because it was his job to make sure the concert began exactly on time. So there he was with the conductor's baton in hand, pacing back and forth like a frustrated lion in a cage as he waited for him to finally get there. I saw the relief on Harry's face when the maestro stepped through the door at the last minute, and then his intense irritation when the conductor quickly turned around saying, "Wait a minute, I have to pee."

As he disappeared through the door, Harry was so aggravated by this conductor's cavalier attitude about time that he threw his baton up in the air. High, too, about 12 feet, I'd guess. I held my breath and was as astonished as Harry was when he caught it behind his back with his left hand. Later, we mused about what would have happened if that baton had been damaged when it hit the floor. This is yet another example of what I meant when I said earlier that Harry often acted on impulse and pushed his luck time and time again.

When the Symphony did a six-day eastern tour in November 1966, and Harry was hired as an extra man, I was once again privileged to tag along to hear concerts in New York, Philadelphia, and Boston. In addition to enjoying the music part of this trip, we got in some fabulous sightseeing and good eating in all three cities. New York was especially memorable because we made a climb to the top of the Statue of Liberty, and this was when Harry realized he had a fear of heights. He was in a near state of panic as we were coming down the crowded narrow spiral staircase because he kept imagining that someone behind him was going to fall and take everyone down like a row of dominos. I also lost a contact lens on the glittery sidewalk in front of Lincoln Center, and half a dozen friendly New Yorkers were down on their knees helping me search for it. Never found it; I ended up with a pair of glasses for the rest of the trip.

I didn't travel with Harry in April of 1967 when the Orchestra did a tour in the Midwest to Cedar Rapids, Des Moines, Kansas City, Columbia, and Peoria, but I did document his expenses for this trip, which are interesting now when you consider the cost of things today. As an extra man, his per diem for the eleven-day trip was $209. Hotel rooms in those cities cost between $7.50 and $12 a night, totaling $98.93. His food costs were $52.49 (and you know how Harry loved to eat). Although he called me every day, sometimes twice a day, his hotel phone bill was just $15.64. He spent his extra per diem on gifts for me.

Chicago's "Killer Storm of' '67"

Now let me go back a couple of months to January 1967, when Chicago suffered the worst snowstorm in its history and, for the first time in the Chicago Symphony's history, two concerts on Friday and Saturday had to be cancelled. It began to snow about 2 a.m. on Thursday and snowed continuously through Friday afternoon, leaving 23 inches on the ground. (One newspaper report said all this snow weighed 24 million tons.) By then, the city was literally paralyzed with no buses, planes, or cars moving. The airports and all expressways and the Outer Drive were closed, along with all schools and 95 percent of businesses. By noon on Thursday, hotels in the Loop were already filling up as many workers decided not to try to brave the roads home. Extra cots were put in many rooms and some people slept in hotel lobbies. Thousands of people who did try to drive home ended up abandoning their vehicles where they sat and taking off on foot. Few got very far because of the drifting snow, low twenty-degree temperature, and fierce winds. Many commuters spent the night in a gas station, school, or church.

Some of the musicians in the Orchestra who lived in the suburbs and took a train downtown didn't get home until Monday because their cars were literally buried in a train station parking lot, and streets were impassable to walk home. They either found a hotel room or slept in Orchestra Hall. The "L" was still running when Harry left Orchestra Hall, but his near-mile walk from the station to our apartment was very difficult due to waist-high snow drifts by then, and the fact that he had a very thin overcoat and wore no boots. (He never listened to me.)

Many commuters spent a very cold night in whatever bus or train they had been traveling in at the time. The airports were jammed with passengers whose flights were cancelled, and many office workers simply stayed in their offices. In one case, some fifteen factory workers spent Thursday night there only to learn the next morning that they were trapped by snow drifts so high in front of all the doors and windows that they couldn't get out. I heard them plead on a radio station for someone to come and dig them out, or at least bring some coffee and food for the duration they might have to stay there. I felt sorriest for people who needed ambulances, mothers who had to give birth at home with instructions by telephone, and homeowners whose houses burned to the ground when fire trucks couldn't get to them. In time, sixty deaths would be attributed to this storm.

Like everyone else, Harry and I figured we ought to go to the grocery store early Friday morning to buy a few groceries to get us through the week. (You know Harry by now—food was always high on his list of priorities.) It wasn't too cold or windy then, so we could really appreciate the artistry of snow drifts that high, still so white and beautiful at that point. People had not yet begun to shovel sidewalks yet, and the alley we waded through had drifts as high as a car. But Harry just jumped into them like a Bohemian jackrabbit and I jumped in after him and we laughed ourselves silly in the process.

I think Harry and I did more walking the first three days after the storm than we usually did in three weeks. We walked to Kroger's each day and brought home a sack of groceries apiece, but some people went overboard. The first day as we neared the grocery store, we saw people in every direction as far as the eye could see, either going to or returning from the store. Their shopping bags, sleds, and toboggans were all laden with groceries as though they were never going to be able to buy food again. Ten and twelve loaves of bread were purchased by single customers, along with gallons of milk. In some parts of the city the food hoarding got so bad that many mothers who desperately needed milk for babies couldn't purchase it. Some stores rationed milk, bread, and eggs, but Kroger didn't. In spite of the circumstances, there was a unique feeling of jollity in the air because this was a once-in-a-lifetime experience for most everyone, and something that put all of us in the same sled, so to speak. Kids were especially happy. Pulling groceries on a toboggan was pure fun for them.

Because there was a growing concern in the city that many oil trucks might not get through to replenish supplies, we bought an electric heater just in case. We didn't run out of heat, but our car was so buried in the parking lot that we could hardly identify it (only the antenna was showing). Even after Harry got it shoveled out, it took several days before the parking lot itself felt the blades of a snowplow and the oil truck could make its delivery to our building.

By Monday, the city had a handle on the storm and the Orchestra took the train to Milwaukee for a concert that evening, figuring the instrument truck could get through by then. The Tuesday and Wednesday concerts were presented in Orchestra Hall as usual, but people would be talking about Chicago's great snowstorm for years to come. (If you Google "Chicago snow storm January 1967" you'll find a lengthy article about this storm, complete with many photos. Of course, the massive snowstorms that swept through the northeast in 2010 now make this historic Chicago snowstorm seem rather mild by comparison.)

Memorable Music Moments of 1967

• For my birthday this year, Harry got a ticket for me to hear Artur Rubenstein, who was kind enough to autograph one of his recordings for us after his performance at Orchestra Hall. After meeting him backstage, I practically rubbed noses with Mitch Miller and Skitch Henderson, both of whom were there that night.

• A couple of nights later, Harry came home with Carlo Maria Guilini's autograph on a record, warmly inscribed "A Harry–*con viva cordialita*," an expression used to convey cordiality and "great warm, loving wishes from the core; the heart." No wonder Harry always said Guilini was a "real sweetheart" and a conductor he loved to work with. (He was 91 when he died shortly after Harry in 2005.)

• In June, one of Harry's friends in the Orchestra got us an invitation to spend the day on his 42-foot Jolly Rogers yacht. It was our first (and only) time on a yacht (a rowboat being our usual water vehicle), and Harry was thrilled when he got to wear the Captain's cap and actually drive for awhile and make a ship-to-shore phone call to a friend.

• On August 15 (Harry's birthday), the *Picasso Sculpture* was unveiled in the Civic Center Plaza in Chicago. Prior to this, the Chicago Symphony played some Beethoven conducted by Seiji Ozawa, and then two speakers dedicated the sculpture. One of them was William E. Hartmann, the Chicago architect who helped persuade Picasso to supply the design for the monument. He began his comments by saying, "It may prove to be a singular event in the cultural history of the world."

When Mayor Daley tugged a white ribbon that loosened the blue percale wrap, the crowd cheered, and a newspaper reporter later noted that "faces in the crowd registered everything from enraptured awe to yawning boredom."

Prior to the dedication, Burl Lane, a bassoonist with the Symphony, made a personal videotape of musicians as they milled around before the concert, introducing each of them as they appeared on camera, and it was here that Harry's imitation of Fritz Reiner was captured on tape. In time, I hope to get this snippet of video on the book's companion website.

• The first year we were married, I learned that Harry had never had an Easter basket in his life, so for that year and a few years afterward until the novelty wore off, I made him a special Easter basket with a handmade card and a special gift inside. For this particular Easter, in memory of his Reiner-triangle stories, I surprised him with a handcarved pink Easter bunny wearing tails and holding a triangle made of a paper clip.

In 1969, Harry was promoted to Stage Manager of the Symphony, and he was hired for this position because management was satisfied that he was qualified for the job. To qualify, he had to list in a letter the duties he felt were the responsibility of a Stage Manager. Since few people probably have any idea of what goes on backstage at the Chicago Symphony, I thought the following excerpts from his letter, written in the fall of 1968, would be of interest to some:

> The Stage Manager's obligations should be to the Chicago Symphony alone. His directions should come only from the Symphony's conductors, General Manager, or Orchestra Manager. A close communication must be kept with the Librarian, Stage Librarian, and Personnel Manager. Orchestra Hall stagehands and Stage Librarian should come under his jurisdiction, as should stagehands or workers away from our home base.
>
> A Stage Manager should be in technical control of concerts and rehearsals at all times. He should start concerts at a time designated by the Orchestra Manager, or at his own discretion, being as close to the planned starting time as possible.
>
> Of prime importance are the engagements away from Orchestra Hall. A full knowledge of auditoriums should be sought and exacting records kept. Investigation of proper trunk space, dressing rooms, stage area, loading facilities, and lighting should be checked as much in advance as possible to remedy any poor circumstances. This information could be obtained by correspondence or personal contact, with the latter being the most effective. The Stage Manager also needs to check the truck driver's itinerary as to arrival times at both towns and halls, and hall managers to verify the arrival of any special equipment needed (pianos, percussion equipment, etc.).
>
> It is important that the Stage Manager have complete knowledge of the Stage Librarian's duties and that he, in turn, be able to handle some of the Stage Manager's work for reasons of illness or spelling off one another.
>
> I also feel the Stage Manager should have something to say in the final decision of hiring or firing Stagehands and Stage Librarians. With the future of our Orchestra at stake, competent, serious and dedicated men are a necessity.

Trouble Ahead

Harry's steady job with the Symphony enabled us to buy our first home in Wilmette, Illinois in the spring of 1969. By then, we had moved several times from one apartment to another to improve our standard of living, and now I hoped we were finally going to put down roots. I had quit my job five years earlier and gotten deeply involved in my arts and crafts hobby. Now I was selling some of my work and beginning to see the growing arts and crafts industry as a place ripe with opportunities for making money.

But it didn't take long for Harry's restless spirit to kick in again. Although he was very happy when he was performing with the Orchestra as an extra man, once he was appointed stage manager, he began to run into problems with orchestra management and personnel. He didn't like to take orders from anyone, especially prima donna members of the orchestra who felt they were too important to move their own chair or music stand two inches to the right on stage. I saw the handwriting on the wall early in 1971 when he put in an application for a job at Disney World, which was scheduled to open in December that year. Week after week, he would come home complaining about "all the crap" he had to put up with at Orchestra Hall, saying that the only thing that would make him stay would be a substantial raise. In June, when that raise was not forthcoming, Harry said the hell with it . . . I've had it, I'm outta here.

I was backstage with him that last night, and I cringed as he slammed the stage door on our way out. We both knew he had just blown his second and last chance for full-time work with the Chicago Symphony, but he didn't seem to care. Because I loved him so much and couldn't stand to see him miserable in his job, I felt I had to support his decision here; but I also felt sick at heart because I could see all kinds of trouble ahead if he couldn't find satisfying work that paid as much as he had been earning with the Symphony.

CHAPTER 10

The Lure of Disney World

I'm too old to pimp, and too young to die, so I'm just gon' keep playin'.
  —Clark Terry, world-class trumpeter

It was 1971, and Harry was getting ready to skip town after having slammed the door on his Chicago Symphony job that would have given us financial security for the rest of our lives. He didn't have a job with Disney World yet, but we moved to Florida anyway because he figured that if things didn't work out at Disney, he'd find something else.

Once again, Harry was "betting on the come" and I was now fully resigned to the fact that he was unlikely ever to be satisfied for long in any one job or place. He would always think things would be better somewhere else. Unlike his pragmatic musician friends with families who believed in pensions and security—as he once did in his youth—he now lived for the moment, giving little thought to saving money or how we were going to live in our old age. Things might have been different if we'd had children, but I had never wanted kids and Harry had already been a father and didn't feel he needed to repeat the experience. So it was just the two of us, which I guess made him feel footloose and fancy free.

A steady income would have been nice, of course, but I didn't marry Harry for money. What I needed more than anything was someone to love with all my heart who would love me back the same way, and I felt Harry was filling that need better than any other man in the world could have done. For some time though, I had been trying to think of a way to make money at home, which is where Harry always wanted me to be. I figured it would be good to have a second income in case he hit some dry spells in the future, but I didn't know then just how important my having a home business would be ten years down the road.

Curiously, it was Harry who came up with the idea of publishing a magazine for art and craft sellers. For several years, my hobby was learning new arts and crafts, and by 1970 I was selling some of my creations in local shops and galleries. This led me to ask a lot of questions, and one day Harry said we ought to start a magazine to help other craft sellers like me who wanted to profit from their creativity. We figured I could do the writing and publishing work and he could help me with mailings, getting ads, and so on.

So, as he was leaving the Symphony, we were preparing to launch the first issue of *Artisan Crafts*. I named Harry as Publisher on the masthead to give his ego a boost, and I was Editor. Of course, neither one of us knew a thing about how to publish a magazine, and I had absolutely no experience as an editor or writer, but writing was natural to me, and what I didn't know, I figured I could learn. We sold our house, bought a new one in Florida, put the first issue of the magazine in the mail, and called the moving van.

Our new home was in Altamonte Springs, Florida, which was near Orlando, where Mickey Mouse and his friends would soon be drawing millions of dollars to central Florida and creating all kinds of traffic problems. Before we left town, Harry wrote this humorous farewell letter to his chums at the Shubert Theatre, with whom he had stayed in touch during his years with the Symphony:

To My Dear Friends of the Shubert Orchestra:

I am truthfully sorry that I have not acknowledged the lovely going-away present you so thoughtfully gave to Barb and me. It is strange how through the course of our life many things leave us, but in this particular case, the memories of the Shubert Gang will stick to me like a Bohemian love for mushrooms. As we all threaten to write books about our musical lives, I am sure I would devote many chapters to the Shubert and Melody Top.

Barb and I will be living in Florida by the time you read this—living in somewhat semiretirement. I think that's appropriate because people have told me I'm the most retiring person they have ever known. Unfortunately, my annual New Year's Eve concert will be forsaken in Chicago, but fear not, for I have already received a booking in a place called the Everglades. It again will be a musical first as I will perform on a flat boat floating through this scenic wonderland. I was told that my audience will listen with mouths agape. The program has not been completed, but many new and original compositions are in the works!

We will be living near Orlando where I have already been offered a job by Disney World. They want me as one of the seven dwarfs, but have not committed themselves as to which one. Barb says she's sure she knows who it is because of the way I act and look.

The Walt Disney World Marching Band

In his application letter to Disney, Harry said he was interested in being a percussionist with the Walt Disney World Marching Band. He also suggested that his experience might lend itself both to performing and doubling as a personnel manager, music librarian, or performance administrator. But Disney was only looking for musicians at that time.

Jim Christensen, a trombone player and conductor of a community band in St. Louis, was brought in to get the marching band started, and he was the one who hired Harry out of the forty or fifty drummers who were vying for the job.

"A lot of the drummers who initially applied for this job thought it was cushy work where they would just sit and play all day," Jim told me. "Many backed out once they learned how hard the work was. This was an eight-hour job that involved perhaps four hours of playing interspersed with walking all over the park to play in various areas for different crowds of people. The marching band would play its twelve memorized tunes in front of the Castle and in Town Square, and then break into four subgroups. During the day, the band members would be in and out of the underground area for breaks and costume changes before moving into a different area of the park to play. There was a lot of walking."

Harry was in the bandstand by the main gate waiting for the crowds when Disney World had its "soft opening" on October 1, 1971. Funny thing, though. There was no *crowd;* just a small handful of people waiting to get in at opening time, and they were probably as stunned as the band members and Disney World management to find no lines in front of the ticket booths. Most people stayed home that day because there had been so much publicity about the opening and the traffic congestion visitors were likely to encounter on the one main road leading to the park. Dick Marlowe wrote an entertaining piece about this for the *Orlando Sentinel* that began:

Disney did it. Just like they said they would.

The $400 million theme park opened more than two hours early Friday morning, climaxing six years of planning and building.

But the biggest news of the day were the things that didn't happen instead of those that did.

Traffic didn't back up to Macon, Ga., as some predicted. It didn't even back up to Kissimmee.

Crowds didn't back up at the main entrance to the theme park and people didn't stumble over each other rushing for the 30 attractions inside.

The official crowd was 10,422, about a fifth as many as are expected at Florida Field today to watch the thrice-beaten Gators play Tennessee.

In another article Harry clipped for his scrapbook, a writer for *Modern Living* humorously reported that "The only untoward incident took place when a somewhat confused woman sought free admission because, she told police, 'I am Cinderella.' The Disney cops, primed for any emergency, lured her away by telling her that their police car was a pumpkin."

Disney World's Grand Opening

After the Magic Kingdom's soft opening, the park was officially dedicated on October 25. On that day, Meredith Wilson, who wrote the book, music, and lyrics for *The Music Man*, led the Walt Disney Marching Band in a grand opening parade down Main Street, playing his famous "Seventy-Six Trombones" signature song from the musical. Later, under the direction of Arthur Fiedler (conductor of the Boston Pops), the World Symphony Orchestra presented a concert in front of Cinderella Castle.

This was not the first time Harry had worked with both Arthur Fiedler and Meredith Wilson. A year earlier when Harry was toying with the idea of moving to Nashville, Fiedler had written a letter of introduction to Chet Atkins, saying, "Presently, Harry is Stage Manager and Percussionist with the Chicago Symphony. He has collaborated with me in both capacities for several years and, I might add, most proficiently in both categories. His plans are to move to the Nashville area, and I would appreciate your talking with him and assisting him in any way you might find possible."

So it was that Harry volunteered to help coordinate the details of Fiedler's conducting of the World Symphony Orchestra to make things as easy as possible for him (once a stage manager, always a stage manager). I have no idea where Harry first met Fiedler, but this is yet another example of how he maintained professional friendships with countless musicians, conductors, and others in the industry.

As for his acquaintance with Meredith Wilson, I know that being in the Disney World Marching Band with him leading it in the Grand Opening parade down Main Street was a highlight of Harry's Disney experience. He may have been remembering then the lovely backstage visit he and I had with him when Harry was with the Chicago Symphony in 1967 and Wilson was conducting a 4th of July concert at Ravinia. When Harry asked him to autograph our *Music Man* album, he wrote, "Love to Harry and Barbara in remembrance of a very happy 4th together in Chicago."

The "76 Trombones" Recording

I always knew Harry had a Disney record album in his collection, and I figured it was because he wanted a souvenir of the band and his bass drum playing in it. In going through his record collection one day, I happened to notice that the copyright date on this album was 1972, and since Harry had left Disney in 1971, I thought maybe he wasn't playing on this album after all—even though they had slapped a picture of him in the Polka band on the back cover. But when John Melcher related the following story, my heart sang.

"I heard this story about Harry right after I joined the band in 1972," he said. "The band had played the piece two or three times, and Harry kept missing a note in the bell part. Now the band is getting hot under the collar. The trumpeters' lips are about shot, and the guys are giving him a hard time for not playing his part perfectly like they're doing. He's clearly under the gun, but he calmly says, 'I'll get it; I'll get it.' And on the next take he plays it perfectly.

"Now I saw that bell part," John added, "which any percussionist will tell you is really tough to play—and I couldn't have played it perfectly even in a relaxed atmosphere. But to play it perfectly when the whole band and the conductor is breathing down your neck? No way!"

As soon as I heard this story, I grabbed the record and put it on the turntable, and there he was—my modest husband who never bragged about his playing to me or told me how hard his job really was at times.

As I listened to him play that wonderful melody line on bells, not only perfectly, but *musically,* I remembered him telling me once that so many percussionists just *hit* the bells, and that there is a real knack to playing a bell part musically.

I don't know if Harry's playing can be heard in any other number on this album because it was a compilation of recordings made over a period of time. But Jim Christensen did confirm that Disney made only one souvenir record album, and they recorded "Seventy-Six Trombones" only once, so there is no question that Harry recorded this particular tune some time after he had marched down Main Street with the "Music Man" himself.

Now that I think about all this, I figure it's likely that Harry *did* tell me he was playing on this recording when he brought the album home, and I just forgot that detail after so many years. But in reliving his Disney World experience in this book, I realize now how much he must have enjoyed making this recording after having been in the marching band with Meredith Wilson conducting it.

It was nearly Christmas 2009 as I listened to this recording and pondered the thought that it had taken nearly forty years for it to wend its way to my ears. Without question, this was the best Christmas present from Harry since our first year together when he gave me that clarinet made of wood.

♪ | Music Sidenote ♪

Should drummers be musicians? Absolutely, Harry said. His reference to playing bells musically prompts me to include these comments he once made to a friend who played euphonium.

"Believe it or not, drummers are (or should be) musicians, too. Anybody can hit a drum, as I demonstrate in my teaching and clinics, but to get a musical sound out of a 'pot' (my favorite nickname for any kind of a drum), and incorporate that sound into the sounds of the other instrumentalists, takes a little bit of doing. One of my pet peeves is triangle playing, or should I say the 'triangle sounds' that come out of high school kids and some professionals, too. The triangle is as much a musical instrument as a euphonium, and yet this instrument is often hit like a player is trying to kill it. (And don't ever get me on the subject of bass drum and cymbal playing!)"

The Life of a Disney Musician

Joe Derrico, now Administrative Dean at Doctor Phillips High School in Orlando, played snare drum alongside Harry in the Disney World Band, so he and Harry became good friends as they marched around the park every day. "He was an awesome professional and real fine gentleman," Joe told me. "I'll never forget a little tip he gave me one day when I was practicing a tricky part of a tune. 'Don't ever let them see you practicing a lick,' he said, 'because it makes them think you can't do it.'"

Many who knew Harry felt he had come way down on the musical ladder to play at Disney World, but he didn't see it that way. After nearly thirty years, he knew his career was winding down but he still wanted to play. Since he had always loved band music, he wanted to give this a shot. And he wasn't the only long-time professional musician to be drawn to Disney World.

As Joe pointed out, "We had several military guys, band musicians retired from twenty or thirty years with the Army or Navy. They fit right in with this kind of music lifestyle because they were used to reporting to work, putting on a uniform, and playing what they were told to play. But given Harry's background, I thought he seemed out of place there."

Actually, I think the kid in Harry just wanted the honor of being in this band when Disney opened its doors, and he loved his red band uniform because it reminded him of his happy days of playing in Morton's high school marching band. After doing the daily parade, the twenty musicians in the band would break up into four smaller groups. At different times, Harry played in both the Dixieland Band and the Polka Band where he played a field drum. He liked his Dixieland costume with its yellow vest and jaunty black hat, but he wasn't particularly fond of the Bavarian lederhosen he had to wear when he was playing in the Polka Band. I thought he looked pretty cute in this get-up, however.

Disney had a very strict dress code, by the way. First, they wanted only those employees with wholesome good looks, and it was said they rejected nine applicants for every one hired. Girls had to keep their makeup light, fingernail tips could not exceed one-eighth of an inch in length, and only watches could be worn "on stage." Guys couldn't have mustaches, beards, sideburns below mid-ear, or hair that went below their ears.

"As a musician, where you're used to doing what you wanted to do with your hair, we kinda pushed the hair limit as far as we could go,"

Rich Sherrill told me. "And then they would come around and tell us our hair was too long, and that would be it—we'd have to get a haircut. The 'face characters' in the park (those that did not wear character masks, such as Cinderella and Snow White), had even tighter dress codes, and they had to watch their weight to stay in character."

You may recall Rich's comments earlier in the book about what it was like to study with Harry, who got him into the Florida Symphony in 1972. After two years there, Rich left because the season was so short (20 odd weeks) and he wanted the full-time employment Disney World could offer him.

"I worked there for the next three-and-a-half years," he says. "I was playing in Fantasyland in a group called The Aristocats. The routine was that we'd play a song, then characters would come out on a stage that came up from underground, and they would dance to the next song we played. Then the stage would descend for a costume change while we played another song without them. This sequence would repeat for about fifteen or twenty minutes. When we first started there, we were playing only four sets a day between 10 a.m. and 5 p.m., which in total was only about an hour's worth of music. Later management caught on and increased our number of performances to seven or eight sets a day."

The public never saw what I always thought of as "the underground," which one newspaper writer called "a cavernous, eight-acre basement and a great place to be in a bomb attack." It's like a city down there, with tunnels leading to all areas of the park that are used by all employees, as well as by maintenance workers who scoot around in battery-powered carts. There's a huge cafeteria, several dressing rooms, the world's largest wardrobe department, a bank, a barber shop, and many workshops where things are repaired or built for the park. Harry only took me underground a couple of times to spend a little time in the rehearsal room where the musicians hung out, so I asked Rich to fill me in on how the Disney musicians saw this underground area.

"Disney didn't just dig a hole in the ground to create the underground world below the park," he explained. "They built the tunnel system and then brought in tons of dirt to build the park on top of it. The underground is considered ground level, which employees call 'the tunnels,' and where tourists are walking around is called the first floor.

"As for the musicians' work routine, depending on what music group you were in, you'd play maybe four or five sets a day, going out on a stage for fifteen to twenty minutes and doing a parade a day. Sometimes you might just go into one of the 'lands' and stay there to entertain the guests. On breaks, the musicians would gather in their rest area, which was a normal dressing room large enough for maybe thirty guys, and it would be shared by several groups of musicians. Then, depending on where we were next scheduled to play, we'd take one of the underground tunnels and come out right where we needed to be."

Rich reminded me of something else the average tourist may not realize, and that is the fact that Disney controls the whole environment for countless miles around the park—more than 27,000 acres, according to one magazine article. "They created their own city, Lake Buena Vista, and it has its own government, rules, and regulations, its own police force and fire department, all run by Disney World people, of course. You're on Disney property for miles before you ever get into the parking lot and then the theme park."

Cinderella Castle

Let me put music aside for a moment to tell you about a remarkable behind-the-scenes experience Harry and I had before Disney World opened, when the band was still in rehearsal. It was my good fortune to be there on the day the last section of the final glass mosaic mural was being cemented into place in Cinderella Castle. Harry and I were then publishing *Artisan Crafts* magazine and, recognizing an opportunity when we saw it, we inquired about the craftsman who had created these mosaic panels and learned that he would be at the castle shortly to supervise the application of the final panel.

And so it was that Harry and I met Hanns Scharff, a distinguished-looking man who spoke with more than a trace of his native German accent. A personable man with a subtle sense of humor, he seemed as interested in me and Harry as we were in him and his work, and he patiently answered our many questions while also keeping a keen eye on the installation work in progress. We did not realize until later that we were talking to a world-famous craftsman, and would undoubtedly never have learned it from him. Extremely modest, he said, "The credit for the Cinderella designs belongs to Dorothea Redmond—I just made the mosaic."

When Harry had to go to work, I stayed on with pen and notebook in hand and ended up with a wonderful feature article for our magazine, complete with photos furnished by Disney World and Scharff's very detailed how-to instructions for creating mosaics.

The five glittering glass mosaic murals in the castle are fifteen feet high and ten feet wide, truly great works of art. Each panel contains approximately 100,000 pieces of glass, some as small as the head of a tack and many that had to be hand-cut and shaped with a power grindstone. More than a third of the glass pieces contain silver or 14–18K gold that was fused into the glass during the manufacturing process. Meeting the artist who created these breathtakingly beautiful murals remains one of my fondest Disney memories.

All That Glitters is Not Gold

Harry had been lured to Florida by the glitter of Disney World, but that glitter began to tarnish as the work days grew longer and hotter and Disney's demands on its musicians became excessive.

"Harry was a wonderful guy, and everyone loved him because his attitude was so good," Jim Christensen told me. "But it didn't take long for him to admit that this job was too much for him physically. Wearing a band uniform and carrying an instrument all over the park in Florida's high heat and humidity got to a lot of the musicians. One day Harry came to me saying, 'I like you and the guys, but I just can't do this any more.'"

It was with regret that Harry sent his letter of resignation on December 11 only three months after he had begun rehearsals. Shortly afterwards, John Melcher connected with Harry, and that was the start of their friendship. He began to study with Harry and, like Rich Sherrill, says he learned a lot from him. After leaving Disney, Rich had a long and satisfying music career before moving into a management position with the postal service. John is a veteran percussionist who has had an active musical life in Las Vegas, New York, and other parts of the country. Currently, he is a freelance jobbing musician on a mission to acquaint more people with the beauty of tubular bells.

Harry and John lost touch after 1974, and it wasn't until John was communicating with someone in the Milwaukee Symphony that he learned of Harry's passing and was able to get back in touch with me. We quickly renewed our friendship and I immediately asked him to help me find Rich Sherrill, who Harry and I had also lost touch with in the late seventies. So John put on his detective hat and tracked him down, and that's how two of Harry's old friends became two very special friends of mine decades later, bringing everything full circle. (God works in mysterious ways.) As his contribution to this book, John made an MP3 recording for me of his remembrances of working with and studying with Harry, and that's when I first heard the "76 Trombones" story I related earlier.

Leaving on a High Note

Harry never regretted his short Disney experience because he made many friends and had a lot of fun performing and hamming it up backstage with the guys in the band. (On the book's website, look for the caricature of "Light-Fingered Harry" in his Dixieland uniform that one of the musicians did to amuse Harry.) When he left, they gave him a big cake with miniature marching band musicians on top of it.

That Christmas, one of the musicians sent this humorous message in a "collective card" to all the guys in the band, which summed up what working at Disney World was really like:

This is a card to all of you to express my most sincere best wishes for the holiday season. I had intended to write and mail individual cards, but my time is valuable. (It's currently valued at $4.90 per hour—except that the cards would be written on overtime, which would be valued at more than $4.90 per hour, depending on how much FICA and whatever else whoever it is takes out of whatever our checks come to each week.)

However, it has come to my attention of late that the personal fellowship of all members of the Walt Disney World Band has been excellent in every regard, and in keeping with company policy, it is my sincere wish that YOU WILL have a Merry Christmas and a Happy New Year, even though we may be marching our asses off in a parade in 90°F heat.

Seriously—the best to everyone in '72. I hope all of you will send a collective card. The savings in cost of stamps will purchase 1.803 packs of cigars, or we could start a special fund for the less fortunate who must play and perform at Six Flags. Should we have an hour or two free to ourselves after January 1, 1972, you are warmly invited to a roaring evening to enjoy Kissimmee night life—at your own expense—before 9:30 p.m.

We stayed in the Orlando area for a couple of years. I was working full time on the magazine and Harry was teaching and performing in the area, often working with the Florida Symphony Orchestra and the Sunshine Pops, a local orchestra John Giattino had launched in 1971. Needing an arranger, Giattino had hired Bill Pape, the composer-arranger for Walt Disney World and also a trombone player in the marching band. It was Bill who introduced Harry to John.

When I finally tracked him down, I learned that John had disbanded the Sunshine Pops in 1977, but gone on to start International Concert Management, Inc. and other orchestras and ensembles that tour regularly, including the Hollywood Concert Orchestra and the new Sigmund Romberg Orchestra.

"Harry was a fine musician who played timpani and percussion in the orchestra," John said. "I found him to be a very interesting man with a good sense of humor; outspoken, too. We had some laughs about Disney, the Florida Symphony, and Orlando, and we shared the same feelings about contractors in both Chicago and New York. We knew many of the same people, and I gathered that Harry knew a lot of musicians all over the country."

Throughout 1972, Harry played regularly with the Sunshine Pops, picked up some hotel dance jobs, and taught percussion at Valencia Community College in Orlando, where he stayed until we left Florida in early 1973. By then, our magazine business was beginning to show a small profit and our mutual desire for fall and a snowy Christmas gradually convinced us that Florida wasn't our cup of tea. Earlier we had bought five acres of land by a lake in southwest Missouri near Branson, and we had planned to rent a house for six months until we could find a contractor to modify the house on that property to our needs. But that plan fell through and we ended up buying a home on the lake near that property in an area called Gobbler's Mountain. It was located close to both Branson and Silver Dollar City, a popular old-time theme park. Harry figured he might find work in one of these two places.

With no money to spare, Harry decided we should move ourselves this time. He had never driven a big U-Haul truck before, or packed a truck for that matter, but little details like that never stopped him. With the help of Rich Sherrill and three of his other students, Harry packed that truck so professionally and so tight we could barely cram in a roll of toilet paper and a box of Tide before closing the door.

Every box, container, nook, cranny, crevice, and furniture drawer was jam-packed with our possessions, as were the front of the truck and every inch of space in the car and trunk. The only thing we couldn't fit in anywhere were two garbage cans and Harry's two timpani, which Rich took care of for him. Because the truck was so heavily packed and now leaning to the right, Harry worried about the axles holding up. Our greatest fear was that if anything happened to the truck and it had to be unloaded into another truck, there was no way on earth we could get it all back in again.

I'm not sure who was the most nervous as we headed for Missouri in March: Harry, because he was worried about driving a 24-foot truck packed to the gills over some very winding and dangerous mountainous roads; or me, because I'd never driven a long distance before and was afraid I'd get lost if I couldn't stay on his heels. I was never more uptight than I was that morning as I followed Harry through Atlanta—in the dark and in the rain—as he weaved that truck in and out of unexpected heavy traffic while trying not to lose me at stop lights. As the trip progressed, I began to think of that U-Haul truck ahead of me as a big old St. Bernard whose tail I was hanging onto for dear life.

Harry said I did a terrific job, however, and a few days later when we reached our final destination safe and sound, got the truck unpacked and found no damage to our possessions, we felt we could do anything so long as we did it together.

CHAPTER 11

A Man of Many Interests and Talents

There are still a lot of books to read and a lot of fish to catch.—Harry

Neither Harry nor I went to college, which worked fine for me, but his situation was different. In his later years he would come to deeply regret his lack of a college degree. Of course his logic for not going to college was perfectly sound. Rejected by the military, he had exciting work waiting for him right out of high school with the Chicago Civic Orchestra. He didn't need a college degree to play percussion in any orchestra, and he believed that once he achieved his goal of getting into the Chicago Symphony he would have a job for life.

At eighteen, however, he couldn't have imagined the agonizing twists and turns his life would take, or that the day would come when his options as a performing musician would run out and he'd have to find another way to earn a living. Without a degree, his teaching options in colleges were limited, and he couldn't qualify for most managerial positions because a degree was usually a primary requirement. It didn't matter that he was smarter than a lot of college graduates, spoke better than most (never saying "ah," "uh," and "you know"), and had excellent managerial capabilities. Without that piece of paper, he was dead in the water.

Of course he didn't need a college education to teach privately, and I often heard him preach "get that degree!" to his private students. But teaching privately was of little interest to him as a job. All he really wanted to do was perform and share his expertise whenever he met a young drummer who needed some help with his technique. He did find a surprising number of places to teach over the years, however, and, even without college, he talked his way into a couple of good managerial jobs. Unfortunately, he didn't hold either of them for long. I think his natural entrepreneurial tendencies always made him feel as though he needed to be the one calling the shots, and he couldn't seem to long tolerate taking orders from those in a higher position of authority.

Without question, Harry was a man of many talents and acquired skills, and one who made learning a lifelong pursuit. He divided his learning time between books and educational programs on cable television. Naturally he loved the shows on PBS, and we both particularly enjoyed British mysteries such as *Morse, Dalgliesh, Poirot, Cadfael, Inspector Alleyn, Sherlock Holmes*, and *Lovejoy*. (In the *Lovejoy* shows, Harry was especially fond of Tinker and laughed heartily when he once said, "Just when things are going smoothly, an angel piddles in your beer.")

Most shows on the Learning, Discovery, and History channels were of interest to him, particularly those on the world's great religions, art, travel, and war, particularly World War II and the Civil War. We both loved the two *Connections* series by James Burke, as well as the programs Ken Burns produced on the Civil War, jazz, and baseball.

For TV amusement, Harry teased his brain with Jeopardy, and we both laughed together during the long seasons of *Mash, Barney Miller*, the *Dick Van Dyke Show*, and of course *The Mary Tyler Moore Show*, where Harry identified with her grumpy boss, Lou Grant (portrayed by Ed Asner). Harry was a faithful watcher of the news every day, but he was annoyed by how the quality of television news and talk radio had changed over the years. "Professionalism has given way to sensationalism and mediocrity," he said in one of his letters. "Everything that made the media so great has gone down to lowest of lows. Nobody speaks well; facts are either distorted or just plain wrong. Pronunciation is frightening, and there is just a complete lack of intelligent personalities."

Always a kid at heart, Harry loved the Muppets, the *Captain Kangaroo Show*, and *Kukla, Fran, and Ollie*. The latter show was broadcasted on NBC between 1941 and 1952, and then on ABC between 1954 and 1957. Somewhere along the line when Harry was working at NBC or ABC, he formed a friendship with Burr Tillstrom. I recall him telling me how he used to chat with Burr, Kukla, and Ollie when he was on break. He said he was always amazed by how natural it seemed to converse with these delightful characters, which seemed so real. Sometimes Fran was there, too. Years later, remembering these good times, Harry bought the entire collection of shows on videotape.

He got a kick out of watching some of the classic cartoons, too, and while I thought this was just the little boy in him making up for things he had missed as a kid, he said what he really loved about them was the music, which was loaded with percussion. (He particularly liked the cartoon music of Carl W. Stalling, who has been called the most famous unknown composer of the twentieth century.)

"Smarter Than the Average Bear"

One of Harry's nicknames was "Harry Bear," so of course he was a fan of the Yogi Bear cartoons and liked the line, "smarter than the average bear." I didn't always agree with Harry, but there was no denying his keen intelligence. I thought I was pretty smart, too, but he was smart in ways that had nothing to do with book learning.

A good marriage is built on both separateness and togetherness; on being alike, yet different. Here's a story that illustrates one of the differences between us. One Christmas I gave him a self-test to determine his IQ, telling him jokingly that now he could find out if he was as smart as he thought he was. But to my great annoyance he put the test away and forgot about it. One day I came across it and decided to take it myself. I was careful to write my answers on blank paper so as not to ruin his test later, and felt rather smug to learn that my IQ was high. I couldn't resist bragging to Harry that I was as smart as I always thought I was. "I can hardly wait for you to take the test, too," I said.

He looked at me as though I were really stupid. "You don't think I'm going to take that test now, do you?"

And therein lies the tale. If Harry had taken the test first, I would have taken the test just to see if I could beat him. But he had no interest at all in finding out whether he could beat me or not. At least that's what he said. I figured that what he really feared was that his score might be lower than mine, and that wouldn't do because he was the teacher, after all, and I the student. That was okay with me, but I still found it amusing. And he really got the last laugh because I was never going to know for sure if I was as smart as he was or not, and *he* was smart enough to figure all that out in the first place, so maybe . . .

As someone who made it a point to learn new things every day of his life, Harry was extremely well educated, and his superb memory for detail made him a fascinating conversationalist. "He had so many interests, and we talked about all kinds of things," says Rich Sherrill. "He had the ability to move freely from one subject to another as easily as he could move from playing a circus one day to performing in the symphony the next. What he was really good at was making some smartass remark that fit the exact situation we were in at the time. This type of story is hard to recreate—you really had to be there to appreciate the wit. His brain always seemed to be running a hundred miles a minute, and every conversation would have some humor in it because he would immediately take all the data, the environment, and the people there at the time, process it faster than the fastest computer, and spit out a humorous quip."

How true! I never knew when the next one was coming because Harry could process any ordinary bit of information and spit out a funny in an instant. Examples:

• One day when we were on the road, Harry (who always had food on his mind) pointed out a sign that said BACON Road, and asked, "Do you think it has an EGGS-it?"

• While driving through the town of Sandwich, Illinois, and seeing a directional sign pointing to SANDWICH HOSPITAL, I thought I was really being clever when I said, "I guess that's where they work on soggy buns." But Harry, who could always one-up me with no effort of all, said, "No, that's where they take care of cold cuts."

• On the news one night when they were talking about how coal was going to have to be used more and more in place of oil, Harry noted, "As I've always said, there's no fuel like an old fuel."

• During a television quiz show the question was, "Is there any reason why you should put peanut butter on your car's bumper?" Instantly Harry said, "Yeah, you might get in a jam and run into a bread truck."

• Reading *TV Guide* one evening, I said, "We've got *Killer Bees* with Gloria Swanson on one channel, and *Lord of the Flies* with English schoolboys on another. "Great," Harry said sarcastically. "All we need to finish the evening is an hour of S.W.A.T."

I had a real gift for walking into situations that just cried for a humorous put-down, and Harry could deliver a clever one-liner faster than Matt Dillon could draw his six-shooter. Like the morning I got up and began to dress, selecting a pair of stretch pants to wear. As I was pulling them on, I remarked that I never could tell the front from the back. "That's the trouble with you dear," he said, "you never know whether you're coming or going."

On another morning, I was looking for a shoe that had mysteriously disappeared during the night. Without realizing it, I set myself up for a joke when I asked Harry if he'd seen it anywhere. "Why don't you look in your mouth?" he said. "That's where you usually put your foot."

Harry always considered it his responsibility to keep my ego under control. I recall the time I walked into his office with a review of one of my books in hand. In a puffed-up voice, I read to him what the reviewer had said: "Marvelously specific, the type of book you'll want to savor slowly, one page at a time."

Harry quickly brought me back down to earth by saying, "What he's trying to tell you, dear, is that your book is hard to swallow."

Now some wives might have been insulted by this, but I loved being Harry's "straight man," and I didn't mind, either, that he was always trying to help me keep my ego under control because I *did* need help in that area. Being able to laugh at ourselves and with each other not only made our marriage more tolerable in times of stress, but strengthened the original foundation of friendship, trust, and understanding on which our marriage was built. As Charlie Chaplin once said, "Humor heightens our sense of survival and preserves our sanity."

Brabec the Bibliophile

Music was indeed Harry's mistress, but he also had a lifelong love affair with books. A quotation by poet Babington Macaulay that he clipped sums up how he felt about reading: "I would rather be a poor man in a garret with plenty of books than a king who did not love reading."

As a youth, his parents couldn't afford to buy books and it was a thrill, he said, when the bookmobile came around to his school. As an adult, he wanted to own as many books as possible, and he treated all of them with loving care. I like to highlight content in my books so I can go back later and find the passages that spoke to me the first time around. But Harry never turned down a page or made a mark in his books, and if I so much as picked up one of them, he'd sass me about handling it with care. He bought some books second-hand if he couldn't get them any other way, but mostly he bought books new, and then kept them in like-new condition after reading them. If a book had a dust jacket, he always removed it so he wouldn't wrinkle it. If the book was heavy, he would read it on a table so as not to damage it. He turned pages very carefully, and I never once saw him lick his finger to turn a page. If the book was a paperback, he was always very careful not to crease the spine. Indeed, here was a man who really loved his books and treated them with great respect.

His collection included many fine books in all of the music and entertainment categories, including big band, jazz, and percussion. (See BarbaraBrabec.com for more about these collections, which I ultimately decided to sell on the Amazon Marketplace. Drummers with old percussion books on their bookshelves might be surprised to find that some are worth a bundle on Amazon. In fact, all but one of Harry's like-new percussion books sold in the range of $175–$295 each.)

Until I began to go through Harry's library, book by book, I had no idea how many signed copies he had in his collection, particularly from musicians who had written books about their lives. I wasn't interested in the books he was buying, just as he wasn't interested in the books I was adding to my collection, so maybe that's why he never brought his auto-graphed books to my attention. In spite of his gregarious nature, he was a very modest man, and maybe he simply thought it would be bragging to show me these signed editions. The only thing I'm sure about now is that he appreciated the special inscriptions in those books because they were clearly written by musicians he knew or had worked with at one time or another.

Lon A. Gault, author of *Ballroom Echoes* (Colophone, 1989) inscribed his book to Harry so touchingly that I couldn't bear to part with it: "For Harry J. Brabec, a stalwart of big band music—may this book remind you of those one-nighters!" (Lon was a history professor who also offered classes about big bands and ballrooms and hosted a weekly program on WDCB in Chicago called "Big Band Ballroom.")

Harry also had a passionate interest in military bands and band books and music, particularly those related to the U. S. Marine Band and the circus. Nostalgic books on his shelves included all of the books written by Norbert Blei, a Czech who wrote about many places and things familiar to him. He also had a good collection of books about Czecho-slovakia, fine art, literature, and many history books, particularly those relating to ships and the sea, the Civil War, and World War II. He was fond of Custer, too, and I recall one time when I came up with an original Custer joke that he liked. "What state was Custer in when he died?" I asked very seriously.

"That's easy," he said. "He died in the Battle of the Little Bighorn in Montana."

"Nope," I said with some smugness. "He died in a state of PANIC."

I usually played the straight man for Harry's jokes, so when I could "get him" with one of my own, he was very proud of me.

Trivia and the English Language

Harry enjoyed all kinds of trivia. He was always wondering why this, or why that, so he was an avid buyer of books such as David Feldman's *When Do Fish Sleep, Who Put the Butter in Butterfly, Imponderables— The Solution to the Mysteries of Everyday Life*, and *How Did It Begin?*, the latter of which is a fascinating study of the superstitions, customs, and strange habits that influence our daily lives. His collection also included *Why Do Dogs Have Wet Noses?, Do Clocks Run Clockwise?, A Hog on Ice & Other Curious Expressions*, and many other unusual books with interesting titles. Clearly, Harry shared Bertrand Russell's belief that "There is much pleasure to be gained from useless knowledge."

Of course books that made him laugh were high on his list, and he especially liked Lewis Grizzard's books, including *Shoot Low, They're Riding Shetland Ponies*, and *Chili Dawgs Always Bark at Night*, whose titles were funny to begin with.

His passion for reading led him to read many books related to language itself, from the origin of words and sayings to how to speak it correctly, such as *Anguished English: An Anthology of Accidental Assaults Upon Our Language* by Richard Lederer (Dell, 1989), and *Is There a Cow in Moscow—More Beastly Mispronunciations and Sound Advice* by Charles Elster (Collier Books, 1999).

In a 1999 letter to Doug MacLeod, Harry shared these thoughts about books and reading:

> The last time we talked, you mentioned you were reading the book, *Citizen Soldier*, by Stephen Ambrose, and I mentioned there was another book that he recommended very highly, and I've enclosed a review of it. You might want to try and get it from the library, which is where I get a lot of my books

that I don't really want to keep. Barb is suggesting that we put a sign on our front lawn telling people that this is the "Brabec & Brabec Bookstore." The house seems to be bursting at the seams with books and magazines we haven't read yet.

We were going to go off on a vacation to a cabin in the woods of Wisconsin, our usual haunt, but physically, I just can't cut it. It's a long drive, and it's too hard now to pack all the books, games, hobbies, music tapes, and other stuff we need to amuse ourselves while we're there. So little by little, although I try to keep as active as possible, I'm becoming a fly on the flypaper of life. Had that cataract eye operation, which scared the hell out of me. For about two weeks I couldn't read because of fogginess over the eyes. It was temporary, however, and I'm back to my usual reading habits, with Barb helping me with the big words.

Word Play

For someone who loved the English language so much, one might wonder why Harry delighted in mangling it to suit his humorous purposes. He made up many variations of ordinary words and phrases that became standard in our household and sometimes may have made people wonder if we were literate. I now think of these as "Harryisms."

One of his favorite word changes was "incidentally." Early in our relationship when we both had so much to learn about one another, we found ourselves constantly saying, "incidentally . . ." before telling one more important thing about ourselves. Harry soon shortened that five-syllable word to just four, giving us "incadently."

Expressions Harry often used included "Time is fluting" (when he was in a hurry), "He's got the personality of a wart," "Don't make with the funny ha-ha's," "Don't be a Mopey Dick," "He's breeding a pimple on the ass of progress," "How's them apples, Charley?", and "You tell 'em, I stutter." I always knew we were in a tricky driving situation—icy roads, bad traffic, or perhaps a reckless driver he was trying to avoid—when he said, "Hang onto your zoobie!" just before he made a dangerous driving maneuver or hit the accelerator to avoid a possible accident. (I might add that he was a magnificent defensive driver who never had an accident in our life together, aside from being hit in the rear once by a truck whose brakes failed when we were at a stoplight with nowhere to go.)

One of my favorite words then and now, which Harry always used to describe any delicious concoction that satisfied his inner cravings, was

"Goopenpucky." Whenever he asked for this for dessert, I knew he would be happy with any cake, pie, or other dessert that was loaded with calories and lots of whipped cream. I always thought he made up this word, but when I found one use of it on the Web in connection with window repairs, I figured he might have picked it up from some construction worker he knew back in the forties, loved the musicality of the word, and simply gave it a new definition.

One of Harry's original words actually won a prize in 1971 when *Yankee* magazine announced the "Name-the-Indian Contest" being run by Hayward's Trading Post in Milford, New Hampshire. A name was needed for the cigar store Indian that had long been the insignia identifying them as "The World's Largest Moccasin Shoppe." Harry won a pair of handmade deerskin moccasins with his name of "Chief Weegotumwatchuwant."

Playing on words was a lifetime game for Harry, who asked:

- "Do you suppose the guys who work in fish hatcheries work for scale?"
- "Is a midget who works on a commuter railroad a metrognome?"
- "Is a guy who builds bookcases shelf-employed?"

To Harry, a crackpot was a "psycho-ceramic." His suggestion for a theme song for King Kong was "Gir-rilla My Dreams." And a motto for snow plough shovelers was "There's no business like snow business."

One of my favorite quips is the one he delivered the day I asked him to unstop the drain in my bathtub shower, where I normally wash my hair. He gave a bad-back grunt as he bent over, reached down and said, "No wonder it's stopped up. There's enough hair in here to start a musical."

An Amazing Collection of Music

Harry began to collect LPs shortly after we married, and he had nearly 5,000 albums when he stopped buying records in the mid-nineties to start his CD collection. Half the records were big band and jazz albums with the rest being an eclectic combination of every other kind of music imaginable, except rock. He used to start at the beginning of his big band collection in his office and play every album straight through (filed in alphabetical order, of course), and he once said it took him about a year to play through the whole collection. Then he'd start over again—or at least he did until the era of CDs, at which point he played only his favorite records.

Harry always maintained that his records were going to be worth a fortune some day, but those hopes were dashed when CDs came along and made LPs obsolete. Or at least that's what we both thought at the time. Today, however, there are still many who collect vinyl albums because they offer a quality of sound that can't compare to that of a CD; moreover, many of the great jazz and big band albums were never reproduced on CD. (Amazon currently lists nearly 30,000 vinyl albums for sale from individual Marketplace sellers.) As one who knew all about making a comeback, Harry would have been thrilled to know that vinyl albums are making a comeback, too. According to an article by Bill Newcott in the January–February 2010 issue of *AARP* magazine, record companies are once again making money from vinyl albums, and retailers such as Borders and Best Buy are reducing their CD space to make room for new vinyl-LP racks.

"Sales soared 89 percent in 2008," Newcott reports, "while CDs, falling prey to Internet downloads, continued to trudge down the road to extinction." Newcott adds that collecting vinyl is not just a generational thing. "Newer acts . . . are finding an LP audience as well, offering vinyl and MP3-download versions of their latest releases as a single package."

When Harry first began to buy CDs, he promised me he would buy only music that he didn't have in his LP collection. Later, when I saw he was beginning to duplicate some of his LPs, I asked him why he didn't just play the records. He had a wonderful excuse: "When I die, I know you will never have time to mess with playing LPs, so from here on, I'm just buying music that I know *you* will want to hear." (How thoughtful could a guy get, right?)

♪ Music Sidenote ♪

Over the years, Harry exchanged many letters with Phil Holdman, a former big band drummer who used to host a jazz radio show and publish *The Browsers* newsletter. What's a Browser, you're wondering? Harry's old drummer friend, Joe Sperry, also a Browser, defined it like this: "A Browser is a dedicated devotee of the truly American art form known as the Big Band. Some years ago, Phil Holdman, founder, often visited record shops seeking rare examples of LPs and 78s to add to his extensive collection. Here, he also met other collectors who sought similar discs or tapes. Phil's wife, Alberta, named the group 'The Browsers' because they were always browsing in record shops. Meetings were held first in member's homes, and then in friendly tavern-restaurants. The roster of Browsers brought to the group a wealth of experience in the fields of music and broadcasting."

Phil Holdman has been in an assisted care facility for a couple of years now, so the old *Browsers* newsletter is no longer in print. But Robert B. Knack is continuing the tradition in a fine newsletter titled *The Great Escape*. In a recent issue Bob wrote, "The Browsers, experts in the big band era, were the creators of an ABC Network big band radio trivia program, hosted by radio legend Eddie Hubbard for 22 years. They also produced a newsletter through most of that period. Some were big band singers or instrumentalists, a few were radio/TV people or journalists. Many were merely rabid fans of that great music and avid record collectors."

The Browsers are still active and meet on the last Friday of every month for beer, pizza, and good conversation at Dino's Restaurant on Chicago's northwest side. Their newsletter is available in both print and electronic formats from DixieSwing.com.

Harry would be shaking his head in wonder if he knew that I had become something of a Browser myself. He never imagined that I would actually be playing his LPs after he was gone, but for the past five years I have been methodically playing all of them to determine which albums I want to dub to CDs for my listening pleasure, as well as those that have some market value and can be sold when I've gleaned all the music I want from his collection. In listening to these albums, I naturally found I wanted more of many orchestras and instrumentalists. Once I learned how to dub a CD from an LP I suddenly found myself looking through record stacks at garage sales, church sales, and Good Will. I continue to find a surprising number of albums for fifty cents or a dollar that play perfectly after being cleaned, and once I dub them to a CD, I send them to Good Will so someone else can enjoy them.

I've dubbed about 600 LPS so far and will probably do a few hundred more before I get through Harry's big band collection, which music I love as much as he did. Then I'll be offering the best of his big band, jazz, classical, and instrumental mint-condition albums for sale on the Web. I laugh whenever I play one of his Big Band albums and see a title on the jacket that amused him, too. Examples:

- *Everybody Wants to Go to Heaven, but Nobody Wants to Die* (Les Brown)
- *Does the Spearmint Lose its Flavor on the Bedpost Overnight?* (B. Strong)
- *I've Never Seen a Straight Banana* (Fred Waring)
- *When the Mush Begins to Rush Down Father's Suit*—subtitled "The Coat and Pants Do All the Work and the Vest Gets All the Gravy" (Hoosier Hot Shots)
- *Some Little Bug is Going to Find You Someday* (Guy Lombardo)
- *Who Threw the Whiskey in the Well?* (Tommy Dorsey)
- *I'm Looking for a Guy Who Plays Alto & Baritone, Doubles on Clarinet, and Wears a Size 37 Suit* (my favorite Ozzie Nelson tune).

For Christmas, as I was nearing completion of this book, my sisters gifted me with an iPod Classic, and I was elated to learn that this little electronic wonder can hold 40,000 songs, 25,000 photographs, or a combination of both. So now I have the technology to get all of my favorite music from Harry's collection and all my favorite pictures of my life with him into a gadget I can hold in the palm of my hand. Granted, the sound won't be as rich as what I hear when I play the old LPs, but if I end up in a nursing home at the end of my life with nothing more than this book and my iPod, I could die happy. I used to hate how technology was forcing me to change the way I worked and lived my life, but now I see only how it is enriching the last years of my life.

Amusing Surprises in the Cassette Tape Boxes

In the early eighties and nineties, Harry and I traveled all over the country for both business and personal reasons. By then he had a good little personal recording studio in his office where he spent countless hours transferring music from his LPs to cassette tapes we could play in the car and listen to in our motel rooms or the cabin in Wisconsin where we liked to vacation. (This was before cars had built-in cassette tape players, but we powered our portable player by plugging it into the cig-arette lighter plug.) He also enjoyed trading voice and noncommercial cassette tapes with a few music friends.

A couple of months after Harry died, I began the arduous task of cleaning out his office and looking through the many boxes of cassette tapes on his closet shelves. The space in his office that once was a clothes closet had long ago been filled with floor-to-ceiling shelves. Thirty-four cassette boxes—each holding about 30 tapes—were stacked three boxes high in three rows on the top shelf, below which were the storage units holding the several hundred CDs he had collected. Never one to throw anything useful away, Harry had saved these boxes from years earlier when it was common for me to order five thousand business reply envelopes at a time. They came in a box the perfect width for cassette tapes, and after I covered each box with walnut-toned Con-Tact paper, he affixed squares of bright orange card stock, neatly labeled in his bold printing as to contents: big band, jazz, classical, circus, percussion, band music, Marine Band, etc.

In addition to all the music Harry had dubbed from his record collection, taped off radio, or gotten in exchange from friends, I found a collection of commercial tapes that included many old-time radio shows. Harry was a great fan of Phil Harris because he always got some good belly laughs from his humor, so he bought all the shows Harris did with Alice Faye that he couldn't capture live on the old-time radio show he always listened to. (You would not believe how many times Harry asked to see Disney's classic, *The Jungle Book*, because Phil Harris did such an incredible job in the role of the lovable bear, Baloo. I have to admit that I loved this film as much as he did, and there is no doubt it was a remarkable tonic for Harry whenever his pain was getting the best of him.)

In one of the tape boxes, I found a collection of miscellaneous tapes that gave me a lot of laughter midst my grieving tears. One was a cassette wrapped in white paper with a rubber band around it labeled "Barb snoring." Harry often complained that I snored, but I didn't believe I snored as loudly as he said, so one night he made a tape of me snoring just to prove he was right. But I had no idea he had *saved* the tape all those years. Maybe for evidence in case I forgot he had a grievance here?

Also in this box was a collection of tapes that included musical novelty numbers such as the delightful "Combine Harvester" (an English song we first heard while in London, which you can hear today on YouTube); the "Go Go Chiropractor," and "Professor" Pete Barbutti's "Kordeen School" stand-up routine (the latter of which is also available on YouTube). The one that amused me most, however, was Misty Morgan and Jack Blanchard's recording of their song, "I'm Washing Harry Down the Sink" (something I felt like doing at times when he was being less than his usual sweet self).

Also in this box was a tape Harry had made from his "Victory at Sea" CD, which includes the real sounds of a ship preparing for battle, with the "Man your battle stations!" command and the "aye-oo-ga" sirens sounding, the machine guns and cannons blasting, and an airplane diving the ship. Harry lifted this particular section and put it on a tape he could play through the speakers down in our guest area. Twice when we had visitors and the man happened to have been in the Navy, he gleefully played this recording as a wakeup call, blasting it in their ears while they were still sound asleep. Once the guest and his wife got over the shock of being scared half to death, they thought this was a pretty funny Brabec joke. Harry only wished he knew more ex-sailors who wanted to stay overnight with us.

He did a lot of things in his office that I never knew about because I was so wrapped up in my own office work and writing. But one tape I found gave me an idea of how he used his little micro-recorder to make notes. He was in his office that day, apparently making a list of song titles he was going to type and send along with a tape he was making for a friend. I was obviously annoying him with the noise I was then making in the kitchen because he was rattling off the titles of several tunes and their composers at breakneck speed and then, without a break in rhythm or speed, he said very sarcastically, "Thanks for rattling the dishes, Barb; I couldn't have done it without you," then immediately went back to his rapid-fire reading of tune titles again.

Later in this tape, probably when he was reading, he stopped abruptly and said, "Look up the word *oracular*, spelled o-r-a-c-u-l-a-r. Also look up *canoodling*, spelled c-a-n-o-o-d-l-i-n-g." Naturally I stopped the tape at that point and got his dictionary off the shelf. I found that "oracular" means "giving forth utterances or decisions as if by special inspiration or authority," which definition made me laugh because one could say that Harry was always acting in an oracular manner about the house. "Canoodling" means "petting or caressing; kissing or cuddling."

It didn't matter that we didn't use words like this in our speech, it's just that Harry loved words, and every time he ran into a new word he didn't know, he'd look it up in his seven-pound $90 Webster's Dictionary—a book he valued so much that he asked me for a quarter every time I wanted to use it. Remembering this, I laugh every time I open it now.

In the middle of another of his microcassette tapes in which he was making a list of miscellaneous things he wanted to do, he interjected, "and order a dozen Dressels cakes" (his favorite store-bought cake).

On another day I found a tape where we were remembering our trip to Moscow back in the seventies. On it I said I remembered how hard he had laughed at one of the acts in the Russian Circus, and he said, "You can probably hear me laughing on the tape I made of that act." As soon as I heard him say that, all I wanted to do was find the tape labeled "Moscow Circus." And when I played it and got to that part of the show, there was Harry's wonderful belly laughter underscoring the hilarious trombone music accompanying this act. Hearing him laugh like that again when I was missing him so much was like finding a diamond on the sidewalk.

There were a few other voice tapes, portions of which, along with Harry's joyful belly laughter at the circus, will eventually be on this book's companion website as MP3 downloads. I am fortunate to have this much of Harry that I can cling to so I'll never forget the rich sound of his voice and the way he delivered humorous quips. He always used to say I never listened to him, but all I wanted to do for a year after he died was play his voice tapes over and over again. I never realized until he was gone how much I loved and missed the sound of his voice. (If you have never captured the voices of your loved ones, do it now because I tell you true, you'll yearn to hear them again when they're gone.)

Seeing Harry through his Files, Notebooks, and Scrapbooks

When we die, each of us will leave something of ourselves behind for others to find and deal with, and some of us will leave much more than others. Unless clear instructions have been left for the survivors, someone will have to try to figure out what to do with all this "stuff." Harry left a *lot* of stuff, but he only gave me instructions for what to do with his drum equipment. We never discussed what I should do with his large collections of books, records, tapes, tools, files, notebooks, and scrapbooks. I guess he figured I was smart enough to know what to do with anything I didn't want, and he was right. But this was a *huge* job, and one that is still unfinished after five years.

The walls of Harry's music room were covered with artwork and photographs that told part of the story of his musical career. His office was also filled with art, pictures, and eight small filing cabinets, all of which I had to sort through to decide what had meaning to me or others. I eventually brought all the things I kept together in one room I now use as a second office and recording studio. (You can see it on one of Harry's pages on my personal domain at BarbaraBrabec.com.)

Harry's office files contained dozens of neatly-labeled manila folders full of carefully trimmed magazine and newspaper clippings of places he wanted to see, restaurants he wanted to try, cities and countries he yearned to visit or revisit again, books he wanted to read, music he wanted to order, and people he wanted to contact. One drawer contained dozens of maps; other drawers and shelves contained no less than twenty telephone books for various cities, some dating back to 1990. Before we had computers, Harry considered his telephone books from every major city in the U.S., and Yellow Pages in particular, to be indispensable information tools. He loved it when I would come to him and say I needed to find this or that, and he'd immediately get out his phone books and play detective on the phone until he turned up a source for the needed product or service.

Stacked in the basement workshop area, I found several boxes of *Civil War Times, American History,* and *National Geographic* magazines Harry couldn't bring himself to throw out, and I couldn't even give away. Other boxes contained years of newspaper clippings he had saved in the belief that, some day, he'd have time to file them in one of his hundreds of file folders. But he simply ran out of time. I looked through every file folder, box, and notebook, and it occurred to me then that anyone looking through these boxes and Harry's files would have known what a thirsty mind he had, and how interested he was in hundreds of topics, places, and things. It broke my heart every time I had to put another box of "Harry's stuff" out for pickup because I felt like I was throwing out little pieces of him along with it.

In bookcases in his music room, I found hundreds of back issues of big band and jazz magazines and newsletters going back to the 1970s (a few of which I found buyers for); a dozen three-ring notebooks filled with programs, circus newsletters, and music-related articles, plus a couple dozen beautifully designed scrapbooks of his life and career, musicians he knew and worked with, obituaries of famous big band and jazz musicians, circus clippings and memorabilia, and hundreds of cartoons that had made him laugh. Here are lines from three music cartoons I liked:

• Two princesses passing a frog by the pond: "I kissed a frog once—but it turned into a musician."

• Wife: "I've had such an interesting life, I could write a book." Husband: "I've had such a ringing in my ears I could write a symphony."

• Funky Winkerbean (rehearsing kids for a Christmas concert, running through it a second time): "This time I want you to play it TWICE as fast! That way the wrong notes won't last so long."

I knew all those scrapbooks were there, but, until I really began to look through them, I had no idea how much time and effort Harry had put into them. One night after looking through one of his circus scrapbooks, I just sat there and cried, not only because it was so beautifully done, but because I didn't remember ever having seen it before. I was often in the room with him working on a project of my own when he was working on one of his scrapbooks, but he never offered to show them to me. I could have looked at them any time, but he never forced them on me, and I let my own projects occupy so much of my time that I never really appreciated them until he was gone. Of course, he never looked at my scrapbooks, either, so I think it's interesting how each of us was wrapped up in our own little worlds to a large degree, not imposing our interests on each other, but merely sharing them when it suited our purposes.

Now I delight in imagining how pleased Harry would be to know that his scrapbooks are playing such an important role in this book, and how much of his music memorabilia is going to be shared on the book's companion website. Without the help of his letters and scrapbooks, I never could have pieced together an accurate timeline of his career—where he was performing, when, and with whom—nor recalled the names of so many of his musician friends.

The Drummer's Workshop and Pack Rat Tendencies

Harry's gifted musical hands were put to practical use around the house. In fact, there was little that needed to be done in the home maintenance department that he couldn't take care of, and this saved us a small fortune over the years. He could do all the simple basic electric wiring and plumbing, install light fixtures and outlet plugs, hang anything on any kind of wall, hook up telephone wires, set up all his recording equipment, and run speaker wires to every room of the house. (Since we moved so often, he got to do these same things over and over again. Thanks to his teaching, I can do many of these things, too.)

He took pride in his workshop, which was as clean and well organized as his office and music room. I still remember how amazed one of his friends was when he was getting a tour of it. "Do you actually *work* on this workbench?" he asked. "It looks clean enough for surgery."

Harry always said I should buy everything I needed to run a great kitchen, and he felt the same way about his workshop, which meant that he had every kind of hand and power tool imaginable, from all the basic tools to power drills, saws, sanders, a grinder, and even a chain saw. He never threw out the original box a tool or piece of equipment came in, and he often stored specialty items in their original boxes, arranging them neatly on a shelf or in a drawer. All instruction manuals were carefully filed, and all hand tools were artistically arranged on the large pegboard over his workbench. And woe was me if I took a tool off the pegboard and didn't put it back *exactly* where I found it. It wasn't long before Harry set me up with my own personal toolbox with the message being, "leave *my* tools alone, thank you."

Harry's old workshop is much smaller now that I've sold most of his tools and equipment, but I still have a nice workshop of my own. (Having a mechanic for a father, my sisters and I have always been handy with tools.) It took me weeks to sort through everything here. In addition to all the tools themselves, several shelves held all kinds of containers, from antique wood boxes, cigar boxes, and metal 3x5-card file drawers to tin cookie canisters, glass jars, and plastic prescription bottles.

In addition to his regular cases of nuts, bolts, screws, and nails, these various containers held thousands of additional items: larger nuts, bolts, screws, and nails; audio, electrical, and telephone supplies; hangers, hooks, chains, old trunk hatches, and several metal items I couldn't identify. In two dozen larger boxes that had served as moving cartons through the years (always saved and stored by my frugal Bohemian for the *next* move), I found bits and pieces of every imaginable kind of raw material, from wood, rubber, tin, leather, plastic and felt to wire, cording, and screening, plus numerous broken household items Harry figured he might salvage parts from. It was a veritable hardware store down there, and my job was to sort out what should be given to friends, sold in a garage sale, or hauled out to the trash.

I wasn't surprised by this, of course, because as early as 1964 I was complaining to my mother about Harry's propensity for collecting junk:

It's absolutely amazing how just Harry and I can accumulate so much junk. He's such a pack rat who won't throw anything away, even boxes, that it gets ridiculous and I have to take the situation in hand once in a while when he's away and sneak some things into the furnace. I throw out a pair of shoes no longer wearable, or a purse with a busted handle, or a coffeepot with a hole in it, and he promptly retrieves all of them for some future use, he says, which I can't possibly imagine.

In a folder in Harry's office titled "Interesting Sayings & Quotes," I found many quotations written in his hand as well as many he had clipped from magazines and newspapers (see Appendix). He identified with this one from Andy Rooney, whom he got a kick out of:

"There are two kinds of savers. The first is the practical saver who keeps string, bags and old aluminum foil as a practical matter. And then there's the sentimental saver. The sentimental saver can't stand the idea of throwing out any memory of his life."

Harry was the practical saver; I'm the sentimental slob who is saving everything relating to my and Harry's life and interests. (I pity my sisters who will have the job of throwing out all *my* junk some day.)

Did I just say Harry was a practical saver? Maybe that's not the right adjective. He didn't have a bathrobe when we married, and every night when he got home from a job he'd strip to his shorts and then sit around until he got sleepy. I was afraid he'd catch cold, so I made him a white robe for Christmas from the plushest terry cloth fabric I could find. He was delighted with it—but "delighted" didn't quite cover it. Harry *loved* that robe, and as both he and the garment aged (with him getting thicker around the middle as the robe wore thinner on the shoulders), he pleaded with me to patch it.

I patched and patched that robe for years, finally buying him a beautiful new one the first time he had to be hospitalized because I was too embarrassed for him to be seen in that ratty old thing. He wore the new robe in the hospital to please me, but the minute he got home, he switched back to his old one. I think now this garment would have qualified for "Ripley's Believe It or Not," because it was still in his closet 43 years later when he died. He simply wouldn't let me throw it away.

Sentimental saver that I am, I couldn't bring myself to throw it away, either, opting instead to cut pieces of usable fabric for my ragbag.

Harry would have approved of that.

CHAPTER 12

Playing Life by Ear

Do what you can, with what you have, where you are.—Theodore Roosevelt

When we left Florida in the spring of 1973 to resettle in Missouri, the tempo of Harry's life gradually slowed from Vivace to Allegro and changed key as well. Now the music was gone, and he was beginning to play life by ear, learning how to do work he never imagined he would be doing to make a living. Like the old timpani player he was, he began to retune his life to stay on key and figure out a new way to roll.

Thanks to having an old music buddy at Silver Dollar City (SDC) in Missouri, plus his credentials as publisher of *Artisan Crafts* magazine, Harry talked his way into the job of Festival Coordinator for the City's annual fall festival in 1973. He had never done this kind of work before, and I was rather surprised to find that he could meticulously plan any event down to the last detail. Once again his natural creativity and imagination enabled him to do this job magnificently.

The Silver Dollar City Crafts Festival

Silver Dollar City, near Branson, Missouri, is an authentically reconstructed village of the 1880s period that has grown and developed over many years. The City's season runs from May through October, and the highlight of each season is its National Harvest Festival (which was called the "National Festival of Craftsmen" in the seventies). An article in a local magazine titled "Specialist Brings Talent to Aid in Festival" described Harry's new job:

Drumming up the best National Festival of Craftsmen we've ever had is the assignment recently undertaken by Harry Brabec. [Then some introductory information about his background that mentioned our crafts magazine.] It was Barb, in fact, who stimulated our new crafts coordinator's interest in the sort of historic handwork which has made Silver Dollar City distinctive. That was back in the days when Harry was still in the midst of what he expected to be a lifelong career as a drummer—which began at the age of 14 with the then widely known Cole Brothers Circus.

In later years, his musical skills were recognized in every sort of setting from lounges featuring the jazz greats of the nation to the huge hall of the National Symphony in Washington, D.C. Harry laughs as he recalls his title with that famous orchestra was "premier percussionist."

Now, though, it's a whole different way of life. "Except," says Harry, "it's still a case of dealing with people. The crafts demonstrators in the Festival are, to a considerable extent, performers, and those who come to see them here are an audience. So actually, I haven't strayed too far from long years of experience as a performer who worked to please his audience."

Harry happily turned in his tuxedo for a pair of jeans and soon became friends with every artist and craftsman in the City. One day during the Festival, I overheard someone directing a stranger to Harry, saying, "Just look for a great big guy in blue overalls with a red handkerchief in his back pocket and a rope belt around his waist." He enjoyed getting to know so many interesting and creative people, and because we had met so many craftspeople during our magazine experience, he brought many new faces and crafts to the show that year.

He liked the lively flavor of Ozark music and was very fond of Violet Hensley, who made her own fiddles and played up a storm. And of course he also loved every exhibit in the City that featured food. One of the craftsmen he brought to the Festival was Horman Foose, a tinsmith we had met earlier in one of our treks to Pennsylvania. Among the various items he made were the special wide-mouth long-handled funnels needed for making traditional funnel cakes. Horman's wife demonstrated the making of this treat, and Harry considered it an important responsibility to "check its quality" every day. He also personally inspected (sampled) all the homemade cheese being made daily, and often brought home huge chunks that were made by City employees to demonstrate the craft but couldn't be sold. Although he was no longer drinking in those days, he took great delight in successfully bringing a moonshine exhibit to the festival, which required more than a little negotiating with the Bureau of Alcohol, Tobacco and Firearms. When my Uncle Ray came for a visit and told Harry he had never tasted real moonshine before, Harry smuggled out a bottle of it under his arm, craftily disguised as a box of Saltine crackers.

Music in the Ozarks

About a year after moving into our house on Gobbler's Mountain, we made the acquaintance of Phyllis Hageman, a neighbor and reporter whose "Down DD" column was about the people and happenings on this road. After reading a letter Harry had written to the editor of *Early American Life* magazine, she was curious to know "who this man from Reeds Spring was and how come he was publishing a magazine called *Artisan Crafts*." Her column reported:

> *Harry told me he had been a percussionist with the Chicago Symphony and later worked in music at Disney World in Florida; looking for a quiet and pleasant place to live, he and Barbara finally wound up here in the Ozarks. Living may be quiet, but their schedule doesn't seem to be. The magazine, Harry tells me, is the result of their joint effort, and it really keeps them hopping. Besides, Harry is head over heels in the Handicraft Show at the City—so there can't be many quiet moments in that household.*

She had that right. We were both putting in long hours with Harry at the City most of the time, and me at my desk, working on magazine articles and dealing with a large volume of mail related to our business. Harry loved his job, but he missed playing. Because his hours at the City were flexible—they didn't care how much time he spent in the office, only that the necessary work got done—he was free to explore his freelance music options. He was very happy when he was invited to be on the faculty of The School of the Ozarks for its 1974 summer term. In addition to his regular teaching duties, he participated in student conferences and did a little conducting, which got him another mention in Hageman's (obviously one of his biggest fans) column:

Was that "our" Harry Brabec mentioned in a recent news story concerning the dedication of the Ernest N. Stafford Horticulture Center at the School of the Ozarks last Sunday? Among items on the agenda for the dedication ceremonies the article said, "The School of the Ozarks Wind Ensemble, under the direction of Harry Brabeck, will play the National Anthem." I suspect that despite the addition of the "k," it really was Harry, whose musical credentials are impeccable, along with his many other talents.

Later, when a local newspaper reporter interviewed him about this event, he said, "My training came by way of hard knocks. They say I'm one of the best drummers in the country," and then he would pause for dramatic effect before adding, "not very good in the city, but really good in the country."

Some time around then, Harry decided to get some of his new music friends in the Ozarks together to play some jazz. When the new Park Central Mall in downtown Springfield was being revitalized, his little group, which he dubbed "The Brabec Six," played a concert called "And All That Jazz." He was amused when Phyllis Hageman once again wrote about him in her column:

There goes our Harry again! Or went, I should say. I happened to hear an announcement on a Springfield radio station and thought, "Oh no, it can't be THE Harry Brabec—not with all he has to do with the Crafts Festival coming up at SDC." But it was our Harry.

The Brabec Six played an afternoon concert called "And All That Jazz" at the Park Central Square last Saturday afternoon. How he found the time with his other exploits, I don't know. I told Harry I didn't think he took vitamins, they took him.

Harry swears he's goin' fishin' as soon as the crafts fair is over, but I really don't think those fish have much to worry about. He's as bad as the bearded wonder: I don't think those two know what it means to rest; sleep is just something they squeeze in somewhere

Later, The Brabec Six performed at the Midwest Attorney Generals Conference Party and was a big hit. And why not? It was a saloon party with dancing—right up Harry's alley.

In our spare time, Harry and I spent some time maintaining the property we owned, which required weekly mowing. One day while we were out there for the afternoon we spied a dog watching us from the woods. Obviously yearning for human companionship, she cautiously crawled towards us on her belly, as if fearful of being struck, and I managed only a quick touch to her head before she turned and ran away. We learned from neighbors that she had been badly abused by her owner, who had recently died of a brain tumor. When his wife left the property, she also left the dog behind to fend for itself. We couldn't stand the thought of this dog's suffering, so the next day we searched for her in the woods, and I was able to lure her to me with some food. She was near death when we brought her back to our home, literally starving and covered in blood-sucking ticks. We planned on cleaning her up and then taking her to the pound so she could be adopted, but she quickly wormed her way into our hearts, and neither Harry nor I could bear to part with her. We named her Ginger, and Harry absolutely adored her.

After two wonderful years at Silver Dollar City, Harry asked for a raise and was stunned to get a letter saying that his request couldn't be met, and they had decided instead to hire his assistant to run the show the following year because she was willing to work for the same salary Harry had been receiving. We were simply flabbergasted when they didn't even give him a chance to negotiate the contract. Later, the owner of the City sent Harry an apologetic letter saying he had been given a different story by the personnel manager, that he thought Harry didn't want the job unless he got the raise.

This was yet another example of the kind of bad luck that seemed to constantly plague him. Even when he did everything right and did a magnificent job, things didn't work out for him. It helped, however, when the president of the company later apologized for this "mix-up," adding that everyone there held him in the highest regard, and were grateful for the outstanding job he had done with the festival for two years.

It also helped when he received many letters from SDC's resident craftsmen, all of whom simply loved working with him. Those letters meant so much to him that he pasted them in his scrapbook. Violet Hensley wrote, "We will always remember you and your good nature." Someone named Smokey (who addressed his letter to "Mr. Harried Bear Brabec) said, "I have really enjoyed working with you and just plain being around you. You are one fantastic person in my eyes." Another wrote, "You made the craftsmen feel like you were one of them."

We stayed in Missouri until the recession of 1975 took its toll on our magazine business and we decided to cease publication and move back to the Chicago area, deciding to rent a house for awhile until we knew what Harry was going to do next. By then, he was more than a little aggravated with me for spending so much of my time on a venture that wasn't yielding a suitable profit for all the time I was giving it. His job had prevented him from being of much help to me, but even with his help I could see I was beating a dead horse. So I didn't give him a hard time when he finally delivered his ultimatum: "It's me or the magazine, kiddo, take your pick."

I closed out the magazine in 1976 with a three-issue *Craftspirit* series that received high acclaim from readers and national recognition by the American Revolution Bicentennial Association. More important, this got me off the hook for having to refund any unfilled issues. We joked to friends that our first business venture was a "literary success but a financial flop," but the experience I gained here proved to be worth gold when it led to a publishing contract for my first book later that year.

Even though Harry's job at Silver Dollar City lasted only a couple of years, we were always grateful that life took us in that direction because we came away with wonderful memories, some valuable work experience and, most important of all, an amazing dog named Ginger that would grace our lives for the next fourteen years.

The International Crafts Exposition

In 1976, after word of his success with the Silver Dollar City festival reached the management ears of Busch Gardens in Williamsburg, Virginia, Harry was invited to produce the first International Crafts Exposition for them. The idea, of course, was that this first-of-a-kind festival would attract thousands of new visitors to the park who would ultimately return again and again. He created a plan to bring together forty highly-skilled traditional American and European artisans and craftsmen who would demonstrate and sell their wares to an estimated quarter of a million visitors, and the first show was so successful that he was hired to produce a second one the following year.

The work for each year's show required two six-week trips abroad to search for interesting artisans who would demonstrate old-world skills. Harry found not only the unusual, but the rare. Many of the crafts he discovered had never been seen in America before, and a few techniques demonstrated at the Exposition were being practiced by only a few people in the world. Invited foreign craftspeople came from England,

Scotland, France, Germany, Austria, Italy, Czechoslovakia, and Poland. (Russia was added to the list of countries for the second year, but at the last minute the two craftsmen Harry had contracted for the show weren't allowed to attend, for reasons that never became clear. But he didn't mind because getting into Russia meant that we both got to see a traditional Russian circus performance few tourists were privileged to attend.)

I was fortunate to be able to accompany Harry on the second of each of those trips in 1976 and 1977, which were once-in-a-lifetime journeys filled with unforgettable people and places. Of course, Harry insisted on flying first class with all expenses paid. When I traveled with him, my travel and accommodations were part of the package, but we had to cover my meals. One may wonder why I even got to tag along for the second trip each year, and I can still remember hearing Harry say to his boss on the phone when this was being discussed, "She no go, I no go." He could barely stand being away from me for that first six-week trip; he wasn't going to tolerate two trips a year like that.

I'm not going into any great detail about this two-year period of our life because this experience would make a book by itself. But I'd like you to know a little about this time in Harry's life because it says much about his intelligence, creativity, and ingenuity. This would prove to be the most challenging management job of his life and one of the most profitable and personally satisfying as well.

This job required work throughout the year, but on a schedule of Harry's own making, which meant he could squeeze in a few symphony and band concerts here and there when he didn't have to travel. For each of the two years the festival ran, he made several trips to Williamsburg and a couple to New York and Washington, D.C. to meet with foreign consulates and embassies to work out the details of importing, exporting, visas, travel permits, tax requirements, and so on.

Each year on the first six-week trip abroad he would find the artisans, then come back and present his suggestions to Busch executives who would select the twenty they liked the best. On the second trip, this time armed with contracts and with me acting as his secretary, he worked out the multitude of details involved in getting twenty people and all their tools and products for sale into the U.S. and through Customs at the same time. (He already had contacts with artists and craftsmen all over America, so finding and signing the twenty American exhibitors each year was a piece of cake.)

The highlight each year was the festival itself, which ran for two weeks in September and required us to spend six weeks in Williamsburg prior to the show. We both walked the grounds of the show every day, talking with all the individual artisans and absorbing their enthusiasm for the show. When I wasn't involved in the show, I was working on my first book or taking Ginger for walks. That kind of stimulation for two weeks took the starch out of us, to say the least. We were on a constant high for the run of the show, and then we literally collapsed afterwards, feeling, I suspect, much like the Chicago Symphony members felt after returning home from an exhausting tour.

As I look back now and see all that this work required of Harry, I think how useless a college education would have been in this case. Instead, this job required the kind of know-how and day-to-day experience he had gained over his lifetime. His knowledge about European history, all the books he had read, and all those foreign travel shows he had always watched really paid off here because he knew a lot about every city and country he would ultimately visit. By my dragging him into crafts a few years earlier, he had also acquired a great appreciation for fine art and crafts, so this, coupled with what he had learned at Silver Dollar City, gave him unique insight when it came to picking the kind of demonstrating artisans that could please the public.

Harry always fancied himself something of a detective, and in this job he had a chance to prove his ability in that area because he had to figure out the best way to move from one city and country to another, get around in each city he visited, deal with language barriers, and then track down the specific individuals, businesses, organizations, and agencies in each of these places that could lead him to the individual artisans he was seeking. His expertise on the telephone was invaluable here, of course. More important, though, were his keen communication skills and ability to deal with strangers in a foreign land who needed to feel at ease with him as soon as they met him. His smiling face and sense of humor was never more valuable than it was here because he was dealing with every kind of personality imaginable, and humor was something everyone could understand, even when they needed someone to translate it for them.

After meeting different artisans in each country, Harry had to decide which ones were the most marketable to Busch in terms of their appearance, ability to communicate, demonstrate their art or craft, and produce enough work for a two-week sale. Basically, he had to know what the public wanted and which products they would most likely buy. As he had said in that interview while at Silver Dollar City, "It's still a case of dealing with people. The crafts demonstrators in the Festival are, to a considerable extent, performers, and those who come to see them here are an audience."

How he accomplished all this still boggles my mind. I couldn't have done this job even if I could have mustered the courage to travel alone all over Europe, England, and especially into Russia, and I don't know another individual (let alone a symphony musician) who could have pulled it off, either. It was simply a once-in-a-lifetime job that required a once-in-a-lifetime kind of guy, and Harry took to this work as easily as he took to the snare drum. *Never before—and never since—has there been an event like this in North America (or probably anywhere else in the world for that matter).*

On one hand, the trips abroad were incredibly interesting and exciting. On the other, from a travel standpoint they were exhausting. It's one thing to travel with an orchestra where all accommodations have been made for you by management; quite another to plan your own itinerary, travel alone, eat alone, and live alone for six weeks, especially when you're ill, as Harry was for most of his second trip alone. (He may have been remembering this when he added this quotation by Will Kommen to his bulletin board: "If you look like your passport photo, you're too ill to travel.")

Our trips took us to many capital cities of the world, including London, Edinburgh, Dublin, Munich, Florence, Vienna, Paris, Copenhagen, Athens, Rome, Venice, Prague, Warsaw, and Moscow—not necessarily in that order. As a small-town girl from a small Midwest farming community, I never could have imagined visiting any one of these cities, let alone all of them not once, but twice. *What a gift Harry gave me here.* Traveling with him was like being on an all-expenses paid honeymoon because we couldn't find a single thing to fuss about during our travels and time in Williamsburg. While traveling, I documented every little detail in my journals which, when typed, totaled more than 50,000 words. In all my years of writing books, magazine columns, and newsletters, Harry never read a word of my business or crafts writing unless I told him I had written something about him. He just had no interest in my business topics. But he read the two books I wrote about our travels abroad and was grateful for all the details I included that otherwise would have slipped from our memories.

Dining on the Way to Germany

The amusing remarks that follow were penned by Harry in 1977 as he was leaving Chicago to fly to Frankfurt, Germany. Once on board, he jotted these comments because I had asked him to make notes about his trip that I could read when he got home.

Well, here we go again! With the usual German precision our plane left its mooring at exactly 5:15, but, with the usual American foul-up, we didn't lift off until 25 minutes later. The first class section is completely filled with a quiet but happy group.

Before we actually departed, over the loudspeaker came the voice of our captain in German, and my first reaction was *by God I'm in the Luftwaffe and we are going to bomb Cicero!* Soon after this we were served a little snack of a small dilled ear of corn, a few celery bits, an olive, and a green onion that went down like butter and then exploded! This was followed by two finger sandwiches. I don't know what they were, but I do know that one was fish and the other wasn't. A girl also came around with Champagne and orange juice, and naturally "contrary Harry" asked for a Coke.

As we became airborne, we were given our slippers and a cute kit with a washcloth, comb, eau de cologne and other stuff. Naturally, if I can, I'll walk off with it (old Light Fingers is at it again). When we started to cross over Lake Michigan, we ran into the worst turbulence I have ever encountered. It really spread the cheeks in my ass and literally gave me a feeling in the legs the likes of which I haven't encountered since having sea legs.

I just placed my dinner order of Venison, which I chose over Roast Beef, Poached Halibut, Ragout of Veal, and Supremé of Chicken. It's getting rough again—I'm willing to turn back for home!

Well, dinner came and went. It started with some hors d'oeuvres of shrimp, foi de gras, or pas de deux . . . whatever. (I passed up the caviar because I felt that was carrying this Russian stuff a little too far.) Then soup laced with sherry, a lettuce and tomato salad, then the venison with lots of vegetables. For dessert I had cheese and washed it down with milk. The food was good, but I thought the service was terrible. Of course, smart guy Harry sat in the back so he could be served first, and these damn Germans started serving from the front—no wonder they lost the war.

The movie was a Charles Bronson thing that was the same old story. So I was listening to the recorded music and the woman announcer said, "People wonder why Haydn called this particular symphony his Oxford Symphony," and immediately my mind answered, because he wrote a lot of footnotes.

I'm sitting now in the First Class lounge in Frankfort and I feel real lousy. If I had to mill with the masses for 4-½ hours, I would really be sick. They woke us (ha ha) on the plane for breakfast. Hell, I just had dinner. But being one not to pass up a free meal, I had grapefruit juice, some cheese and ham and other sausage stuff, and milk. I was a good boy, though, because I passed up the fruit, bacon, and eggs.

Forced to Move Again

We would always consider the two International Crafts Expositions a major highlight of our lives, and Harry was justifiably proud of the job he'd done here. His ability to find unique European artisans and showcase their crafts to an American audience while transcending language differences and maneuvering various governmental policies was undeniably one of his greatest life accomplishments.

And yet . . . because this work did not revolve around music, something important was missing in his life. He had been doing his "entrepreneurial thing" since leaving Silver Dollar City and playing only now and then since leaving Disney, so the "music hole" in his life was growing larger. That, plus his concern about what he could do next to bring in a buck, was getting to be a worrisome weight on his shoulders.

After returning from the Busch Garden's show in late 1977, we learned that we had to immediately move from the house we were then renting in Libertyville. We had originally been guaranteed by the realtor that the owners, then in Australia, would give us three months notice, so we panicked when we were given only a month's notice to get out. Already exhausted and in need of a rest, now we had to move the contents of our four-bedroom house. Since we had the money to buy a house, we went shopping, found one we liked, and applied for a mortgage. As usual, we were fearful of being refused. In those days, if you were self-employed—or worse, "a musician"—lenders often looked at you as though you were the world's worst credit risk. But Harry's credit record was excellent, and when his income qualified us for the mortgage we needed, his heart soared.

Then the appraisal came in. On a house that should have appraised much higher, they put it $15,000 lower in value, and now we couldn't get the full mortgage and came up $5,000 short in cash with nowhere to get it. We tried other lenders who flat out refused to lend to a self-employed individual without 20 percent down, three great years of income behind them and proof of the next year's income as well. We agreed to take a second mortgage when the seller offered it, but he backed out at the last minute and everything fell apart. Once again, Harry saw this as just more of the bad luck that had been plaguing his life since his Reiner days. With our backs against the wall, we had no option but to move to another rented place, which was like sticking a knife in his heart.

Real estate was climbing, interest rates were rising, and neither of us had a clue about what we were going to do in 1978 to earn a living. We had owned three homes in the past, but now we believed we might never be able to buy another house, and Harry just couldn't come to terms with that on top of all his other personal and work challenges. With no other options available to us, we moved into a very nice rented condominium in the next town over, even though we knew we could have it for only six months. By the time we got resettled, both of us were nearing our physical and emotional limits.

It helped when Harry picked up an easy consulting job related to his crafts business expertise that paid him well for little more than brain work. In December of 1977, when he was working again with the Milwaukee Symphony, he got a call from a head honcho with Marriott's Great America theme park in California who had heard about his great success with the Busch Gardens festival. They were interested in a three-week crafts show in California to be presented the following May, and perhaps one in Illinois as well later on. Harry agreed to coordinate the show for a good fee and expenses, and I was hopeful that 1978 would be a good year for him.

But it wasn't to be.

CHAPTER 13

Dark Days in Brabecland

*The light is at the end of the tunnel, and you have
to walk through the dark to get to it.*
—*Linda Lavin, Actress*

When we left Florida in 1973, it marked the end of Harry's very
successful thirty-year career as a full-time musician, as well
as the beginning of his life as an entrepreneur who was
trying to find another way to use his unique skills and talents to make a
living. The work with Silver Dollar City and Busch Gardens that followed
was a blessing in our lives in more ways than one. But things really went
downhill when he learned in January of 1978 that Busch wasn't going to
do a third festival. In terms of drawing a larger crowd to a park, a festival
of this magnitude simply cost more than it was worth. Harry saw this as
just one more door closing for him.

It helped that he had the Marriott job because this income would
cover six months of living expenses. We flew out to California in February
of 1978 to get things rolling, then went back again in May to do the show.
This time, because we had to be there for three weeks, we drove so we
could take our dog Ginger with us. (She was a great traveler who
journeyed with us to more than forty states before she died.) We had a
good time on that trip, turning it into a paid vacation for us, but as soon
as we were home again and Harry had no other work to look forward to,
he became morose and difficult to live with. The Marriott show didn't
prove to be profitable enough for them to have one in Illinois, so yet
another door had closed and there wasn't a thing he could do about it.
With little hope for his future prospects as a breadwinner in or out of the
music industry, I think he must have felt like a tired fighter who was
wobbly on his feet and about to go down for the count.

Harry's Deepening Depression

Harry knew I was on his side, but all the disappointments in his life, his sense of insecurity about his future, and the intensity of his back pain from a calcified spine (spinal stenosis) and degenerating disks, was making him increasingly restless and irritable. In spite of all the happy times I've described from 1973 on when Harry's career path changed, there were some periods in between when he had to battle his fears about how he was going to make a living as he got older. Now he began to lash out at me for no apparent reason I could understand, and sometimes it just cut me to the quick. How could this be happening to the beautiful couple we once were, I wondered? Could the lack of work actually destroy a creative person like Harry?

In these down times he often suggested I would be better off without him. More and more he seemed to be deliberately picking fights with me to see if I'd tell him I wanted out of our marriage, almost as if he were testing me. And I eventually figured out that was exactly what he was doing. Since I was the only one he truly trusted and loved, it was only natural that he would test that relationship, believing that sooner or later it would be destroyed like everything else he valued. After all, his first wife had walked out on him after he lost the Symphony job and couldn't find work, so it was no wonder that he worried I might leave him, too, if he couldn't take care of us financially.

Harry often told me I was the only friend he had in the world, and if I deserted him he would have no reason to live. And I believed that. I thought that turning Harry out into the world would have been like taking our dog into a strange area and dumping her. Someone might take her in and care for her, or she might get hit by a passing truck. He seemed so lost and devoid of dreams at fifty, but I couldn't seem to help him because I was going through a terrible forties identity crisis of my own at the time (*who am I, where am I going, and how do I get there from here?*). I knew Harry loved me and wanted me in his life, but it was hard to deal with his verbal put-downs when he was feeling depressed about his life. I'm sure he hated himself at that point for failing me as a reliable provider, and I coped by telling myself it was only logical that as long as he had no use for himself, he couldn't have much use for me, either.

Harry was a fun-loving man when he had his sticks in hand, but when he couldn't find places to play, or any other work he could do to bring in meaningful income, he brooded about all the mistakes he had made because of his bad luck, his impatience, or his intolerance of one thing or another. Because his guilt at times must have been too much for him to bear, he then tried to lay some of the blame for his failures on me.

I remember now something that Gordon Peters told me that summer when we were dating. In talking about his passion for music, he said that it was as if music had possession of his soul, and that he knew he would always have to strive to understand the power it had over his life. He also said that when music went badly for him, he got very moody. I know Harry felt the same way about his music, but he didn't just become moody when he wasn't playing; after awhile, he began to believe that if he couldn't perform at least once in a while, he had nothing left to live for.

Men's egos (and some women's as well) are so tied up in their career that if they lose their job and can't find other satisfying work—or any work at all—dealing with it is indescribably difficult. But what one may not realize is that their depression at a time like this is equally hard on their spouse. I never stopped loving Harry, but there were many times during the late seventies and early eighties when he wasn't all that likeable, and I was grateful for an opportunity to be away from him for a little while, whether it was lunch with a girlfriend, a three-day trip somewhere to do a speaking engagement, or a visit to see my sisters and mother in California.

Situation Desperate

By this time, noise had become the bane of Harry's existence, and the list of noises he could no longer tolerate included everything from vehicle traffic, trains, and airplanes to barking dogs, screaming kids at play, basketballs being bounced on a neighbor's driveway, the booming bass of a radio in a passing car, lawnmowers, kitchen noise, the clatter of my electronic typewriter, even the swishing sound I made when I turned the pages of a book or magazine. But he wasn't just being difficult about this. On top of tinnitus, he had a serious hearing problem no doubt brought on by years of playing percussion in close quarters. Instead of diminishing, however, his hearing had intensified to the point where even the smallest sound apparently seemed twice as loud to him as it did to me, as if all the normal buffers in his ears had been destroyed.

Of course doctors could do nothing to help him with his noise sensitivity problem (except to suggest using earplugs), and he was only more aggravated by the fact that noise didn't bother me. This was partly because I had grown up alongside a railroad track, and partly because I had learned in the corn canning factory how to close my mind to noise that I found intolerable. When Harry needed to rant, and I had to be there to listen to him but really didn't want to *hear* him, I developed another mental skill that I likened to pulling down an imaginary window shade in my mind that buffered the gloom of the moment.

What I found so curious about this time in our lives was how Harry could say one day that he had nothing to live for, then play somewhere the next night and come home as happy as a lark, as if nothing were wrong in our lives. We could have a very upsetting or hurtful discussion one day, and the next day he'd come home from the post office with a bouquet or a box of candy. It was as if he lived only in the extremes of life—either he was supremely happy or so miserable he wanted to die. We often live in the mid-range of life, but there seemed to be no middle ground for Harry. That's how he felt about people, too. He either loved them or wanted nothing to do with them. Perhaps this explains why I now see my life with him as one that was filled with measures of both supreme happiness and heartbreaking grief, with nary a moment of boredom in between.

Time and time again when he was without work, he would test me by saying, "Any time you want out of this marriage, just let me know and I'll be gone." When he couldn't get a rise out of me with that one, he began to threaten suicide. I didn't believe for a minute that he'd actually take a gun and shoot himself or slash his wrists, but I did worry that, given his daredevil risk-taking nature, one day he might do something foolish while driving and hit a truck or a tree and end up crippled, if not dead.

I finally put a stop to his suicide threats by telling him that his life insurance policy wouldn't pay off if he killed himself, and if he really wanted to take care of me he'd forget that idea. Thankfully, he never thought to check the policy to see if this were true. Of course that clause applied only to the first year of coverage.

By early 1978, Harry's pot of despair was nearing the boiling point. He was now in constant pain from his back and, work-wise, everything was going badly for him. He had just had a big job interview that fizzled. Then he lost two music jobs tentatively promised to him that would have paid a couple thousand dollars. Three resumes he sent in response to ads for convention managers yielded bupkis. One disappointment after another was literally making him sick because he could see absolutely no hope for his future as a wage earner. Frankly, I didn't see much reason for hope, either.

He was no longer the joyful man I had married, and of course I was no longer the sweet and lovable wife I was when we married. Sixteen years of following Harry from here to there as he tried to find work, all that moving, and then my five years of trying to build a business that proved to be unprofitable in the long run had taken its toll on me. So there we were—Harry without work and with a wife who was stressed beyond measure. I was still trying to learn how to write well as I worked on my first book (a lot different from writing articles for a magazine), and also trying to figure out a business I could start that we could run together, one that might actually support us some day.

From the very beginning, Harry had given me the responsibility for paying our bills since money management wasn't one of his strengths, so now I was doubly stressed because there was less income than before and we were going into debt. And of course I still had to do all the regular "wifely things," like doing the laundry, cleaning, shopping, and cooking. "That's not my job," Harry was fond of saying.

It was common now for him to constantly speak in depressing tones about his work situation and his life in general. He was unhappy with everything, including me. I felt as though he saw himself in a pool of quicksand about to go under, and I was trying really hard not to be sucked down with him. I understood what he was going through, but it infuriated him that I would not let myself become as depressed as he was. He got angry with me when I insisted on remaining optimistic in the face of impending tragedy, but this was the only way I could live.

Hitting Bottom Once Again

I will never forget the day when Harry hit bottom again, and I believe it was a bottom as emotionally heart wrenching as the one he had experienced after his divorce. It was April 1978, and he was just 50 years old. That black day began with a discussion about a serious financial problem we were then facing because our hospitalization insurance was not going to cover an outpatient surgery he needed, and it was going to make a serious dent in our savings account for a house. This conversation unleashed a torrent of emotion in Harry, and then a bitter tirade against himself with some verbal attacks on me as well. I had long before learned when to talk and when to just listen, so I let him talk as he gradually worked his way up to the heart of the matter.

"We can't afford a house, and now I can't even afford to get sick or go to a hospital," he said, near tears. "Don't you realize I'm a *failure*? I've *lost*. I've played the game of life, and the devil, or whoever, has won. *I GIVE UP!* I don't know what to do. I have no training for anything but music, and I can't get back into music. I've explored all the possibilities and no one is calling me for work. I've just about run the gamut on the theme parks. Another show or two, maybe, and then what?"

He was slumped in a chair by the table with a pile of newspapers in front of him, scissors in hand, cutting out articles for his many files and scrapbooks. He kept working at this task throughout his long volley of negative talk, and now—not knowing what else to do—I just went to him and hugged him tenderly while trying to think of what I might say to make him feel better.

With incredible sadness in his voice, and without looking at me, he said, "If you were smart, you'd get the hell out of here. The ship is sinking and there's no sense in you going down with it. If I were you, I'd be looking for a way to get out of this whole mess."

I turned him toward me and looked him square in the eye. "LOOK AT ME!" I commanded. "You may think you've lost just about everything you've always worked for and wanted, but you're *not* going to lose me. I will *never* desert you. Surely you know that? *I LOVE YOU.*"

"I don't know why," he said, completely whipped.

In searching, I eventually found the right words to soothe Harry's troubled soul that day, but our life would only get more difficult and complicated from this point forward as his job opportunities and health declined, his back pain increased, and I gradually became the bread-winner—a reality he found very difficult to accept. For the next few years, whenever he wasn't playing somewhere, or when he felt he wasn't contributing enough to our support, he would play a variation on the above theme while also picking at me for every little thing I did that annoyed him. It's true that at times I found myself feeling angry because he couldn't give me the financial security I had always longed for, but I loved him so very much and understood that he was a unique individual, a*nd I was glad.* I knew that if I had to do it all over again, I'd choose Harry to spend my life with, even in a sinking ship.

In August of that year, he applied for the position of Personnel Manager of the Milwaukee Symphony, but he lost that job to someone else who had a great deal of experience in that area. But at least he was still trying to find work, and I often wondered how he kept finding the emotional strength to keep getting up and trying once again every time life knocked him down. It spoke highly of his character, I thought. At least this latest rejection had nothing to do with him as a musician because the Symphony continued to hire him when they needed an extra percussionist.

Meanwhile, I was trying to figure out what to do about our poor hospital insurance. One serious illness or hospitalization would have wiped us out, and that thought scared the hell out of both of us. All our earlier attempts to get good insurance had failed because of Harry's pre-existing conditions. Thankfully, I lucked out when I was able to get into a prestigious writer's organization with a good group medical insurance plan that did not require a doctor's examination, and this eliminated one of the things that had been stressing us.

More Disappointment in the Eighties

As my first book was nearing publication in the fall of 1979, my publisher asked me to come to work with him as his assistant, and Harry reluctantly agreed to my working three days a week. Emotionally, he needed me to be at home with him, but someone had to bring in some regular money. A few weeks later in November, my publisher was killed in that horrendous DC-10 crash at O'Hare that took the lives of 273 people. When I realized that my book was never going to be published in this one-man publishing division if I didn't do something about it, I volunteered to take over his job until a new person could be hired. The company was thinking about just closing the book publishing division until I convinced them I could do the job. And that's how I found myself with a full-time job as publisher and general manager of the book division of Barrington Press, Inc., and the person responsible for the publication and sales success of my first book. This job solved our financial problems, but my getting it only made Harry feel worse about his inability to be the primary breadwinner.

Shortly afterwards, the Ft. Meyer Symphony offered Harry a job as a percussionist, but the pay being offered was less than half what I was then making. He was happy that someone finally wanted him, but upset that the pay was so little. They said it might double in time, but I knew he was grasping at straws here. Now that I had a good-paying job and could see a future as a corporate executive if I wanted it, I couldn't encourage him to accept this job offer. It broke his heart when I said I couldn't keep chasing rainbows with him if it meant another costly move back to a state he hadn't liked the first time around to a job that wouldn't support us. But I didn't want to hold him back, either, so I suggested he take the job and rent an apartment for awhile until he was *sure* he was going to like the work and could guarantee me that he would do everything to keep this job. But he simply couldn't bear to be apart from me. In truth, I was the glue that was holding him together, the only stable thing in his life. He simply couldn't function then without me by his side.

He picked up several miscellaneous concerts and jobs that year, including a couple of weeks of extra work with the Milwaukee Symphony, but he became very despondent in November when his close friend, Jim Lane, died. He was a much-loved percussionist in the Chicago Symphony, and I'm sure there was a large turnout for his funeral. But Harry and I weren't there and it fell to me to explain this to his widow. In a letter to her, I wrote:

> *"Harry could not bring himself to come, and I was very reluctant to come without him since we always do things together. The reason Harry couldn't—or wouldn't come— had nothing to do with Jim or his love for him or you, but rather with the fact that in coming he would have had to face so many of the men from the Symphony, and he said he just couldn't do this. This will tell you, perhaps, how upset he is for screwing up his whole professional and personal life by leaving the Symphony after he had gotten back into it a second time as stage manager. It's a mistake he'll regret to his dying day, and going to Jim's service would only have made him face this fact once more at a time when he only wants to forget it."*

Shortly after this, Harry queried the Los Angeles Philharmonic Association in regard to the position they had open for a production coordinator, something at which he would have excelled. But he didn't have enough experience to get this job, and they sent him a standard rejection letter. How many more rejections could he take, I wondered?

After two years of working full time and seeing how hard this was on Harry, I took a big chance and quit my job, which was then paying twice as much as I had ever earned in an office before. But one day I suddenly realized that everything I was doing for this company for a salary could be done at home and possibly for greater profit. It was a simple quote in *Reader's Digest* by Frederick B. Wilcox that actually spurred me to action:

"Progress always involves risks.
You can't steal second and keep your foot on first."

By then I had learned a lot about how to publish, promote, and sell books, and had in fact quickly made my own book one of the company's best-sellers. So I took courage in hand and set up a publishing and mail order book-selling business at home, basing it around my *Creative Cash* book and a companion subscription newsletter, both of which were all about how to make money at home by selling art, handcrafts, and related products and services. It would prove to be the smartest life decision I ever made.

A Symphony Fiasco

Harry got another shot at a job in November 1981. After a grueling interview that he passed with flying colors, he was offered a job as General Manager of the Springfield Symphony Orchestra in Missouri. It paid a salary we thought ridiculously low, but I encouraged Harry to take it. Since our moving expenses were to be covered, and our business looked like it might fly, we figured if the job didn't work out we'd be okay financially. Of course I didn't like the thought of yet another move and I was still wondering if and when we would ever find a place where we could put down roots, but I wanted Harry to have another chance at work he might like. He flew down in February to find a house for us while I took care of packing for the move. (House prices in Missouri were lower than in Illinois, so his new job qualified us for a mortgage on a beautiful four-bedroom home.)

After settling in, and with Harry on the job for a month, it soon became clear that things weren't going to work out. I supported him completely when he resigned two months later after being presented with what we both considered an impossible "demand list" of a dozen major things the Symphony expected him to accomplish in just thirty days.

Basically, they were looking for a miracle worker—not only an expert fundraiser and advertising manager, but someone who would manage all the other departments in the office, write detailed weekly progress reports on what everyone was doing, and much more with little assistance from the orchestra's office staff. Although Harry had some great fundraising ideas, the orchestra had done these things a certain way for many years, and they weren't at all receptive to his "big city" ideas. Frankly, I felt the mistake was the Symphony's for not making their needs clearer in their initial interview with him. I doubt they could have found anyone who could have done all the things they wanted for the little money they were offering, but this was just one more thing gone wrong in his life that he found difficult to deal with.

Thankfully, the business was growing, and my career as a writer really took off when I got a contract for my second book a short while later. I finally convinced Harry that if he would give me some serious help with the mundane aspects of the business so I could have more time for writing, we could eventually live on our business income, and then he could continue to play part-time without having to worry about being the sole breadwinner. So it was that he began to work full-time with me as I worked on my new book, which I titled *Homemade Money*. Together, we dealt with a growing volume of reader mail and orders and the mailing of thousands of direct mail packages to get book orders and newsletter subscriptions.

Until that time, I had always managed our money from a joint account, but now I encouraged Harry to open his own checking account, saying anything he made playing would be his money to spend as he wished on books, records, art, dinners out, whatever he wanted. Since I was in control of all the business and household income, this gave him the sense of financial control that he needed.

Things were uncomfortable between us for some time, however, because we both knew that the power in our marriage had shifted. Whereas I always used to defer to his wishes, now he had to defer to mine because I was the boss of the business and he was my helper, or "office flunky," as he called it. In years to come, he would often be torn between being proud of me for all my writing and business accomplishments and resentful of my successes because they only reminded him of his failures. In the end, however, he always did what needed to be done whether he liked it or not.

As our life calmed down and he began to play more for the fun of it than to make a living, his sense of humor came back, though at times it was rather ironic. He often joked to friends on the phone that "Barb's the brains and I'm the brawn," or "I'm in charge of the S-Details: Stapling, Sticking, Stuffing, Sealing, and Stamping."

♪ Historical Sidenote ♪

In recent years—and especially in 2009 when millions of men and women lost their jobs and even their homes in an economy gone crazy—many couples have been forced to make uncomfortable adjustments in their lives and marriages due to financial difficulties or breadwinner role reversals. Today a growing number of men and women are starting businesses of their own because they can't find a job, and by itself this is a stressful undertaking at best. Countless thousands of stay-at-home dads whose wives are now bringing home the bacon—and the health insurance protection their family needs—are also struggling to make adjustments in their personal lives. Damaged egos and depression are simply part of this package as couples learn how to adapt to their changing life circumstances.

Back to Chicago Again

We stayed in Missouri until early 1984 when we both agreed it made sense to move back to the Chicago area. Now the business we had both been working on full time for the past two years was profitable enough for us to buy a four-bedroom home in Naperville, even with interest rates at 12 percent. My second and most successful book, *Homemade Money,* was published that year, and I suddenly found myself in demand as a speaker at home-business conferences across the country. Whenever I had a job anywhere within comfortable driving distance, Harry would drive me there with Ginger in her first-class accommodations in the back seat, and we'd always squeeze in a mini-vacation with a few days of hot-tubbing, trying new restaurants, and generally having some fun.

When Ginger died in 1986, we felt as though we'd lost a part of ourselves. In those years when Harry and I were struggling so hard to get through the darkest days of our marriage and his work disappointments, Ginger could always bring a smile to our faces. She was the one stable thing in both our lives for fourteen years, the "child" we'd never had, and often the glue that held me and Harry together at times when our marriage seemed to be falling apart. She gave us immeasurable joy in the darkest of days and was as important to Harry's emotional stability as I was. When he and I were "on the outs," she was a bridge between us, and he would often communicate with me through her when I was within earshot, saying such things as "Ginger, mommy is mad at me, and I don't know what to do about it. Do you think we should all go for a walk together?"

The minute Ginger heard the word "walk," she would come bounding to me with "yes, yes!" in her eyes, and the three of us would come together as a joyful family. While her death pained us terribly, it also brought me and Harry closer as we grieved her loss together. For years afterward whenever we were in the car, we felt as though she was still there in the back seat, ready to give Harry a lick on the ear, or patiently waiting to lick the milkshake container when we stopped at a drive-in. I dreamed about her for years. She was such a perfect companion for us that we could never bring ourselves to get another dog.

"No other dog could measure up to Ginger," Harry always said, and I agreed. She was as much a one-of-a-kind dog as he was a one-of-a-kind man.

Harry's whole attitude about life and work began to improve about the same time his health began to fail. It seemed the pattern of his life was always going to be "out of the frying pan and into the fire."

"But at least we ain't got locusts"

In the summer of 1987, we were both stunned to learn that Harry needed immediate bypass surgery. For some time he had been having minor chest pains, and when a treadmill test was inconclusive, the doctors suggested an angiogram. Like many men, Harry hated going to the doctor, so he had been resisting this particular test for weeks. I didn't press him about it because neither of us believed he had a serious heart problem. Overweight, yes; in poor physical shape due to lack of exercise; yes. But arteries that were 90 to 95 percent blocked, with a heart attack likely to occur at any moment? No, this certainly was the farthest thing from our minds.

The worst might have happened if we hadn't learned on the first of May that our major medical insurance plan was being cancelled, which news almost gave *me* a heart attack. While there would be some kind of automatic hospital conversion, the major medical portion of the policy was not convertible, and the thought of being so financially vulnerable again made me an emotional wreck for days. With less than thirty days before the bell tolled on our policy, I made arrangements to have a test for a strange symptom I'd been having (which proved to be nothing), and again pressed Harry to have the angiogram, if only to prove there was nothing wrong for insurance purposes.

Thus it was that he reluctantly entered the hospital on May 7, literally forced there by the insurance cancellation notice, and thinking that we'd be off on our vacation the next day. You can imagine our shock when we learned he had to have quadruple bypass surgery *at once*. (As one of his friends told him later, "that Czech food catches up to you in time.")

When he was doped to the gills with Valium and all the other pre-surgery drugs, he kept trying to stay awake, saying he wanted to know everything that was going on. "Knowledge is the most important thing," he told me in his semiconscious state, slightly slurring his words, and he was still sleepily asking questions as they wheeled him through the door into surgery. I couldn't help but laugh at that.

It was no surprise to me that he proved to be a great patient. Doctors, and especially nurses, loved him because he relieved their stress by making them laugh. He was released from the hospital after only five days when most heart patients at that time stayed for at least seven. He hated hospitals, and his cardiologist, Dr. Mark Goodwin (whom Harry loved because he had a great sense of humor), finally just got tired of arguing with him and let him go home early with his promise that he'd take it easy for awhile. Of course he paid no attention to that advice, and no amount of prodding on my part or the doctors could get him to complete the six-week course of physical therapy all heart patients were prescribed. Halfway through, he said he felt fine and he quit going simply because he couldn't stand the loud rock music being played in the exercise room. Since they wouldn't play the good march music he brought with him, that was it as far as he was concerned. There was no arguing with this Bohemian when he had his mind made up.

All costs related to the surgery were covered by the old insurance policy, but after that, we would have only a 120-day Blue Cross hospitalization policy with limited benefits for doctor bills until he got on Medicare. During this period I had to cancel three of my speaking engagements, the next issue of our newsletter was delayed, my computer crashed, and the book I had been working on was set back six weeks. It was a very stressful time for both of us, but Harry bounced back very quickly, even without all the physical therapy, and went right back to playing Grant Park that summer. Except for his growing back pain that now required heavy daily doses of Vicodin (which gave him no noticeable side effects and did not affect his playing), he was pretty much his old self. In fact, I had trouble keeping up with him as we walked across the green to the stage for the first Grant Park performance he played that year.

If May 1987 wasn't exactly the best month we ever had, it wasn't the worst either. The worst could have been a heart attack for Harry with no insurance to pay the bills. In trying to look for the bright side of things, he reminded me then of the Oriental philosophy Jack Soo had delivered in an episode of *Barney Miller* years before:

> *"Many things look bleak at their moment of occurrence.*
> *But at least we ain't got locusts."*

Lifestyle and Attitude Changes

Both of us were now trying to adjust to the new lifestyle that had suddenly been thrust upon us by Harry's heart condition. Dr. Goodwin said he would be fine so long as he gave up his old way of eating and exercised regularly.

"For how long?" he asked, and the doctor said, "Forever." We agreed that "forever" seemed like a very long time, but now we knew we were getting down to a matter of life and death, and that the fun and games of eating anything and everything our hearts desired was over. It was a hard transition, but Harry soon lost twenty pounds as I learned how to cook a new and more healthful low-calorie, low-fat, low-cholesterol way.

Of course his new diet severely restricted eggs, which just broke his heart. It wasn't so bad, giving up sausages and other fatty meats, but the egg-substitute products just didn't make good sunny-side-ups. For a long time he suffered their loss, eating them only on special occasions, and he also reluctantly gave up eating commercially-made cookies, most of which at that time contained "bad fats." But later he decided he'd rather die early than give up everything. Until the end, eggs and Oreo cookies remained his weakness. Once, about his low-cholesterol diet, he rhymed poetic:

> *Harry, Harry, quite contrary,*
> *How does your cholesterol grow?*
> *Bacon and eggs, and ham and Spam,*
> *And 21 Oreos, all in a row!*

Fighting overweight and dieting would continue to be a challenge throughout Harry's life, and he could always come up with a good excuse for going off whatever diet I had him on at the time. One Tuesday before Thanksgiving, his favorite holiday, he announced he had to go off his diet because eating our Thanksgiving dinner with all the trimmings was comparable to running a marathon, and he had to warm up for it by gradually eating more for a couple of days beforehand. Of course that meal always included everything ordinary people had for this meal *plus* sauerkraut and dumplings. Second helpings were a given.

As the eighties wore on, Harry continued to play whenever and wherever he could, but now, in addition to his back pain, arthritis was playing hell with his hands. He still joked about his condition, however. In a letter to Doug MacLeod in January 1987, he said he wouldn't be going to the Windjammers meet in Florida that month, adding, "I'm into 'Cokecane' now. All I drink is Coke, and I walk with a cane."

I accompanied him to a concert in Milwaukee at the end of 1988 because he needed some moral support. He wanted the money, and he hated the idea of having to lay down the sticks, but he was also getting concerned about the quality of his playing and beginning to think he ought to quit playing professionally before he got a bad reputation. He had always wanted to go out in a blaze of glory, and now he could see that his time for playing was beginning to run out.

I continued to write more books and do an increasing number of speaking engagements. Early on, I began to endear myself to audiences by sharing Harry's humor as it related to working at home. On returning from one conference, I told him that his jokes in my keynote speech got a lot of laughter and made me look good as a speaker.

"Since I'm contributing to your success as a speaker," he said, "I think I ought to be paid for the jokes I write." And that's how Harry launched his new sideline business as a gag writer. He said I had to pay him $5 for each humorous story I published or used in a speech. Either that, or he'd quit being funny. Since I couldn't stand to live with an old grouch, I didn't have much choice here. I just tried to figure out how to deduct that expense on my Schedule C tax return.

CHAPTER 14

Nostalgic Music Remembrances

When I get too old to drum, I'll still have you to marimba.—Anon.

arry wrote interesting letters, and he could have written a great book about his life if he had put his mind to it. But just as I thought one musician in the family was enough, perhaps he figured one writer in the family was enough. Prior to 1993, I never read any of the letters Harry wrote to friends or the replies he got, just as he did not read my personal correspondence. We each had our own interests and friends, and valued the privacy of the other.

When it began to get difficult for him to write letters by hand or type them himself, I encouraged him to start dictating them to me for typing, at which point I began to save them on computer. Only then did I realize what interesting and amusing letters he had been writing all his life. Even so, what he said in those letters didn't mean much to me at the time I typed them, because I was always so selfishly focused on my own writing and in a hurry to get back to my work. However, when I reread all of his letters in total after he was gone, I realized how much music history he had documented in them, and I was touched by his own gift for writing.

Good writers try to avoid the use of exclamation points, striving instead to add excitement or emphasis with the right choice of words. But Harry just loved them, and never wrote a letter or even a little note to me or to himself without two or three exclamation points at the end. Rather than edit them out, I've left his exclamatory punctuation in all of his letters in this book so as not to ruin his style.

The following excerpts from several interesting letters to favorite correspondents include Harry's musical remembrances, opinions, and often some humor as well.

Joe Sperry and Harry's Old Drum Set

Although Harry was an outstanding percussionist and musician, he always thought of himself as "just a drummer," and he jokingly called drums "the tools of ignorance." He got his first drum at the age of seven, and when he died he still had a little note on his bulletin board that read, "The first thing a child learns after he gets his first drum is that he's never going to get another one."

In a letter to Joe Sperry in November 1997, he reminisced about his old drum set, writing:

> Been thinking about our friendship. We go back a long way. It was in 1946 right after the war when we first met, and we have been friends ever since. You might be interested to know that I still have that set of drums you sold me. I haven't used them in some time because my health, like yours, has really deteriorated. I can't get it through my thick head that this mind of mine is inside a 70+ year-old body. Just remember:
>> "When I grow too old to drum,
>> I'll still have you to marimba."
> (It's an old joke, but then again, I'm an old man.)

Harry was trying to get rid of his drum equipment that year so I wouldn't have to worry about this when he was gone. Earlier we had found appreciative buyers for my marimba and his beloved "Black Beauty" snare drum, but the rest was a problem. As he told a friend, "Nobody is interested because of all the advances that have come about in the percussion field. I can't even give the stuff away to the Shrine band because they are down to a couple of drummers who are not that competent to play mallet instruments, so I'm stuck with my good but old equipment. Thank goodness there isn't that much of it."

Harry's old drum set can be seen on this book's companion website, along with an article he wrote in 1985 but never tried to publish ("Tips for Show Drummers" on learning the trade and designing one's setup). Like the drummer who played it, this old set of drums was truly one of a kind, with the bass drum having an unusual hardware setup Harry designed and had made especially for his jobbing needs when he was playing many hotel jobs.

Harry finally sold his bells and xylophone, but his old drum set was still in his music room when he died, along with a couple of Ludwig snare drums, some Zildjian cymbals, many sticks, stands, pedals, and other small percussion instruments and equipment. I worried for a couple of years about what to do with the last of his equipment until Harry's good buddy, Joel Cohen, helped me determine the value of everything. I was happy to eventually connect with Steve Maxwell of Vintage and Custom Drums who bought the last of Harry's equipment and just took the old bass drum off my hands as a favor. He said it had no market value, but would make an interesting display in the shop's museum area.

One never knows about drummers, however. In time I learned that Harry's old bass drum had been sold to a young drummer who had come along, found its hardware fascinating, and asked if he could buy it. I have no idea how old this drum set was when Harry bought it from Joe Sperry in the mid-forties, but I know both Joe and Harry would have been delighted to know that the bass drum from the drum set they both used for decades is still being used professionally by a young drummer somewhere (who I hope will find this book's website and learn its history).

In a January 1998 letter to Joe, Harry shared his opinions on a couple of other topics, writing:

> Thanks so much for sending the tape of the "Kraft Tympani Concerto." Ron Holdman did a nice job. It's just unfortunate that it was not a studio recording so we could hear all the intricacies, especially of the second movement. I made several copies of it and sent it on to some of the kids here in town. I was really surprised to find that these up-and-coming percussionists had never heard of this piece. I remember seeing the music on it, but inasmuch as my love was always in playing percussion, I made no attempt to try to perform it. It's just as well. I could have set timpani playing back a hundred years!
>
> I'm sure you're aware that Orchestra Hall is no more. It is now called Symphony Center, and it seems like every night they have something going on there. The day of the Chicago Symphony ruling the roost is long since gone. I haven't bothered going down there to see the Hall, and have no interest in what's going on there at all. That feeling seems to run through a lot of the guys that are no longer connected with the Orchestra.

Harry mentioned Joe Sperry's passing in a May 1999 letter to his Browsers pal, Phil Holdman, saying:

I'm really sorry to hear about Joe Sperry. He and I go back a long way, fifty years to be exact. We were both in the Civic Orchestra, and we split when he went to the Columbus Ohio Symphony and I went to the National Symphony in Washington, D.C. Our paths next crossed when he went to NBC as a TV floor manager and I was doing the *Wayne King Show*. In fact, I bought a set of drums from him then that I still have. We lost contact when I went with the Chicago Symphony, but renewed our friendship about ten years ago.

It seems so sad that a guy like him who had so much drive and energy gets knocked for a loop by Parkinson's disease. But then again, all of us in our mid- or late seventies have slowed down a lot. I'm sure all of us have a mind that says "let's go!" but a body that says STOP. I know I'm slowing down faster than I thought I would, but I'm going to try to keep on going till I wear out my last pair of 2B sticks."

Ollie Zinsmeister, Xylophonist Extraordinaire

Ollie Zinsmeister, who was with the Marine Band for twenty years before retiring in 1955, was a faithful correspondent of Harry's in the mid-nineties and beyond. (You may recall my earlier mention of him and his outstanding xylophone playing. He continued to play solos into his eighties, and in his later years wrote marches for the Marine Band.) Following are a few of Harry's letters to Ollie, and a very special one from Ollie to Harry:

January 1994: I played a concert with a new kid in town and he wanted to study with me. I told him I didn't want to be tied down to a schedule, but if he would like I could coach him at my convenience. I wouldn't charge him anything because I would like to pay back some of the courtesies that were extended to me when I was breaking into the business. I told him to contact me after the first of November, and he was so happy and double-checked with me during the concert that I would be sure of seeing him—and that's the last I heard from him. So much for the young drummers of today! If he ever does contact me, I will charge $100 per half-hour and that should scare him away forever.

I was very happy to hear that you were remembered by Harry Breuer's son and that he sent you those mallets. I would love to have a pair of his sticks providing they made me sound like him. (Dream on, dream on.) As you say, he was certainly a fine fellow and a true artist. Everything I heard him play was so relaxed. It's unfortunate that we don't hear his type of playing anymore coming from the kids of today. I always found that the greater the musician, the nicer the person, which sure was true of Harry.

I won't be coming down to Sarasota this year for many reasons. It comes at a bad time of year for us and I don't feel that great. Don't get me wrong, my condition is not life threatening, but it is uncomfortable. Also, with three bands going now, you don't have a chance to play alongside the people you would like. In fact, I have been thinking about resigning from Windjammers altogether. I belong to many organizations but am not active in most of them. Doug MacLeod is trying to talk me out of it, but I just haven't made a decision. I have many friends in the group and I consider you one of my favorites. It's really a pleasure knowing you and having played alongside of you, and I only wish we lived closer together so that we could visit.

So till next time, keep going. Our society needs young fellows like you!

♪ Music Sidenote ♪

The above mention of Harry Breuer reminded me of something John Melcher told me:

"A couple of times when I'd go for a lesson, Harry would have a Harry Breuer album out on top of his record collection. He often emphasized in his lessons the importance of getting to know the right people whenever you hit a particular city, and more than once he told me that Breuer was the man in New York to get to know. Years later, I was excited to finally get to meet him there, and it was all because Harry told me this was an important contact I needed to make to get jobs in New York."

Breuer was a remarkable percussionist and xylophonist Harry obviously held in high esteem, and his *Mallet Magic* and *Mallet Mischief* albums are among my favorite percussion records. I don't know where Harry worked with him, but his letter suggests he knew him personally. Breuer worked in vaudeville and television, performed with Paul Whiteman and Benny Goodman, and was a percussionist with the NBC Orchestra in New York. He died in 1989 at the age of 87.

Continuing Harry's letters to Ollie Zinsmeister:

December 1994: Thanks for those pictures of the Marine Band musicians, and especially the drummers. I don't know if I ever told you that I have a great love for history and these pictures will really enhance my collection. Those pictures and the Marine Band photo will soon be framed and put in a very conspicuous spot in my music room/den. How can I show my appreciation for the recordings of the Marine Band you are sending? When someone goes out of their way to help me, I think they deserve some kind of a favor returned. Please let me know if there are any recordings of any kind of music you might like. What I don't have, I may have access to.

January 1995: Those Marine Band recordings are just wonderful! You have no idea how touched I was to receive them from you. That was one of the nicest things anyone has done for me. I will cherish them always.

I'm sorry I didn't get back to you sooner but I was waiting for the tape from your Naperville concert. It finally came and while listening to your solos, I could just picture you performing. It sure sounded good!! You mentioned that you made a mistake. I caught it, but it wasn't noticeable. I do feel the band could have given you a better accompaniment in the "Czardas." They seemed just a little bit too heavy. Your playing will go into my archives of great mallet players.

I really appreciated that picture of the service bandmasters you sent. Did that bring back memories! I so remember listening to radio broadcasts with them conducting with Walter Damrosch. I remember being herded in a large room in our grade school to listen to his symphony shows. I can still hear that trumpet call from the "Leonore Overture."

Since I last wrote, I have had a couple more incidents with my heart, but again, it's nothing serious. I'm going in next week for another series of tests. This has something to do with nuclear medicine. I kid Barb about my glowing in the dark so she can use me for a night light.

June 1995: It was nice to hear from you again, and Barb and I are especially glad that you have decided to continue with your solo work. There is such a shortage of good musical mallet players that you only wish the kids of today would put some of that experience into their performing. They play a lot of notes but with no heart. Have you noticed how many play like they are chopping wood? Where are the teachers who taught you play with the wrists, not the arms? You are probably the last of the great musical mallet players. What I hear from the kids of today is just plain unmusical; lots of notes but no feeling. I'm glad I was lucky enough to hear and know the great ones.

I was wondering, Ollie, maybe we could play duets—you play the marimba and I'll turn pages. (I'm not so dumb!!)

I was sorry to hear that Sammy Herman is blind. What a player! At least we have the memories (and recordings) of his playing.

I have finally decided to quit playing. It's just too much for me physically. I can't take the chance of playing a concert and having my heart kick in, and sometimes the pain from my back and torn rotator cuff is strong enough to hinder the use of my arms and wrists. Rather than play badly, it's best for me and the fellows around me to give it up. Of course I still overdo things when I work around the house, and after I rest for awhile I can hardly move. I sat down and did some snare drum woodshedding a few days ago and noticed my left hand has lost a lot of its control. It flopped around like a fish out of water. I never thought I would go out this way.

At least I have the memories of a good career of playing and meeting some wonderful people such as you and Marge. Of course I have my records and tapes, so at least I have good music around me all day.

Thanks for asking about Barb. She's feeling fine. Her breast cancer appears to be totally gone, but she has the aches and pains that are present in most senior citizens. Of course her biggest pain comes from the guy she's married to, but she is a strong woman!"

Note: Harry had a heart attack and a second bypass surgery in September of this year (see Chapter 16). That effectively put an end to his playing.

January 1998: Thanks so much for that *PAS* magazine with your interview. I often wondered how close to the original Sousa marches those snare drum parts were, and you've answered a bunch of questions that were in the back of my mind. I'm going to make copies of that and send them off to some so-called "concert drummers" who couldn't play a march to save their neck (or any other part of their anatomy).

I remember when I was at NBC, we used to do a radio show every week that ran for an hour and we always played three marches. This was a lot of fun, and I must say that I took some liberties playing them. An accent here, crescendo rolls there, just something that would give a little bit more spice to the band. Even though there were forty men in this studio band, these added drum parts seemed to add just a little more spice to the final product. Just as in your article, where you stated that playing loud accents doesn't necessarily make for good music, I tried to keep everything down to a musical minimum. So I will always treasure this article and your explanations.

I understand you're still going great guns, and I thought you said you were going to quit playing xylophone solos. You're like an old fire horse . . . when you hear the bell, you come out running! That's great!

I haven't been feeling too good, which is a combination of a couple of things. I have to go in to the hospital the middle of February for a colon operation which they say is not cancerous, but should be taken care of as soon as possible. (They know me so well at the hospital where I go for all my tests that I have my own private parking stall.) I figure this will give me an excuse to be lazy and have Barb baby me just a little bit more.

October 1998: I can't thank you enough for sending those tapes. What a wonderful gift! You know how much I treasure all the recordings I have of the Marine Band, and these last ones were the icing on the cake. Of course, the highlight of this musical surprise was the duet you played with Chris Williams.* It was so nice to hear that duet again by two very good players. It was clean and musical with just a touch of humor to make it sound like you two boys were having a good time. You know how I feel about your playing, so adding Chris made it that much more enjoyable to both Barb and me. Send my compliments to Chris. I also wanted to play that duet, but never found anyone who would share my interest. These young kids!!!

My health is beginning to show wear and tear and it's getting a little rough getting around, but I keep plugging along. It's a good thing I have Barb to keep me on the right road. We are both sorry to hear that you are retiring from solo public performances. Just remember how much musical joy you have given people all these years. There aren't many people who have even come close to accomplishing that. I know you have made my life a lot nicer.

* According to a page on the Web, Chris Williams was appointed principal percussionist and assistant timpanist with the Baltimore Symphony Orchestra's in 1978. Since 2002, he has also been a faculty member of the Asian Youth Orchestra, traveling to Hong Kong in the summer to coach the percussion section. In 2005 he went on tour to Europe as a soloist with the Baltimore Symphonic Band under the direction of Christopher Wolf. The tour was highlighted by the fact that two of his sons performed alongside him.

Five Famous Russian Composers

Immediately after receiving the above letter from Harry, Ollie sent the following reply. I know he would have been tickled to give me permission to print it, but since he's gone now, I'm taking the liberty of publishing it here. Harry thought so much of it that he saved it behind the picture of five Russian composers Ollie included with this letter. Among other interesting musical tidbits, it includes historical information about this rare photo (which can be seen on TheDrummerDrives.com website). This letter certainly explains why Harry enjoyed his correspondence with Ollie so much.

Dear Harry: I know we just corresponded, but I would be remiss if I did not thank you for your kind words. I have never received anything like that before from anyone.

You will recall we met when Windjammers was at Naperville several years ago now. You seemed to take a liking to me and me to you, and we have been dear friends ever since. Lord only knows if we are ever to meet again, so our friendship continues through correspondence and phone calls. I had the same kind of friendship experience with Harry Breuer. Getting back to Windjammers at Naperville, I remember you brought your lovely and attractive wife Barb to hear me play. Until we met I did not know that she was a marimba player. You are blessed having her to take care and watch over you. I have been fortunate too with Marge who has looked after me for 62 years.

Now for new business. I do not know if you are a member of Percussive Arts or not. If you are, you saw the enclosed article about Sammy Herman. If not, it might interest you. Came out in 1997. I will always be grateful to you for that

Sammy Herman tape you sent, which I will cherish forever. The enclosed photos have nothing to do with the Marine Band, but I thought you would like to have them for your various collections.

I have been corresponding with G. Butov, a Russian marimba player, for the past couple years. I purchased his 24 etudes for marimba and have included a few for you and Barb to look at. He said if you do not follow directions, they are of no value. You must play each one first with the left hand alone, then the right hand alone, and then together.* Try them. They are hard as heck. I just bought his xylophone solo, "Russian Rag," and the tempo mark is 208. Anyhow, he sent me the enclosed photo of the five Russian composers. I gave one to Buster Bailey, and this one is for you. I would be willing to wager several thousand dollars that the three of us are the only ones in the U.S. to have one of these pictures. I think it is priceless and I wanted you to have one.

The other photos speak for themselves. It is hard to believe the drummer Johnnie Williams is the father of Johnnie Williams of the Boston Pops and the great composer for the screen. I sent John Williams this photo along with another one I had with his dad, who played with Eddie Duchin. I received a very nice thank you letter from him and put it alongside his photo in my conductor's album. Thought my Sibelius note would also interest you.

Boy, I am really wound up today and better sign off. Thanks again for your kind letter. My feeling towards you is mutual and we love you both.

---

* I chuckled when I read Ollie's comments about how to play the Russian etudes, because this is exactly what James Dutton made me do once when he gave me a Musser Prelude to learn. And it really works. Twenty years after I quit playing, I could still visit my marimba in Harry's music room and play without music the one piece I had mastered using this technique.

November 1998: Boy, Ollie, you are really keeping me in musical history information! As you know, I have a love of history and especially things pertaining to our craft. What makes all that you send me so great is that I have a connection with every photo, article, or piece of music. I can remember listening to the Marine Band's radio broadcasts. I always like to tell the story of my dad not being too pleased that I was in Washington with the Symphony, and didn't quit and switch over to the Marine Band. Sometimes I think I should have listened to him.

The photo of the Russian composers you sent is priceless inasmuch as I played so much of their music and actually played a couple of weeks with Khachaturian. (He might have been a great composer, but he was a real prima donna. Not much talent as a conductor, but a lot of ego.) I also worked with Prokofiev.

I looked at those Etudes by Butov, and had no trouble with them at all. Yessir, I picked them up, took one look and immediately put them down. I'll say one thing though: just looking at them gave me the ambition to try them (with not much luck).

Well, Ollie, thanks again for thinking of me with those valuable gifts. Give our love to Marge. We think of you often.

June 2000: Thanks much for sending the program of your concert down in Naples. I'm glad your marimba found a good home. I just hope they take good care of it.

Under the category of "isn't it a small world," on that program I noticed you did a thing called *The West Point Symphony* by Robert Dvorak. Bob and I went to the same school, at different times, however. He's just a little older than i am and I can't remember if he was conductor or assistant conductor of the West Point Band, but I remember that, during the war, he played French horn in the band.

I knew Bob very well. He later became conductor and head of the music department of Morton High School in Cicero, Illinois. Now the other funny part about this is that the guest conductor on the program, David McCormick, was also conductor at Morton High School. However, he came after me and I never did know him, but I think it's kind of ironic, you sending a letter to me with this information in it.

After meeting Ollie when he played in Naperville, it was easy to see why Harry loved him. He was then in his eighties, full of good humor, and still playing up a storm. After Harry died, Ollie, who had recently lost his wife, helped me through my grieving period by staying in touch with me and talking about his own grieving experience. He would phone every so often, and the last time we talked, he was telling me how much fun he was having with his new girlfriends who always wanted to lunch with him. A very sweet and loveable fellow, he died in 2008 at the age of 97. I often listen to his playing on the CDs he sent Harry.

A Twenty-Year Correspondence with Doug MacLeod

Harry corresponded with Doug MacLeod for twenty years, from 1980 to 2000, after which time they communicated only by phone. Doug saved all of Harry's letters and then gave them back to me after he died, which was a gift worth gold to me because I'd never read any of them and they contained a lot of Harry's dry humor. Most were little handwritten notes with a few being typed on his electric typewriter. The complete collection was too long to include here, but the few brief excerpts below were selected because of their interesting bits of music history or notes about Harry's miscellaneous music activities and witty one-liners. (Check the book's companion website for more of his letters.)

> **April 1981:** I played with the "Easter Bunnies" Band from Illinois State University just before Easter. Bob Hoe called me at the last minute to help out 'cause one of the drummers couldn't make it. Boyd Conway was there. He's one fine guy and one good drummer. We got along well and had a lot of fun talking over old times. He was in the Marine Band while I was in the Symphony in Washington, so we had a lot of mutual friends. He told me Charlie Owen was leaving the University of Michigan this year or next. He had a Gladstone snare drum that sounded beautiful. If I'm going to be playing more march and band music, I better start looking for a more appropriate drum. If you come across a deep (8" x 14" or 10" x 14") drum, let me know. Price is no object—I'll spend as much as $11 or $12. That's providing it comes with an instruction book, sticks, and case.

> **May 1984:** Just a quick note to accompany the enclosed article about Jo Jones, taken from a book on Count Basie. Jo Jones was his drummer just before the war and then returned after he was discharged. He was a good drummer and a good friend.

February 1988: I'm feeling about the same, which is not too bad. Playing is keeping me busy with a ballet and some recording. The Symphony is on tour in Australia so I'm picking up all their excess work. Actually, what I'm really doing is keeping their chair warm till they get back.

April 1990: I'm going to send a note to Windjammers saying I want to be a conductor at Columbia this August at the "disorganized meet." But then, I have been told that I have a head like a hard piece of oak, so I guess that makes me a non-conductor.

P.S. By the way, I found the notes for "The Lost Chord"—would you like them for your library? If so please send cash!

November, 1990: I figure if you could have read all those poorly-typed letters from Merle Evans through the years, you shouldn't have any trouble reading mine. Due to my hand problem, I find it really hard to hold a pen or pencil now, so all my friends have to suffer through my whacking away at this infernal typewriter.

I'm enclosing a tape marked "Fucik Conducting." This is the old man himself conducting a Czech Army band. (I can't figure out why the song titles are written in three languages—English, Italian, and German.)

Notice how differently he does some of his own works. The Moravanka Band is a Czech group of folk artists who are highly respected over there. The leader of the band is also first trumpet in the Brno State Opera. I thought you might get a kick out of it. The "Sousa for Orchestra" is made up of music I'm sure you're familiar with, but it has an entirely different sound when played by strings. The second part of that tape is Sousa's music used for the Broadway show, *Teddy and Alice,* which I think is great. The Allentown Band is from the CD I told you about. You can see what I mean about the bass drum and cymbals not only being overbearing, but done in bad taste.

I'll close down the drum shop now and hope to hear from you. I hope you realize how much I value your friendship. I sometimes think we are two peas from the same pod.

Give our love to Mary. (Did you ever notice how the nice ladies always end up with questionable characters like us for husbands?)

P.S. Don't forget to practice. There's no sense in both of us forgetting.

February 1991: Here's that music I told you about. The Stone exercise I play four times each at a tempo of about 120 beats per minute. I try to start at the top repeating each one and going all the way to the bottom without stopping. It not only gets your coordination together but also keeps your mind from wandering.

The "Doubling the Downfall" is a real backbreaker if you take it at a good up-tempo. I want you to practice this one real hard and maybe we will send you to contest next year.

March 1992: Thought you might like the enclosed article. It doesn't really tell the whole story. What it boils down to is that, by 1996, Ringling will be traveling with its own band and using nary a local musician anywhere. Our illustrious Union president said that even though this wasn't good for the local musicians, Ringling still used Federation players. What a dunce!

October 1992: I will try to make this letter short as I'm trying to cram two pounds of —— in a . . . well, you know the rest. Excuse all the typo errors and goofy spellings. Let's just say I'm a student of the Merle Evans "Scool" of Typing.

About the enclosed tape . . . you have no idea how hard I had to work to get the first three tunes on this tape recorded just for you. I stayed up all night several times writing the music and then arranging it. Then I had to talk to a lot of my musician friends to record them for free. Also had to get the singers. (I, of course, sang all the lead parts, so I had to practice that in the bathtub.) So, anyway, I dedicate these bits of musical history to you with the hope that you remember me as one who will suffer anything for a friend!!!!!

I'm feeling about the same, which isn't saying a lot, but I always figure it could be worse. (When you consider the alternative, it could be a LOT worse.) I'm on a self-imposed diet. It's going pretty well as I have lost about fifteen pounds. Of course that's like taking a cup of water out of Lake Michigan.

Talk to you soon. Meanwhile, keep your heads dry and your bird whistle wet!"

November 1992: Enclosed is the list of records I don't have. If you can get any of them, that would be great. If not, I will straighten out your triangle.

I sure appreciate all our phone conversations. I always feel better after speaking with you. I'll call you soon and then we can solve the world's problems.

Note: The above letter was signed: "Pig Sty Harry," in response to a phone conversation he and Doug had earlier. Doug said they often tried to outdo one another with creative insults, like two old Vaudevillians. He sent me this example:

Harry: Hello you old goat!
Doug: Say, Harry, you know, the other day I stood up for you.
Harry: Yeah, how so?
Doug: Well, someone said you weren't fit to eat with the pigs, but I said you were, too.
D&H: Yuck, yuck.

August 1993: Here's that article from the Union paper. Sure looks like the Union is going down the drain. It will be interesting to see how soon.

I'm looking forward to that Czech music you are sending. I have decided to get up very early every morning and run three miles before I start my vocal exercises so I can give you the full treatment of my singing expertise.

April 1995: You might find the enclosed article of interest. How many more bands will be cut, or just cut down in size, I wonder. And yet, I still see ads for Army bands.

Can you believe the war has been over for almost fifty years? That seems like such a long time ago, and yet it seems like only yesterday (and you know what a rotten day yesterday was). Got a letter from Ollie today telling me about a dear friend of ours who is in bad shape—Sammy Herman, the great mallet player. He is blind, which we are both saddened about. Ollie also said that he's not going to quit playing xylophone and marimba solos yet. More power to him!

August 1995: Here is the definitive translation of that Kmoch music—or at least it's close. I somehow believe this would lean to being more accurate than the one you sent me. That one seems just a little militant and stormy compared to the one I received. Of course the Czech language, like so many others, will have many definitions for the same word. Also, like most Slavic languages, there are usually three classes of the spoken word—the well-schooled, the city working class, and the peasants. So I suppose whoever does the translating determines the wording. Like I said, this material is a song/ march, which I suppose was sung at parties.

I hope I haven't muddied the waters any more than necessary. But think of the fun we had with this. (We're lucky you weren't looking for the translation of a Wagnerian Opera.)

Thanks again for the Czech band tape. I really enjoy it. I think you're right about some of those cuts being a commercial recording. About the third, fourth or fifth cut is that Kmoch march. Listen to it and then you send me a recording of you singing it in both Czech and English, now that you have the words.

February 1999: Finally, after all these months, I'm getting this tape to you! On the Buffalo Bill side, I omitted the "Grass Dance," which is nothing but an Indian tom-tom beat for about three minutes. If you really want it, I'll send it on to you, or I could play it for you over the phone.

I added a little something from a southern California Salvation Army Band festival. It just goes to show you how far you can go if you practice your tambourine!

The following letter was written in June 1992. I've put it at the end of Harry's correspondence with Doug because it's a touching letter that sums up his feelings for this dear friend of his. It's the kind of letter more people should send to the people they love.

I would just like to tell you how much I value your friendship More than ever. It looks like my playing days will soon be coming to a halt—a lot sooner than I hoped or figured on. Inasmuch as we both love music so much, it is doubly hard to think that I may not stand alongside you again. So many people who play an instrument do not have the burning desire to play just for the sake of playing. But you do, and it can be seen in your playing.

To have to give up playing hurts me as much as I'm sure it will for you. I think what's so bad is that it's really not of my choice. I'm going to fight it as hard as I can, but it sure looks like a losing battle. It happened so fast. But at least I will have you to continue on.

My good luck is that I have had your friendship all these years. It always seems that when one of us is down, the other manages to pick up the other one.

I don't want to sound down about all this, but I would like to tell you how much better my life has been, knowing you. Thanks, friend, for that phone call and all the other niceties you have shown me.

I'm not down yet, and don't expect to be for some time. But it's not for me to say.

All my love to Mary.

Harry's Most Amusing Letter

What better way to close this chapter than with one of the funniest letters Harry ever wrote? We were living in Springfield, Missouri at the time, and this letter was a thank-you note to his Italian friend, John Violetta, who had a great sense of humor. He had sent Harry his favorite recipe for Polenta, and we both loved it. (I tried but could not locate John after so many years.)

Dear John:

What have we done!!! Your recipe for Polenta came and has been made several times; relished each time more than the time before. Barb thinks it's the greatest thing since Herbert L. Clarke.

But, we are in deep trouble. Let me explain. We made the mistake of giving some of this Italian ambrosia to our neighbor, he being second generation hillbilly, the kind of folks who say, "Mah fanger hirts, so ah'm goin' to Sprangfield to get it done rat."

Well, anyway, we gave these people the recipe and here's where the trouble started. They thought it was delicious, and they started spreading it around the area. It has taken over! Everywhere you go, you see nothing but Polenta, Polenta! There are bumper stickers that say "Polenta Power," Chinese restaurants that serve Egg Foo Polenta, and a local Polenta Shop that is now serving 33 delicious flavors.

Polenta has replaced grits! You can't buy corn meal for at least a hundred miles. It is only sold in darkened doorways, musty basements, or inside of a famous building that features a half moon on the door. It sells for about $7 a pound, and that's cut by a third with whole wheat. Rumor has it that there is a place in town where you can buy the finished product upstairs, and where, downstairs, an upright piano is found in the corner played by an old Italian who knows only one song: "Polenta Leaf Rag!"

I can only hope that, in the future, this obsession will die down and we will all be back to normal.

P.S. I am currently looking for a spaghetti sauce not made with tomatoes. I had this in Florence and was told that it was a Neapolitan recipe made with olive oil, basil, fennel, garlic, and black olives. It was delicious, and I would give my best pair of 2B sticks for the recipe.

CHAPTER 15

Winding Down a Long Musical Career

It occurs to me that music, with the possible exception of riding a bull, is the most uncertain way to make a living I know. In either case, you can get bucked off, thrown, stepped on, trampled—and if you get on at all, at best it's a short and bumpy ride.—Gene Autry, cowboy singing star

Just as you can take the boy out of the country, but can't take the country out of the boy, one could never take the love of performing out of Harry. Although his career as a full-time musician ended when he left Disney, he continued to play whenever and wherever he could in the seventies and eighties, and into the early nineties until his severe back pain, arthritis, and heart problems finally forced him to lay down his sticks for good.

But it wasn't just age and physical limitations that were making it difficult for him to find work. By 1980, the music industry he had known in the sixties and seventies had changed considerably. Today, it is so different that it's nearly impossible for freelance musicians to find enough work to make a living in Chicago unless they're also into teaching, writing, arranging, conducting, or recording.

Joel Cohen, a freelance percussionist who remains active in the business today, was one of Harry's closest music buddies at the end of his life. They played together occasionally and talked regularly by phone about how things were changing in the music business. When I asked

Joel to give me some perspective on how things are today, as compared to when Harry was in his prime, he summed it up like this: "Basically, there is much less work now and more percussionists vying for the few jobs still available."

Chicago's Music Business Then and Now

"So many of the places where Harry once found work are either gone now, or much more difficult to break into," Joel explained. "Theatre work in town has pretty much dried up because shows coming in from New York are under the jurisdiction of national union rules for touring musicians. When a show leaves New York to do a tour in several cities, they bring with them a core of musicians, and about 95 percent of the time this includes the drummer. The rest of the musicians are hired locally to fill out the book, and there may or may not be need for an extra percussionist."

In Harry's day, different contractors booked musicians into a variety of theatres and hotels. Now, says Joel, there is just one contractor who represents all the theatres under the Broadway in Chicago umbrella. "If he likes you, you're in."

This umbrella covers the Oriental Theatre, Cadillac Palace, Bank of America Theatre (formerly known as the Shubert), and occasionally other venues. In the sixties, one show after another would come into the Shubert and run for a few weeks or several months—up to a year. But today, Joel says, "Shows coming in from New York run continuously in one place for a long time, such as *Jersey Boys* and *Wicked,* which ran for about three years. Things have changed with other groups as well. There are some local performing organizations that have garnered 'exclusive' arrangements with various contractors (or theaters) that present touring shows, and if you are not a part of that particular Chicago-based performing group, your chances of being hired are greatly reduced."

Joel pointed out that when Harry was in the Chicago Symphony in the fifties, it was still not a full year's job. "The Lyric Opera in Chicago was just starting up and would eventually expand to a ten-week season in the mid-1960s," he remembers. "By then, the Symphony finally reached full-year status; the opera season gradually grew to about a half year by the late 1980s. Of course there are no American touring opera companies today. A few ballet companies still tour, but very few use live music. The Arie Crown Theatre doesn't put on shows anymore. Moreover, a lot of the jobs once played by musicians have now gone to DJs. (With the right software, I could have five days' worth of music; just get an amplifier and a couple of speakers and a flashing light, and I'm in business.)

"I know Harry used to play a lot of hotel jobs, but there are no hotel jobs these days. Through the late sixties and seventies, a lot of the hotels had house bands that they paid for. But there are no groups like that any more in any of the hotels. As for the kind of dinner music you used to offer on your marimba, the only place now that might have something like that might be the Drake—a harpist, perhaps, playing background music.

"There are still some recording studios in town," Joel continues, "but the recording business is extremely limited now. It used to be that some musicians did nothing but recordings, but the commercial recording industry Harry knew in the sixties is pretty much gone now with most recordings being done in New York or Los Angeles. Actually, it's so easy for musicians to produce a commercial CD and sell it themselves that no one really needs to record in a studio any more. Even the Chicago Symphony has its own recording label now (CSO Resound), or they can buy performances as iPod downloads. They no longer have agreements with any of the major recording companies they once used, such as RCA and Mercury."

Symphony orchestras will always need good musicians, but orchestras everywhere have been having financial problems for years, and today's bad economy can't be helping the situation. Joel believes some chairs are sitting empty today because of an orchestra's budget deficit.

"It costs a lot to run an audition one chair at a time (judges, mailings, etc.), so some orchestras are delaying hiring musicians, sort of doing this on a triage basis as they try to figure out which opening has to be filled first. When Harry was in his prime," Joel concluded, "majoring in percussion at a major university was a rarity because music wasn't considered a good career path then. Today, however, hundreds of universities offer degrees in music and percussion, so now we have an overglut of people with degrees in music and no place to play. It's another whole world from the one in which Harry once made a living."

Playing *A Chorus Line*

Harry played his last musical shows in 1979, doing *Cabaret* when it came to Theatre East in Milwaukee that year, and then *A Chorus Line* when it played for a couple of weeks at Milwaukee's Performance Arts Center in June. I have no special memories of *Cabaret,* but I'll never forget *A*

Chorus Line.

Harry was nervous about playing this show because he was older now, and he knew his "chops" were a bit rusty. He hadn't done a Broadway musical since leaving the Shubert fourteen years earlier, so he was naturally uptight when rehearsals began. I remembered that this was a difficult book to play, but I didn't realize just *how* difficult until I talked to Joel, who had played this show at the Shubert before Harry played it in Milwaukee.

"This show had a completely different percussion book than any percussionist had ever seen before," he said. "In traditional Broadway shows, about half the time you're just sitting around counting rests. Prior to *Chorus Line,* the percussion parts in most Broadway shows were usually 16-measure parts on bells or xylophone, and then you might pick up a tambourine or cymbal, hit it and then put it down and rest a bit before you might play a chime note, timpani roll, or some other instrument. But in this show there was virtually no downtime. You were playing almost every minute of the show, going from one tune to the next with no pauses between. This show really changed how percussionists played in a Broadway show, even more so than *West Side Story* did, which till then was probably the most intricate book for a show, and here you'd usually have two percussionists.

"You really had to know the book well, and Harry might or might not have received it ahead of time. It called for about 40 different instruments, including vibes, xylophone, chimes, timpani, bongos, and all sort of toys. Because every pit was different, with a different set of instruments, each percussionist had to come up with his own solutions for how to set up everything to fit the available space while keeping all the instruments within arm's reach. So many instruments naturally required a variety of sticks—several pairs of mallets for the keyboard instruments and chimes, and three different sets of timpani and drumsticks. At one point, one needed a double-headed mallet with a soft head on one end and a bell mallet on the other because you had to play vibe and bell tree notes at the same time. Another time, the cowbell and tambourine had to be played together. This meant that each percussionist also had to plan ahead for how he was going to pick up sticks, put them down, and pick up the next ones."

Harry's scrapbook revealed additional details about this show, which traveled with a conductor and four instrumentalists (keyboard, guitar, drums, and lead trumpet). The pickup orchestra included fifteen musicians. Most touring shows rehearsed the pickup orchestra for only a couple of hours, but this show had an eight-hour rehearsal, then a two-hour sound check, then a complete run-through, and finally another rehearsal to smooth out any problems that were evident in the run-through. After Harry had done the initial rehearsals, he got permission for me to hear the show backstage during the final rehearsal. I was blown away not only by the number of instruments he had to play, but how he moved from one to another, sometimes playing two at the same time. He changed sticks constantly, pulling some of them out of his belt and back and side pockets. (See pictures on the website.)

The orchestra for this show was hidden beneath the stage so the audience never saw it. This musical is about a bunch of dancers rehearsing for a big show, so it has no intermission. (To me, all that dancing overhead sounded at times like a herd of elephants on the rampage.) The producers didn't want the orchestra to be a distraction to the audience, so the rehearsal piano player on stage was the only visible musician. As soon as he began to play, the whole orchestra came in, just like in all the great movie musicals where a guy and his gal are in the middle of a park or on a desert island, start to sing, and a symphony orchestra magically begins to play in the background.

> *"If ever an orchestra deserved applause for what it contributes, this one does," said associate conductor Bell. But, as he noted wistfully, "the audience applauds the dancers—and most reviewers never mention the orchestra. Out of sight, out of mind." - from a review by Dominique Paul Noth*

We didn't know it at the time, but this would be the last musical Harry would ever play. He still had years of playing ahead of him yet, but as he had always hoped, he left this particular arena in a blaze of glory. I saw the show from out front on another night, but it wasn't nearly as interesting to me as the night I watched him play on this lidded stage.

I've often wondered how many other musicians' wives ever had this kind of theatre seat, or were even interested enough to want to see their husband's professional life from this perspective. Although many wives traveled with their husbands when an orchestra was on tour, I don't recall ever seeing any of them backstage in all the years I was tagging along with Harry.

He gave me quite a gift by letting me see all the shows and concerts he played from both the front and behind the scenes backstage.

The Bensenville Concert Band

A very social person by nature, Harry was always the happiest when he was able to mingle with other musicians, especially those who appreciated his professional advice and humorous stories. This was the atmosphere around him in the Bensenville/Wood Dale Concert Band, where I know he felt privileged to perform from 1982–1992. Here he had the opportunity to play both classical and pop music as well as marches. He played whatever instrument was needed, but usually he was on snare drum or traps.

This Band has been conducted by Fred Lewis since 1953. Although the trust fund money for musicians has run out, band members love the band and Fred so much that they continue to play without pay for their loyal audiences. Through the years, Fred has brought together some of the best professionals and top amateur musicians in the Chicagoland area. Represented in the band have been musicians from the Chicago Symphony, Lyric Opera, Grant Park Orchestra, Shubert Theatre, the NBC Orchestra, and former members of the Army, Navy, and Marine bands.

Harry's friend, Scott Thomas, a clarinetist in the band and the rich-voiced announcer of a classical music show on WFMT (98.7 on the FM dial), told me how much he and all the musicians in the band loved Harry. "He was like an uncle or father figure to us. For all his great experience and all he had done musically, he always treated everybody as an equal, and I never heard him say a bad word about another musician. He was always telling us stories of jobs he played, and he particularly liked to talk about playing with the Windjammers Circus Band and his experiences with Merle Evans. He never cared what instrument he was asked to play, but I think he was happiest when he was playing snare drum in a march. He always helped the band with his playing."

In reminiscing with Fred Lewis as I was writing this book, I asked if he had any special memories of Harry, and he laughed. "We still talk about Harry, recalling our memories of him and some of the stories he told us. Just the other night when a bunch of us went out for beer and pizza after the concert, I was telling them how Harry used to razz me about the kind of music I was programming. I've always tried to program everything from soup to nuts, but once in awhile I wanted to go back to my classical heritage and program some serious classical numbers. That's when Harry would say, 'Fred, why are you playing all this classical stuff that we used to play in the Chicago Symphony? Why don't you play something the people might *like*? Always remember that you should play for the *audience*, not for yourself.'"

I found that funny because Harry gave me the same advice when I was writing my first book. "Don't write what you want to write about," he said, "write what your readers want to read." (In our marriage, he was always the teacher and I the student.)

It is Fred's custom to chat with the audience during a program to announce some of the music being played, or to tell a little story. He said he has shared Harry's comments with them from time to time when he's announcing a number he knows the audience is going to love. Fred chuckled when I told him the title of this book, saying it described Harry to a T.

"Often when we were rehearsing a march in which Harry was setting the beat on the snare drum, he would jokingly say to the musicians, 'Remember now—follow me, not Fred,' and then I'd come back with 'There's only one conductor here, and it's me. If you don't like it, get your own band.' Then we'd all laugh and play up a storm."

As Harry got older, Fred said he didn't always play the music exactly as it was written, but often added his own special flourishes. And sometimes he missed a note or played something wrong in a passage. "What I found amusing about this," Fred says, "was how innovative he was then. When that same passage of music was repeated later, Harry would play it the same way he played it originally—with the missed note or error—so it all matched up. The audience didn't know the difference, and he and I were the only ones who knew this wasn't the way the music was written."

Harry had aggravating vision problems as he aged. At one point, he had four pairs of glasses, one for each type of reading job, and the lenses usually needed to be changed twice a year. In 1980, he told his buddy Doug, "I got a pair of those half-glasses like you have and they are just great. I was surprised to find how many more notes there are on a page. I guess my days of faking are over."

In another note to Doug five years later, he joked again about his failing eyesight. "Incidentally, we played the 'St. Louis Blues March' at the last Bensenville concert, and it made a big hit. I'm glad we did it, but next time I'm either going to have to get the part enlarged or get a seeing-eye drummer."

Failing health problems naturally made Harry a little cranky in his "old musical age." In a letter to Tommy Wetzel (timpanist, Milwaukee

Symphony) in 1997 he wrote, "I'm not doing much playing for several reasons. One, I just don't want to haul drums around, although one group I work with has everything there, and the second reason is that all the drummers I have worked with lately are young and inexperienced. Now I don't mind that, inasmuch as I was there a long time ago, but so many young drummers today have such high opinions of themselves. I finally told one kid to 'shut up and count your measures.' You can see with all my illnesses, I still have retained my sweet and loveable personality."

Harry kept a notebook of all the programs he ever played. In looking through them, I was reminded of the many enjoyable concerts I heard during the years Harry was with the band. One I especially loved was the 1985 presentation of Handel's *Messiah* with the Bensenville Orchestra and Chorus. And for that year's Gala New Year's Eve Concert, Harry played percussion alongside his friend Joel Cohen on timpani. Another terrific program was the "Circus Ring Concert" the band played in May of the following year. During this concert, Fred told the audience that Harry and another band member, Ron Grundberg (who played euphonium in the Windjammers band), had played with Merle Evans, the world famous circus band conductor.

This program reminded me to call Ron to chat about Harry, who then told me this little Fritz Reiner story Harry had told him about playing *Bolero*. "Harry said Reiner didn't give a good prep beat, and I can still see him in my mind, standing there, literally on tiptoes, leaning forward so he could hit that first note exactly when Reiner wanted to start. After that, I always thought of him as on-the-beat-Harry."

One of the boxes in Harry's cassette tape collection was labeled "Bensenville Band," but I didn't realize the treasure I had here until I turned up the above-mentioned notebook with all the Band's programs in it. Thus began a project that literally took me a hundred hours or more. Once I could identify the concerts in which Harry was playing snare drum or the drum set, I began to listen to each tape to identify tunes I wanted to dub over to another tape, then spent hours dubbing selections to several different tapes, keeping categories of music together. I picked only tunes I liked and where I could hear Harry playing his heart out. Later, when I learned how to burn CDs, I began to dub these tapes to CDs and then duplicated the CDs for family and friends. (Yes, I know these were third generation recordings by that time, but I had bought a new tape dubber and CD burner and the CD quality was quite good.)

Downloads of recent concerts are available on the Web at Archive.org (search for the Band's name). As soon as possible, several music downloads of my favorite drummer playing his heart out in this Band will be offered as MP3 downloads on the book's website. Featured will be some marches, classical numbers, show tunes, and the "St. Louis Blues March." I am very grateful to Fred Lewis for allowing this reproduction of his Band's music, and his permission to offer the complete 1986 "Circus Ring Concert" as well.

I also greatly appreciate that the Band's February 27, 2005 concert was dedicated in memory of Harry, who Fred called "an exceptional percussionist that will be greatly missed by all." The program included some of Harry's favorite music by Dvorak, Fucik, and Arban.

The Windjammers Circus Band

Windjammers Unlimited is an historical music society dedicated to the preservation of traditional music of the circus. Circus musicians are traditionally called "windjammers" because they "jam wind into cornets, clarinets, trombones, baritones, etc. for six to seven hours a day," according to Merle Evans, who was the most famous windjammer of all.

I believe some of the most musical fun Harry ever had came when he was playing in the Windjammers Circus Band from 1981 to the early nineties. Each year the organization presents a winter convention in Sarasota, Florida and a summer meet in a different part of the country. Harry and I attended several of these meets and always had a delightful time. Here, he regularly played snare drum alongside Doug MacLeod on bass drum.

"Once at a Windjammers meet somewhere," Doug recalls, "a man joined us in the drum section who said 'I don't read music but I'll just play along.' It turned out he had no sense of rhythm and his playing distracted us very much. Someone had to speak to him, and the rest of us elected Harry to do that job. He very diplomatically asked the man to take a seat and enjoy the rest of the music. He did. Another time in Indianapolis, our conductor had difficulty starting a march. Harry suggested a drum roll-off and it worked. Harry admired my bass drum playing and was very supportive when I landed the job with the Detroit Concert Band. We talked drumming in our many telephone conversations over the years. I admired his playing and his experience in percussion. We made several Windjammers meets, and I always enjoyed playing alongside him."

Harry especially enjoyed the Windjammers meets when Merle Evans came to conduct the band. Merle was a lovable soul with a good sense of humor, and he and Harry naturally became friends and occasionally exchanged letters. Evans had retired in 1970 after fifty years as bandmaster for the Ringling Brothers and Barnum & Bailey Circus, but he continued to conduct for many years after that, staying active into his nineties. He introduced the Windjammers organization to his wide circle of friends and established the contact with the Sailor Circus that would become so much a part of the annual Windjammers conventions. Harry was thrilled to be in the band in 1984 with Merle conducting when the Sailor Circus once again put on "The Greatest Little Show on Earth."

This circus was established in 1949 as a public demonstration of tumbling and acrobatics, but over the years it has developed into a full-fledged circus that is the pride of Sarasota. It's unique in that it is performed by young people of the Sarasota County School System, grades four through twelve. So high is the standard of training and dedication of instructors and student/performers that some have gone on to professional circus careers.

Harry said he first played with a circus (Cole Brothers) when he was just fourteen years old, but I never thought to ask for details about this. Frank Kaderabek said it was common for the circus to come into town and stay a week, and Harry probably just got a chance to sit in with them for awhile. I figure that playing in the Sailor Circus at the end of his life must have been like coming full circle once again, just as playing in the Disney World Marching Band had surely taken his mind back to his high school days at Morton.

He had always wanted to play in a circus bandwagon, and he finally got that chance in 1981. Granted, it wasn't in the Ringling Brothers Centennial Parade in Baraboo we had always enjoyed watching, but it was the next best thing—a small wagon owned by Bob Barnes, a tuba player and fellow Windjammer. The wagon was part of the parade for the annual "Western Days" celebration in Chatfield, Minnesota, and riding and playing in it that day was a highlight of Harry's life. Doug was sorry that there was room for only one drummer on the bandwagon. Harry played snare drum with a foot pedal on a small base drum, and he and the other musicians were crammed into the wagon like a fat lady in a girdle two sizes too small. After we returned home from the parade, Harry got the following letter from Bob Barnes:

To all those "cats" willing to risk life, limb and buttocks to ride and play on a Circus Bandwagon in Chatfield, Minnesota:

> *We had a terrific time and hope you did also. Harry Brabec and I proved that you CAN get three gallons of crap into a two-gallon bucket. I know you were equally cramped in your respective spaces, but I hope it was worth it for the experience. You were just great! We played to good sidewalks and that made it worthwhile.*

Harry's Windjammer days had other great benefits as well, for it also brought him back together with Boyd Conway, Charles Owen, and Buster Bailey, three old percussionist friends he had known for most of his life. I knew Boyd Conway was an old friend of his, but until I researched his life a bit, I didn't realize that he had been in the U S. Marine Band for 29 years. This acquaintance had been formed during the years when Harry was in the National Symphony in Washington, D.C. and got interested in the U. S. Marine Band. At the same time, he also struck up a friendship with Charles Owen, a marimba soloist and timpanist with the U.S. Marine Band and Orchestra for twenty years and later principal percussionist with the Philadelphia Orchestra.

Elden "Buster" Bailey was a percussionist with the New York Philharmonic, and it's easy to see why he and Harry were friends. They shared not only a special love for the snare drum, but also the circus. By the mid-eighties, all of these old drummers were retired and playing together for the first time just for the fun of it, often making music under the direction of Merle Evans, the "Toscanini of the Big Top." Harry and all his great percussionist friends from the "old days" are gone now, but their legacy endures. One can only hope they're all still making music together in Heaven.

Masonic Musicians

Harry was a Mason, and in a letter to Brother Norman Lincoln in December 1995, he was discussing the research Lincoln had done on Masonic musicians:

> In your listing of musicians, you have a blank for Arthur Pryor as to his Blue Lodge. I have scanned all my books to come up with his lodge but cannot find anything. I know I read somewhere he was a member who came from St. Joseph,

Missouri. Along with Arthur Pryor, there were, and are, many band conductors and composers who took the degrees. Merle Evans, who was with Ringling Bros. Barnum and Bailey for over fifty years, Leonard Smith, conductor of the Detroit Concert Band, Patrick Gilmore, Herbert L. Clarke, Frank Simon, Karl King, and Henry Fillmore are just some of the bandmasters that come to mind. Of this bunch, only Leonard Smith is still living.

I joined the fraternity almost fifty years ago. Let me preface this by saying that I was a professional musician. I never became an active member because of my traveling, but managed to make as many meetings as possible and to visit as many lodges as I could. Here in the Chicago area we had a daytime lodge that was called St. Cecelia, who is the patron saint of musicians. Needless to say, it was made up almost entirely of professional musicians. Whenever we had degree work, live music was performed, and at their installations a forty-piece orchestra would be there. It was quite impressive. They have since merged with another lodge that meets in the evening. My mother lodge has had three other lodges merge with it and finally they merged with still another. I guess it's the sign of the times.

♪ Music Sidenote ♪

Harry had a couple of CDs of the Arthur Pryor Orchestra in his collection. Pryor (1870–1942) was a ragtime pioneer, once one of America's most important musical figures. Called the world's greatest trombonist, he was a celebrated conductor and the composer of some of the most popular tunes of the early 1900s, including "A Whistler and His Dog," which one writer on the Web calls a tune that's "perfect to skip to."

Sitting In with the Carson & Barnes Circus

Harry would have played for nothing just to play one RB&BB Circus, but that opportunity never came his way. However, when the Carson & Barnes Circus was playing only three miles from our home in 1982, he knew the opportunity to sit in with a circus band was at hand since the conductor of the band was Bill Reynolds, a trumpet player and Wind-jammer friend.

We went over early that morning hoping to see the tent go up and meet some of the musicians. We missed the tent setup but walked about the grounds for awhile and then went back at 12:45 so we could get in without a ticket on the shirttails of a band member. (Harry often joked that his name was Crime, and Crime never paid.) His strategy not only worked, but got us the best seats in the house—right alongside the bandstand and just around the corner from where all the acts and animals came into the tent.

I've been to several circuses, but I never *felt* them as I did this one. Unlike the rest of the audience who saw only the glitter, I was close enough to see the finest details and touch the animals if I had dared. Imagine nineteen elephants trotting past you, their trunks swaying as the tassels on their colorful robes bounce against their hide; and then the big cats, as they come rushing through the chute into the cage in the center ring. I have always yearned to just touch a Bengal tiger, and on this day I was sitting within arm's reach of them, close enough to see the texture of their fur as they streaked past me. As I wrote in my journal that day:

Before the circus began, Harry was invited to sit in on the pre-show warm up, which was a thrill for him. While conducting the band at this time, Bill was holding his one-and-a-half year-old daughter on his lap—a tiny armful as cute as any kid I've ever seen. She was "born in a trunk," so to speak, and the circus is all she knows and she obviously loves it. Even at her tender age and size (about two feet tall), she is already doing acrobatics, hanging from things, jumping over ropes, etc., and next year she'll actually start training on the trapeze. She thinks nineteen elephants, several camels, horses, bears, tigers, and lions are normal fare, not to mention a rhino and other assorted animals. The Carson & Barnes Circus is the largest animal show in the world, so the child is really getting an education. (It would be delightful to follow her life; what a book it would make.)

Her mom is a circus performer, having only learned this life three years ago after marrying Bill (who is obviously divorced, with two children elsewhere). Bill's mother plays organ in the band, and his dad also plays, I believe. Bill made an interesting statement about the circus as a profession for musicians. He said that great musicians have never been found in circus bands because good musicians can always make more money elsewhere. So the circus is traditionally a place where kids start to get experience, and older men end up when they can't get work elsewhere. But oh . . . this is a hard life—living in small trailers and moving almost daily to some new spot. And when you sit as close as I was to the performers coming into the tent, you see the telltale signs of this life—the torn costumes, grease spots on glittery garments, the chipped paint on all the equipment, and the "tired lines" on the faces of some of the performers. One would simply have to love the circus life more than anything else in order to stand it as steady fare.

The circus acts, per se, were not very good—in no way as classy as the Ringling Brothers and Barnum & Bailey Circus acts—yet I enjoyed this particular circus more than any other I've seen to date because I felt a part of it, having had a special glimpse of circus life before the actual performance.

The real highlight of the day, however, was the rainstorm's effect on the performance and the elephants. We've been having a monsoon season lately, just one rainy day after another, and naturally it had to rain on the day of the circus. The heavens opened about three-quarters the way through the performance (much like that night at Melody Top when its tent began to leak).

I had to move to avoid a bad drip, but it was nothing compared to what the poor drummer had to endure. Frankly, Harry was glad to be sitting in the stands with me then instead of behind the drums, because a big tear in the canvas let in a virtual cascade of water that poured, as if from a spout, directly onto the cymbals and snare drum, which further splattered the drummer as he continued to play. But he was very good natured about this, as were all the other performers who were obviously following in the tradition of "the show must go on." The trapeze artists did not move to avoid the water, even though it drenched their heads. In all, it struck me as terribly funny and I found myself enjoying the show all the more as a result of this unexpected surprise.

When the show ended, the rain did not—it even picked up in intensity. So we all stayed in the tent (it was a small crowd), and while Harry gabbed with the musicians, I joined several people near the opening to observe the elephants who were having a field day—literally. Imagine nineteen elephants chained in two rows in a grassy area strewn with straw as a downpour of rain is turning the area muddy. The grass is now being destroyed by the elephants' heavy feet.

The more it rains, the more they all strain at their chains in an attempt to get nearer to the little puddles of water now collecting around their feet. One finally manages a trunkful and sprays it over itself in ecstasy while others try to lie down and roll over (which is very difficult to do with a chain on one hind and one front leg). Now two or three are pushing against each other, all of them vying for the choicest and muddiest spot to roll in. The elephants were putting on quite a show for us, and they seemed as happy as pigs in slop as they threw muddy straw all over themselves, swaying to and fro, their trunks delighting in this newfound joy.

As it continued to pour, I could only imagine the mess there would be for the evening show only three hours later. It rained again about seven, and I still wonder how the handlers managed to put the fancy sequined garb on these wet hunks of flesh to get them into the big parade. This is the stuff of circus life, and the kind of thing few in the audience would ever wonder about.

It so happened that this day was also our twentieth wedding anniversary, and I gave Harry a collector's circus plate with a card that read:

This Collector's Circus Plate was originally meant to be a Christmas gift, but since we're going to the circus on our 20th Anniversary, it seems to be appropriate for today.

It's doubly appropriate when you consider that our life together has been very much like a circus—populated with interesting people (and a couple of rare animals) . . . filled with music and travel . . . and laced with surprises and a sense of expectation as to what the "next act" will be.

Like circus people, we've had our share of laughter and tears . . . good times and bad . . . and there's one other thing we share: Regardless of what has happened—or may happen in the future—we both know "the show must go on." And we're SOME show, my friend. Here's to the next twenty years, and a toast to more laughter and less tears.

CHAPTER 16

The Last Difficult Decade

Getting older isn't so bad; it's trying to maintain your oldness that wears you down. —Harry

In September 1995, prior to going on vacation to our favorite cabin in the woods of Wisconsin, Harry had been expressing concern about his health. He hadn't been feeling "right" for a couple of months, and he'd been having some feelings of pressure in his chest. He didn't think they were related to his heart because he'd just gone through an intensive series of tests a couple of months earlier and the doctor saw no problem then. Yet he was concerned enough that he made a map for me and a list of all the towns on the way up and back that had hospitals, just in case he had a heart attack or something during our vacation. (He always joked that I couldn't find my way out of a paper sack, and a map in my hands was a lethal weapon.)

I prayed that we would have a safe trip up and back, and I asked God especially for this happy time with Harry because I knew it would be the last vacation of this kind we could take—loading the car with lots of stuff to amuse ourselves for two weeks in the woods was a hard physical job. In fact, I had to load and unload the car both going and coming because Harry just didn't have the strength for it.

For a month prior to this, he had been in constant pain, more than ever before from his back, arthritis, fibromyalgia, and torn rotator cuff, the latter of which had been giving him pain for the past eight years. (By the time he realized how serious it was, he no longer had the will power or physical strength to do the weeks of follow-up therapy the repair surgery would have required.) Although food had always been one of Harry's greatest joys, he now had no interest in eating. When I'd ask what he'd like for dinner, he often said, "I don't care." It was then, as a serious student of the Bible, that I began to reflect on a particular verse that spoke to me of Harry:

> *For God does speak—now one way, now another—though man may not perceive it. In a dream, in a vision of the night, when deep sleep falls on men as they slumber in their beds, he may speak in their ears and terrify them with warnings, to turn man from wrongdoing and keep him from pride, to preserve his soul from the pit, his life from perishing by the sword. Or a man may be chastened on a bed of pain with constant distress in his bones, so that his very being finds food repulsive and his soul loathes the choicest meal.*
>
> – Job 33:14–20 (NIV)

We *did* have a lovely time together on that vacation, but Harry had a growing feeling that we ought to leave early, so we did. A week later, he had a heart attack. Had this occurred in that cabin in the woods, miles from any medical facility, he might have died. Once again, we learned the importance of heeding our gut instincts.

Nine Days That Changed Our Lives

I woke up at 8 o'clock that morning to find Harry sitting on the bed, saying he'd been up since 6:30 with pain in his chest that was going down his left arm. He didn't want me to call 911, so I called his cardiologist, who told me to get Harry to his office immediately. Of course the drummer always drove, so I didn't argue with him about this since the doctor's office was just five minutes away in the hospital complex. As soon as we walked in, the nurse got him hooked up for an EKG, and only a couple minutes later Dr. Goodwin checked him and said, "We've got to get you into the hospital because you're having a heart attack right now."

He ordered his nurse to call an ambulance, but Harry, who didn't believe he was having a heart attack, was still trying to call the shots. "I don't want an ambulance with sirens blasting," he protested. "Can't you just wheel me over in a wheelchair?"

The doctor knew Harry well enough not to waste precious time arguing with him, so he asked his nurse if she thought she could do that, and I think she said yes simply because she knew and liked Harry. She was a woman of modest size, and Harry probably weighed 280 pounds at that time, but she put his wheelchair in high gear and literally ran across the large hospital complex to get him into the ER. Given my bad knees, I couldn't keep up with her, and later she said that pushing his weight all that distance and up a couple of steep inclines almost gave *her* a heart attack.

A couple of hours later Harry was in the cath lab getting an angiogram and then an angioplasty. By this time, blood was flowing through only one-and-a-half veins into his heart. Prior to surgery the following morning, and for a day afterwards, he was on a "balloon machine" to ease the load on his heart, and the noise of the motor and the loud kerthumping every time his heart beat just about drove him nuts.

After his first bypass nine years earlier, he said he would never go through this operation again. But when push came to shove and he learned the alternative to going home without treatment, he looked at me, looked at the doctor, and said, "I've got a pretty good marriage, and I'm not through with her yet, so let's do it."

Humph! Not *through with me* yet? That remark echoed the one he had said years before when he was ordered to quit drinking and smoking or die, but this time I thought he might have found a better choice of words.

Talking to God

The morning before surgery I asked Harry if he wanted me to pray with him, and he said, "No, I talked to God last night, but I don't think he heard me." By then, I had dozens of people praying for him, from friends and family members to hundreds of people on my business mailing list where I had been sharing his humor for some time.

Even though a redo of a heart bypass is always a lot trickier the second time around, Harry came through the surgery with flying colors. In fact, the next morning after surgery he had all the nurses in the ICU in stitches as he cracked jokes and told all of them he was going to be out of there in five days (as had been the case the first time around). No one could believe that anyone could come through open heart surgery with this kind of attitude on waking. Of course the next day he was like a whipped puppy because he hadn't sleep a wink that first day, and the combination of morphine and other drugs had him more than a little high by dinner time, and quite grouchy as well. When I could no longer stand him, I kissed him goodbye and went home. As always, we took this in stride. The next morning he apologized for "coming on strong" and things were back to normal (not that anything about our life had ever been what one could call normal).

When the fifth day came and went and Harry thought he ought to be going home, he began to give the doctors orders to "get me outta here!" with no results. His medications were not yet properly balanced, and when they told him the next day that he still couldn't go home, he didn't handle the news well. I prayed then that God would give him patience to endure this whole experience, and I saw that my prayer had been answered when I went in the next morning and found him to be surprisingly calm. He said he had finally accepted the fact that he was sick and no longer in control, and that he would do whatever the doctors told him to do.

Just when he seemed to be making gains, his heart went into an irregular beat, his pulse and blood pressure climbed, and his blood count dropped to the point where he had to have a transfusion. The longer he was in the hospital, the more hours I spent with him—as many as twelve hours at a stretch—because I knew he needed all the moral support I could give him.

Shortly after surgery he had looked at me differently, saying, "You're a very strong person." Another day when I went in, he grabbed my hand saying, "I just need to hold onto you for awhile." I liked that he seemed to be seeing me in a new light and was perhaps beginning to wonder how I could have been so calm and collected throughout this whole experience.

Of course it was all about my faith in God. In all the years we had been married, God and faith had never been a topic of discussion, although we both had a reverence for our Maker. We did attend church a few Sundays after we married (which was when I learned Harry couldn't carry a tune in a bucket), but we soon stopped going when he began to work seven nights a week on one job or another, often not getting home till after midnight and then being unable to go to sleep for hours. After awhile, we decided that since I was working days and he was working nights, we would just skip church so we could sleep in on Sundays and relax together. Like so many others, once we stopped going to church, we never went back.

But God had plans for both of us. He had brought me to my knees about a year before Harry's heart attack, and as soon as I stopped worrying about trying to save his soul and simply put Harry in His hands, I felt more at peace. Prior to this, I had tried several times to make Harry understand how my personal encounter with God had changed me, but he always cut me short, saying, "Don't preach to me. God and I have our own understanding."

There in the hospital, I saw that my faith had not been misplaced, and that my prayers were being answered, one by one. At every opportunity, I commented on how fortunate we were to have one another, how good God was in his timing—letting us have our vacation, even giving us time to get caught up on our work before he had his heart attack. I also emphasized how many people loved and cared for him. Harry showed great concern for what I was going through then, but he could see I really meant it when I said I was doing just fine.

While he was still in the ICU, I asked the hospital chaplain to visit him. After she prayed for him, he took her hand and said thank you. Later when she was walking the corridor outside his regular hospital room, he said, "Isn't that your pastor friend? Tell her every little bit helps."

Inside I whooped with joy because I saw then that Harry was seeing the power of prayer for perhaps the first time in his life. (It's one thing to see prayer working in the lives of others; quite another when you see it working in your own life.) The chaplain stopped by again later, and this time I asked her to pray for both of us. Afterwards, I moved away from the bed, and when I turned back to look at Harry, he had tears in his eyes. He was still holding her hand when he said, "My wife doesn't think so, but I'm a believer. It's just that I'm a Mason and her views and mine are a little different."

Shortly after that, I went back to church for the first time in thirty years, and I was in such an emotional state that I cried throughout the service. When everyone in the congregation was invited to take communion, someone took my hand and led me to the altar. I kneeled, took the bread, and when the cup of wine was passed, I just collapsed in a heap of sobbing. *How I needed this release then.* I was very embarrassed by my outbreak, but the pastor put his hand on my shoulder and a lovely woman next to me gave me a hug.

I didn't tell Harry that I had gone to church because I didn't want to stress him needlessly. I figured God would let know when the time was right, and He did. The first evening home, Harry told me how much he loved me and how much he had needed me throughout this whole thing, and I told him then that my strength had come from God and that I wanted to get back into church. I could never get him to go to church with me, but I knew that a man didn't have to be in a church to communicate with his God.

A New Perspective on Life

The best part of this really difficult life experience was that it brought a special sweetness and tenderness to our marriage. All the while Harry was in the hospital, he kept telling people he couldn't have gotten through this without me at his side. Every time he was ready to give up, I would just give him a hug and say, "Together, dear, we can get through anything." He also began to tell others that he was seeing me in a different light, too. Once when a nurse saw me working in the room and asked what I did, I said I was a writer and quickly dropped the subject because I didn't want to give the impression I was bragging on myself. But she persisted until I finally told her the name of one of my books, at which point Harry interjected, "Actually, she's written five books and her newest one is just off press. She's known all over the world as an expert on homebased business."

That just blew me away because, except for my cooking, Harry had *never* bragged on me in the belief that my ego was too big to begin with. He later explained that, since I'd been so good to him through this whole experience, he thought I deserved something extra myself. Over the nine days he was in the hospital, both of us came to realize once again just how much we loved and needed one another.

When he finally learned he could go home, it took more than two hours to get all the paperwork done. As he was sitting on the edge of the bed waiting for the release papers and the wheelchair to take him downstairs, he said with humorous sarcasm, "I hope it's easier to get into Heaven than it is to get out of this hospital." Later, at home, noting that his hair needed cutting, especially his eyebrows, he said, "I feel like I'm looking through the hanging gardens of Babylon."

Hmm, I thought, he really *is* hearing God's voice now.

The next morning as we snuggled in bed, I was fingering the big scar down his chest and commented that I could hardly believe that beneath the thin line of invisible stitching there was a row of metal staples holding his chest together. All of a sudden I got the giggles, and told him it was because I suddenly envisioned the surgeon with a huge office staple puller having to pull out all the old staples from the previous surgery before they could cut him open again. He got tickled, too, looked heavenward and said, "Lord, why me?"

Later that day when I once again brought up the topic of God, Harry showed some resistance. When I knew he was about to say, "Don't preach to me," I quickly said, "I'm not going to preach to you, Harry, but I just want to show you the connection between God and all the things that are happening in our life now."

"You're bound and determined to make me a Christian, aren't you?" he said. But this time it was said in love and not with irritation as it had been before.

I never thought I'd see the day when I'd thank God for giving Harry a heart attack, but I did. In all this, I had seen an exciting example of His perfect timing and how He always "works all things together for good," how the Holy Spirit moves in people's lives, and how prayer works. The man I brought home from the hospital was not the same man that went in. He had learned a very painful but important lesson in the hospital; namely, that he was no longer boss, and that he had to rely on a lot of other people to get him through this ordeal. By making Harry face the possibility of death if he didn't have the surgery, God literally brought him to his knees and touched his heart in more ways than one as he brought him back to his former happy self.

One day while we were out running errands with me driving because he was still not allowed to drive yet (although he was driving me nuts with all his "helpful" driving suggestions), he referred to a guy in front of us by saying, "Oh, great, now we're stuck behind Sleeping Moses." When I asked what he meant by that, he said, "Actually, the expression is 'Sleeping Jesus,' but since you don't like me to take the Lord's name in vain, I changed it to Moses."

I saw this as evidence that he was beginning to feel guilty about taking God's name in vain, and that he and God had probably been communicating quite a bit lately.

In December of that year when we were both listening to radio and someone made a remark about going to a nightclub, I said, jokingly, "You know, I've never been to a nightclub in my life. Do you think I've missed anything important?"

Harry stunned me with his quiet response. "Do you know what I've never done in my life?"

"No, what?" I asked, quite curious.

"I've never taken communion."

Out of the blue, it seemed that Harry had been doing some serious thinking here. I told him then that, while he was in the hospital and recovering from his surgery, I had gone to church to pray for him and taken communion again for the first time in thirty years. I told him I'd just fallen apart then because the experience was so emotional for me. He didn't say anything after that, but he didn't have to.

A Hard Row to Hoe

Harry's heart attack effectively put a stop to his playing, even for fun, and his continuing health problems and inability to help me with the business soon prompted me to close our mail order activities and cease publication of the newsletter I had been writing for fifteen years. By then, the bimonthly publishing deadlines were simply getting to be too much for me to deal with on top of my new care giving responsibilities. I also stopped traveling to do speaking engagements and focused on writing full time so I could be there for Harry when he needed me.

Before the turn of the century, his "medical repertoire" included hospitalizations for blood clots in his legs, pneumonia, and a partial bowel resection. Adult-onset diabetes followed soon afterwards, along with two cataract surgeries and two knee joint replacements, each of which required weeks of physical therapy. For some time now he had been working with a pain specialist who was giving him spinal injections and trying to control his back pain by testing every known type of narcotic pain killer in existence. Yet he tried to make light of his situation, as this comment in a June 2000 letter to Ollie Zinsmeister proves: "I'm having serious pain problems, and the doc just put me on an opium patch. God knows I'm squirrely enough—I don't need outside help!"

None of the pain meds helped much, and his attempts to deal with his pain made it a constant topic of conversation, to the point where even I began to feel consumed by it and often felt guilty as well because I had no physical pain myself. It wasn't that he was complaining about it, but it seemed we were always *talking* about pain management strategies, new medications, dosages, treatment options or results, on and on. Anyone who has ever had to personally deal with a huge level of pain or watch someone else cope with it understands that PAIN is an invader in one's life that demands constant attention. Just dealing with it is exhausting.

At this point, Harry no longer had much physical stamina for anything beyond sitting in his office for a couple of hours a day. Playing drums was the farthest thing from his mind, but music continued to play in our home whenever he wasn't watching educational television or trying to read with eyes that allowed only brief periods of reading pleasure before blurring.

Journal entry, a Sunday in May, 2001:

> *As usual, Harry sits at the table, eyeglasses down on his nose—the better to see the fine print through the bottom of his bifocals—scissors in hand, looking at a newspaper page for that article he read earlier and now wants to clip for his scrapbook, or perhaps for me to read.*
>
> *In the background, his Sunday jazz program is playing on the radio, delivering tunes that kindle his memories of happier days when he was young and healthy, never imagining then that one day he would actually be too old and infirm to play drums.*
>
> *Now 74, he lives with a daily load of pain he has endured with little complaint for the past ten years—one that would bring most people to their knees or put them in such a state of depression that they would never be able to get out of bed and face another day. But his mind is still young, and somewhere deep inside I know he believes that if he just keeps going, the next day will be better, even though history has shown it never will be.*
>
> *I sit across the room from him, a stack of reading material in front of me, jotting these random thoughts on paper as I think about how my whole life has always revolved around this man, without whom I never would have become a writer or done any of the things that have made my life so interesting, challenging, and, yes, difficult.*
>
> *I think as I watch him now that he could have another heart attack or stroke one of these days when he least expects it, and I try to prepare myself mentally for this possibility. All things being equal, I will outlive Harry by a couple of decades or more, and after 40 years together, it's almost impossible for me to imagine my life without his powerful presence in it.*

Harry's health problems were now monumental. It had been a long time coming, but, by the fall of 2002, the drummer who had always called the shots was no longer driving, but merely riding, impatiently waiting to reach his final destination. He now knew he could never drive again without fear of an accident. From that point on, he would be fighting "cabin fever," going out only to see a doctor or have another medical test or surgical procedure. Sometimes, just to get out of the house, he'd ask to ride along with me and wait in the car as I ran errands or did grocery shopping. We'd hit a drive-in for some fast food and pretend life was normal.

One day he said he had never been afraid of dying, but now he was afraid of living. He added that when he thought I couldn't take it any longer, he would simply kill himself because he couldn't stand to take me down with him. Again I had to insist that he stop with the suicidal thoughts, saying that *if and when* I ever felt I could no longer "take it any more," we'd look for some other option at that time. Inside, however, remembering my promise to never put him in a nursing home, I was very concerned about my physical ability to take care of him if he became completely disabled. By then, I also needed knee joint replacements myself, but there was no way I could have surgery and take care of Harry at the same time.

"I love you very much, and I'm so sorry to be putting you through all my problems," he said. He often expressed his love for me in one way or another, but he didn't always verbalize it as nicely as this, and just hearing such words always gave me a surge of strength. Although his medical problems had pushed romance out of our lives a long time before, the love and friendship we always had for one another only grew stronger in these last difficult years when I'm sure we were both remembering our marriage vows:

> To have and to hold,
> From this day forward,
> For better, for worse,
> For richer, for poorer,
> In sickness and in health,
> To love and to cherish,
> 'Till death do us part.

At this point, we were clearly in the latter stages of "for worse." As if all the above weren't enough, in the last two years of his life Harry was diagnosed with sleep apnea and Parkinson's. When he was told he needed to start sleeping with a CPAP machine and learned that it made a noise, he refused to even consider it. As for the Parkinson's, we were grateful that it didn't cause any noticeable hand shaking, but it did weaken his hands considerably, affected his memory and speech at times, and left him with feet that seemed glued to the floor. By then, his bad back made it nearly impossible for him to get up out of bed without assistance, and a walk to the bathroom from the bed could take up to thirty minutes, even with my help every step of the way.

After reading that some Parkinson's patients responded to rhythmic patterns, I began to sing march music, doing a "ta-da-ta-dum, ta-da-ta-dum" melody to see if he could get his feet moving to the beat I was setting. And it worked! He got awfully tired of hearing my terrible singing, but it helped with the walking and gave us something to laugh about.

♪ Music Sidenote ♪

Many musicians are among the millions who get Parkinson's disease every year, and there are several discussions on the Web about the connection between music and Parkinson's. One article I found explained why the above "musical exercise" might have worked for Harry. It quoted Dr. Robert Melillo, co-founder of the Brain Balance Achievement Centers. "Different areas of the brain need to be coordinated from a timing standpoint for the brain to work completely as a whole," he says. "Music, because it has a rhythm to it, can actually cause the brain to change the speed in different areas so that the timing becomes better."

As always, music played in the background of our lives, and humor remained the best medicine we had. It was always there, like an invisible friend riding the choppy waves of life with us, ready to splash us with a dose of laughter as we struggled through the last two and most difficult years of Harry's life. One day while talking to one of my sisters, he joked about the amazing team we had become, with his being all crippled up from arthritis and Parkinson's, and me being dippy from lack of sleep in caring for him. He cracked me up when I heard him say, "Just call us Cripp & Dipp."

As his medical problems continued to worsen, however, it was a struggle for him to find anything funny to laugh about, or even come up with one good reason to keep on living. By December 2004, he was truly at the end of his rope and quite depressed because he had now been confined to the bedroom for the past two years, and couldn't even leave the room without the use of a wheelchair. When we had a doctor's appointment, I would wheel him to the kitchen and he could still walk up and down the six steps to the garage (which, curiously, was easier for him than walking straight ahead). But I was becoming increasingly worried about how I was going to take care of him since my own health was suffering now. Shortly before Christmas I had a chair lift installed on the kitchen stairs, but he never got a chance to use it.

I had prepared his usual Christmas dinner of duck, sweet-sour sauerkraut, potato dumplings, and mincemeat pie, but he had little appetite then or the day after. He went to sleep at 9 p.m. on December 26 and when I couldn't waken him at 10 o'clock the next morning, I called 911. He was quickly admitted to the hospital because his blood pressure and oxygen level were extremely low and his heart was racing, which was very dangerous given his A-fib condition. I almost fell apart that evening when I was told he might not make it through the night because his heart could give out at any time.

But Harry was a lot tougher than any of his doctors thought, and apparently he wasn't "through with me" yet because, time after time in the next few weeks when everyone was sure he was at death's door, the "comeback kid" would make yet another astonishing medical comeback.

Dancing with Death

How a man dies says as much about him as how he has lived, so this book wouldn't be complete without some information about the last weeks of Harry's life.

Of course I'm not going to go into detail about all the truly miserable days he and I spent as he went in and out of the hospital and nursing home from December 26 through January 17 when I was finally able to bring him home on Hospice (about which I cannot say enough good things). I'm not going to elaborate, either, on how difficult it was for me to be his full-time care giver for the last five years of his life, and especially the last couple of weeks under Hospice. Anyone who has ever taken care of a disabled loved one who is dying knows full well the kind of physical stress and emotional distress this causes to both the care giver and the one who is dying. (If you have not experienced this yet, count yourself lucky.)

Unless we're extremely fortunate, most of us will suffer at the end of our lives, either from physical pain or emotional distress, or both, as was the case with Harry. In the end, many of us may find ourselves saying, "I never thought I'd go out this way." The point I want to make here is that while we may have little or no choice about what's going to finally take us down and out of this world, we *do* have a choice about how we're going to face our own death. And Harry faced his with a peaceful and stoical acceptance of the inevitable that amazed me. He never once moaned "why me?" or asked me to do anything for him that wasn't absolutely necessary. In fact, he was more concerned for what his illness was doing to me than what it was doing to him. I was never more proud of him than when he was dying, nor more thankful that we both still had a sense of humor.

Now, with some summary paragraphs and a couple of excerpts from my journal, let me tell you something about how Harry died, and the role his humor played in our last days together.

Journal entry, January 8, 2005:

Beep-beep, beep-beep, beep-beep. Every six seconds, another beep-beep as Harry's IV monitor responds to the restless movement of his arms, now covered with black and blue marks from the many blood draws that have been taken since he was brought back into the ER from the nursing home yesterday.

The nurse comes in to check the IV machine and the beeping stops for the moment but begins again as soon as Harry moves his arms. The incessant beeping plays against the quiet soothing sounds of the music that is now playing on our portable CD machine. It's sub-titled "The most relaxing classical album in the world—ever," and it is helping to calm me and, I hope, also speaking to Harry as he drifts between consciousness and sleep.

There was a time when the beep of a monitor drove me crazy, but I've come to accept it now as something I can't control, and thus must not fret about. I've come to accept many things in the past two weeks, but I'm totally exhausted by the emotional and physical rollercoaster ride I've had as I first put Harry in the hospital two weeks ago Monday, and then had to face the possibility that his death might be imminent.

When the doctor coldly asked me that night if I wanted them to "use extreme measures" to bring Harry back if his heart stopped in the middle of the night, or just let him go, it was like getting a bucket of cold water thrown in my face. "Of course!" I said.

"Are you saying we should put him on a ventilator?" the doctor asked, as if this were a ridiculous idea for someone as old and ill as Harry, and I almost screamed, "YES! Do everything possible to revive him because I haven't had a chance to say goodbye yet."

As he flailed about in bed last night, his temperature spiked again and I wondered if the stroke they thought he had could have impaired his brain to the point where he wouldn't be able to recognize me or talk to me without slurring his speech. I didn't sleep much, what with worrying about him and the beeping IV going all night, plus the constant stream of nurses and aides coming and going. Imagine my surprise and joy when, at 6 a.m., Harry opened his eyes, looked at me, and weakly said, "Hi."

"Hi yourself," I said. He didn't know I had been there by his side all night, and I am so grateful that this new Heart Hospital wing offers patients a private room with a comfortable bed and chair for their spouse, which means I can be here all the time. He was clearly glad to see me and I knew his sense of humor was still intact when I went over to him, bent down, and said "Give me a kiss."

"Hell no," he said, turning his head aside, and it broke me up. He did kiss me, of course; this was just typical Harry humor.

"I love you," I said, and he smiled and said, "What's not to love?"

"I'm playing one of your favorite CDs. Do you know what it is?"

"Yeah; Dvorak's 'New World Symphony.'"

That he could recognize the music being played told me that any stroke he may have suffered the night before had not impaired important mental faculties.

After several more tests some time later, we learned that a minor stroke while eating breakfast had caused him to aspirate food into his lungs, so now he had pneumonia again and, worse, a serious problem in swallowing, which meant no more food or drink. When he learned he had failed the swallowing study and would have to be fed through a tube in his nose or stomach for the rest of his life, that was a terrible blow to this man who had always had a passionate relationship with good food, one who looked forward to each meal with all the anticipation of a child waiting for Santa Claus. After being force-fed through the nose for a couple of days, he said he wanted no part of living like this. When he demanded that the tube come out and he be given something to eat and drink—knowing full well this could kill him—the doctors and I agreed that we should let him live and die as he chose.

After Harry had cheated death that first night, I told him we needed to talk about the Power of Attorney he had given me years before. I needed to hear him say once again that it would be okay for me to "pull the plug" if it came to that, and he said yes, he didn't want to live if his brain was gone or if death was imminent and a machine would only delay the inevitable. Of course I cried like a baby, but Harry, always a realist about this topic, was calm and undisturbed.

"There are some CDs I'd like Joel to have," he said, "and I have some tapes that need to be returned to Fred." And then he paused and said, "You should probably get a cat," and I just lost it again. I loved cats and had been yearning to have another one after we lost Ginger, but Harry's remembrances of our two early cat experiences had soured him on bringing another one into the house. With all the things in his life he was dealing with, I chose not to press him on this subject, so it meant a lot to me to know then that he wanted me to have a pet for company after he was gone.

Is That Jimmy Stewart I See There?

Even when one is ill and flirting with death, there can be moments of fun. One of those came one day when an orderly walked into the room, took one look at Harry and said, "Wow, I see your name on the door is Harry Brabec, but there for a minute I thought I was looking at Jimmy Stewart himself."

Harry just looked at me as if to say, "You've *got* to be kidding." It was a wonderful moment for me that made me laugh aloud, and then Harry had to laugh, too, because we had an inside joke here. I had always had "a thing" about Jimmy Stewart. He was always, and still is, one of my favorite actors. Many years earlier, I decided I just had to write and tell him that. Jimmy remains the only movie star or celebrity I've ever felt so personally drawn to. I won't bore you with the details of my letter, but suffice it to say that he responded with a sweetly autographed picture and a handwritten note saying, "I'm very grateful to you for your wonderful letter. It's just about the best letter I have ever received, and the things you said about my life and work mean a great deal to me."

When I showed Harry his note and picture and offered to let him read the letter I had sent, he just grunted, and when I put Jimmy's picture on my bulletin board, I think he was actually jealous. Earlier, I had joked with him that maybe I had fallen in love with him on first sight because he subconsciously reminded me of Jimmy, whom I'd loved all my life. As he and Jimmy aged, I continued to point out the physical resemblance between them, but he couldn't see it. So when that orderly walked in and confirmed what I had always told him, he knew he no longer had a leg to stand on and then he found it very funny.

Maybe you had to be there to appreciate it, but to me it was one of those delightful I-told-you-so moments that still makes me laugh when I think of it.

While writing this chapter and working in the kitchen before Christmas, I decided to once again watch *It's a Wonderful Life*. Suddenly I saw another parallel between Harry and Jimmy that hit me when I was about halfway through the movie, and this one made me cry. When Harry's symphony dreams were shattered, he had to keep going, eventually doing things he never thought he would have to do, always feeling disappointed that his life hadn't turned out the way he had intended, and feeling like a failure when he couldn't find work. More than once when he was seriously depressed and believing he had nothing left to live for, I saw a look on his face that mirrored the desperation and pain I saw on Stewart's face as he portrayed George Bailey getting ready to jump off the bridge. I had seen this movie several times before, but this time it was almost too painful to watch because for the first time I was seeing Harry's life mirrored in it.

Like George Bailey in the movie, Harry also made an impact on the lives of many people, but he never realized how important his teaching, personal encouragement, and professional connections had been to the careers of so many of his old school chums and musician friends. There was no angel to come down from Heaven and point out that the world was a better place because Harry Brabec had been in it. There was only me, and although I did all I could to encourage him, I knew nothing about all that he had done to help and encourage his friends because none of them ever told me these things until after he was gone. I'm sure he never knew, either, that he was so loved, respected, and fondly remembered by so many whose lives he had touched.

"Strange, isn't it," Clarence the angel said in the movie, "how each man's life touches so many other lives. When he isn't around, it leaves an awful hole." But the one that really got me was the card on the Christmas tree at the end of the movie, with the line that read, "Remember, no man is a failure who has friends." I just wish Harry had realized how many friends he actually had when he was going through his darkest days at the end of his life.

I hope this little story will be a reminder to you to *always* tell someone if they have made an impact on your life, whether it's a letter to a famous person you have admired from afar, one of your old teachers, your parents, siblings, or an old friend you're taking for granted because he or she has always been there for you. Even something you consider insignificant can have a sweetness to it that the recipient will appreciate, such as what Rich Sherrill told me when he was sharing information for this book.

"Something I've always remembered about you, Barbara, is when I came for a lesson with Harry, you always made us a grilled cheese sandwich for lunch, and you put a slice of fresh tomato on it because that was how Harry liked it. To this day, I've never made a grilled cheese sandwich without that slice of tomato on it, and that sandwich always brings back a flood of happy Barbara and Harry memories."

Special Blessings and Small Miracles

With Harry so near to death's door, I had a growing concern for his soul. Although he had appreciated the hospital chaplain's prayers when he stopped by, he wouldn't take communion when it was offered. I'm guessing he passed on this because to him it must have seemed like a last-ditch effort to get into Heaven. He was holding true to his promise to "never use Christ as a crutch." He once told me that he caused his own problems, and he alone was responsible for them. "I won't beg for mercy from anyone, least of all Christ," he said.

When Harry learned that he had to go back to the nursing home for awhile because I was then too ill to bring him home, he naturally became very despondent. He had always told me to just give him a shotgun and be done with it because he couldn't tolerate a nursing home, and I promised to never put him in one to die; yet there I was, physically unable to care for him. So all I could do at that point was pray:

Oh, Father, I'd like to have the opportunity to regain my strength so I can care for Harry at the end of his life. And I pray that you will not give up on this man whose feet seem as solidly planted against coming to Christ as they are glued to the floor when he tries to walk. Lord, please open his heart, let him hear your knocking. And then ask your angels to stand by to escort him to Heaven so he'll be there when I get there. In Jesus' name I pray. Amen.

God would not only answer that prayer but astound me with His graciousness in the last weeks of Harry's life. For the next couple of weeks, he would be going back and forth between the hospital and nursing home, and once I realized I had been "officially relieved" of the responsibility of caring for him, I allowed myself to get sick—*really* sick. I ended up in the hospital for three days, totally dehydrated with my potassium level at rock bottom. For the past two years, my greatest fear had always been who would take care of Harry if I had to be hospitalized. I had no family in the area, and the cost of round-the-clock nursing care was simply a financial impossibility. But I needn't have worried because God had it all figured out. He simply put both of us in the same hospital at the same time. We were like ships passing in the night that day as I was wheeled down to Harry's room to give him a kiss before they took him back to the nursing home a week after he had been admitted.

Another amazing thing that happened while Harry was in the hospital was that his pain suddenly diminished. They had taken him off the narcotic pain medications when he was admitted, and we were waiting for the pain consultant to come in and prescribe whatever he needed at that point. But when asked if he was in much pain, Harry said no, he had no pain to speak of, and from that point on he required nothing more that a few Tylenol tablets each day. To me, this was nothing less than a miracle, and a confirmation that God was showing Harry some mercy even if he hadn't asked for it.

Back home again, I had a hard time getting my strength back, but I woke up on Monday, the 17th of January with a terrible sense of urgency that told me I had to get Harry home at once, whether I was well or not. I had been told that he could die quickly or live another few months, but I have always followed my gut instincts, and now I sensed that time was quickly running out for him.

As I was writing this and referring to the calendar notebook in which I had jotted thoughts for this period of time, I suddenly saw that, starting on this day and counting, Harry had just 18 days to live. *Could it be merely a coincidence, I wonder now, that God gave us the exact same number of days to say goodbye as it had taken us to say hello, fall in love, and marry?*

A couple of days before I brought Harry home, Fred Wickstrom had called to tell me he was going to fly up from Florida to see Harry on this particular day. Because I wasn't yet well enough to drive, he picked me up and we both went over to the nursing home to surprise him. As we entered the lobby, I was puzzled when Fred spied a big tin container and asked the attendant if he could borrow it for a bit. He stayed outside as I went in to greet Harry, and then he began to beat a drummer's routine on the tin. Harry couldn't figure out what was going on, but suddenly he didn't look sick any more. As Fred waddled into the room, continuing to beat on the "drum" he was carrying between his legs, Harry beamed as though he had just won the lottery. I'll never forget that moment and the joy I saw on his face at seeing one of his oldest friends again at the end of his life.

Later that day we set up the arrangements for Hospice, which moved with incredible speed. I spent the rest of the afternoon and evening tearing the bedroom apart to make room for a hospital bed and other medical equipment, and two of Harry's friends came over to take the bedspring, headboards, and mattress out to the street for garbage pickup the next morning. Everything was in place before noon when Harry was brought home. He was so happy to be there with me that he didn't even ask what I'd done with his bed.

We had one good week together with him eating well, although less and less each day. I was so grateful to be able to take care of him at home, to prepare some of his favorite meals, play the music he wanted to hear, and to read to him that week. He didn't complain about his condition, which was heart wrenching to me, but asked only that I stay with him as much as possible. I had some part-time help now, but I rarely left his side.

A phone call that week from his friend Doug made him chuckle. Sam Denov and his wife came by for a visit on Thursday, bringing some pictures of Harry playing in the Symphony that I hadn't seen before. He was still alert and able to talk a bit that day, but that would be the last day he could express anything in full sentences. Scott Thomas came by for a visit the next day, but Harry was pretty much out of it by then. I asked the Hospice chaplain to come by later that day because I sensed it would be the last opportunity for anyone to talk to him about God and have him understand it. With Harry's permission, the chaplain prayed for him and said all the right words I wanted him to hear. I felt comforted when he asked Harry if he was afraid to die, and he said no. At that point I believed he was communicating with God because no one could have faced his Maker so calmly and peacefully otherwise.

When he could no longer take food or drink, he began to sleep most of the time. My sisters Mary and Mollie arrived the following Monday, and I wept because I so wanted them to have a chance to say goodbye to Harry, and now he appeared to be in a coma. But once again he surprised all of us when, after being asleep for four days, he suddenly awoke on Tuesday morning, alert and happy to see me. He had difficulty talking, but he enjoyed visiting with my sisters, and we all got kisses that day.

Knowing how much Harry loved dogs, and especially the therapy dogs who always visited him in the hospital, I believe God arranged it so Harry would get a visit from *three* dogs in the last week of his life. When I accidentally learned that two of the Hospice workers had dogs, I convinced them that they needed to bend the rules a bit and bring them into the house on two separate days. When Harry experienced a brief surge of energy on this particular day, I asked Scott Thomas to come back again, this time bringing his dog Caesar with him. When that big, fluffy white dog walked through the bedroom door, Harry said softly, "Oh my goodness," and gave all of us his last big smile. We mere humans couldn't make him smile like that then, but his deep love of dogs and the memory of our own beloved Ginger did the trick.

I was at his bedside the next morning when he woke up for a few minutes. "I love you," I said, and asked him if he could speak. Very clearly he said, "I love you." Those would be the last words I'd ever hear him say. I couldn't have asked for more.

Going Home

Harry was adamant about not having a formal memorial service, but a day before he died we took solace in the private service we held in the bedroom. It was led by the Hospice chaplain, who read two Psalms of my choice (100 and 103). Although Harry was in a coma by then, we believed he could hear our special prayers for him, and we hoped he appreciated the loving, humorous memories of him each of us shared at that time. I know he would have laughed uproariously at our off-key rendering of "Amazing Grace," which we all agreed was amazingly graceless. Nevertheless, this unusual service gave us a lot of comfort.

Long before Harry became ill, I had asked him if there was any special music he wanted me to play if he were near death or in a coma, and he said yes, he wanted to hear Dvorak's *New World Symphony*. So that's what I was playing that night in the hospital when he nearly died, and it was this music that I continued to play in the last days of his life as he lay in a coma. I didn't think about this then, but only as I was writing this chapter. He had only one CD of this music, and it was the recording he had made with the Chicago Symphony and Fritz Reiner in 1956 in which he played triangle in the third movement.

How strange, I thought—*how ironic*—that the last music Harry wanted to hear was a recording he had made under the baton of the man who had dealt a death blow to his professional life so many years before.

Harry died at 4:30 a.m. on February 3, 2005. If we could all choose the way we died, one could not choose a more peaceful death than he experienced, in his own bedroom, with Dvorak's music playing in the background and his wife and sisters-in-law there to hold his hands and caress his brow. His breathing and heartbeat simply slowed over the last half hour of his life, much like an old Victrola machine winding down until there was no power left, and his soul was released into the arms of God, the great Composer, Orchestrator, and Conductor of all our lives.

"Harry was a musician to the end," my sister Mollie noted, "with his heart going from prestissimo to a peaceful adagio ending."

I believe this Showman's Prayer, which Harry had on his bulletin board for years, indicates how he may have felt about God throughout his life, and especially at the end:

> *O my God, I believe in you, I trust in you, I thank you for all of my blessings. I love you and ask forgiveness for all my sins. Guide and protect me and all those dear to me. Make me mindful of my privilege as a showman to bring joy and happiness to all people . . . especially the poor, the lonely, the less fortunate. And when my last act on earth is completed and the final curtain falls, take me to yourself to be happy with you forever. Amen.*

CHAPTER 17

A Widow's Ponderings and Regrets

"He was always difficult, but he never was a bore."
—Harry's suggestion for an embroidered pillow

I still remember the day decades ago when Harry and I were driving around Chicago and passed a tombstone factory. As we began to muse about what our own headstones might say about us, I had a rare flash of genius. He laughed heartily when I said to him, "If you should precede me to the great beyond, I know exactly what I'll have inscribed on your headstone: *"Here lies Harry Brabec. He finally took his drum and beat it."*

Years later when we were on vacation in Gatlinburg, Tennessee, I learned just how much he had appreciated that remark. In one of the craft shops, Harry was fascinated as we watched a metal spinner make a brass spittoon. Having played in more than one saloon in his day, he just had to have one of them, and the craftsman was more than happy to inscribe something he wanted on the bottom. It read:

"Old saloon drummers never die.
They just take their drum and beat it."

"No Fanfare, Please"

Not wanting to be a bother to anyone or the center of attention at a funeral or memorial service, Harry's last wish was to be cremated without fanfare. I had cried so much in the weeks before he died that when it was finally over I had no tears left. I was simply numb from stress and exhaustion. But perhaps Harry's spirit was still hovering in the room when the two men came to take his body for cremation, because something happened then that made me smile. In one of my grieving letters to him, I spoke about this experience:

> *The cremation guys told me to stay out of the bedroom while they put you in the body bag, saying this wasn't something a widow should subject herself to. But I told them I belonged there, that I had watched over every minute of your care through your many years of illness, and I wasn't about to abandon ship now. They were struggling as they gently lifted your stone cold, spiritless body and began to put you in the body bag. One of the men looked at me apologetically and said, "This is a really big man; I'm not sure we can get the bag zipped." And I smiled and said, "I think Harry would have laughed about this because he always said 'The world is round, but I am square.'"*
>
> *So they had to leave part of your head sticking out of the bag as they took you down the hallway, through the kitchen, and down the stairs into the garage. This turned out to be a good thing for me to have done, because I felt I had fulfilled my commitment to you to never leave you, even when you no longer needed me there. But my heart lurched when they stood you up to take you through the door to the garage because your head bobbled with no support, and my immediate thought was that this would have hurt you. Funny, my concern for your physical well-being even after you were dead."*

I had often joked with Harry that I was going to put his ashes in his ornamental brass spittoon, but after looking for a special urn and finding nothing that suited his unique personality, I suddenly realized I had the most appropriate container right in the bedroom. It was a leather-lined box I'd made for him one Christmas in the sixties that was ornamented with my wood-burned drawings of Civil War soldiers on the sides and a hand-painted drummer boy on top. He treasured this gift and gave it a permanent place on the top of his chest of drawers, where it still resides today in my bedroom. Above it is another gift of mine that he loved—a framed collage of photos of him playing drums in different places and at different stages of his life.

I'm sure he would be very happy to know that he is going to be near me always in his very special box, and it gives me great comfort to pat that box occasionally and talk to him a bit.

Harry's Estranged Daughter

Earlier in the book, I told you about Harry's failed first marriage, but I gave you only half the story then. It wasn't until after he died that I really began to study his life from a different perspective and began to understand the implications of all the emotional baggage he had been carrying around with him for our entire married life.

He didn't want to talk about his life with Doris, and I really didn't care to know all the details of what went wrong because we were so happy together. There are many reasons for why marriages fail, and we agreed there was no sense in dwelling on something that was over and done with. Because Harry had shared some of his fatherhood stories with me, I knew how much he had adored his daughter Bonnie. He maintained a personal relationship with her as long as we were in the Chicago area, but her mother had full custody and Harry and I could never get more than an hour's visit with her in her home once in a while.

Harry paid child support long after it was no longer legally required of him, and even increased the amount. After we moved to Florida, he and Bonnie stayed in touch by mail and phone, and we were hopeful that they would eventually have a relationship as adults. However, when he was financially unable to put Bonnie through college, as she and her mother expected him to do, their relationship quickly went downhill.

Bonnie was a young adult when she and Harry and I last met at a family funeral. I was at Harry's side when he approached her and tried so hard to engage her in conversation. But she merely answered his questions about her life with as few words as possible, making it clear to both of us that she wanted nothing to do with him. Already a wounded spirit who could take only so much rejection, Harry never had the heart to force the relationship after that. To my deep regret, they remained estranged throughout his life, never speaking to one another again.

After he died, I got to thinking about Bonnie, tracked her down, and learned that her mother was gone, she had never married, and was now retired from an apparently very successful career. I reached out to her with a carefully written letter telling her about her dad, how much he had loved her, how he was so admired by his peers and friends, and how proud I was of him. I included a package of his pictures and voice and

music recordings, and offered her some of his most cherished possessions, but she never responded. I still weep today when I think of all they
both missed by not knowing one another as adults.

As Harry lay in a coma the last week of his life, he thrashed about a
great deal and cried out frequently, calling my name. The Hospice social
worker told me that people often do this when they're dying because
they're trying to resolve unresolved issues in their life. I feel certain that
Harry's relationship with Bonnie was a major unresolved issue in his life,
and I so regret that I did not hound him relentlessly about trying to
contact her one more time. I can only pray that she will read this book
when it arrives on her doorstep, and will finally know the wonderful but
troubled man her father was.

Of course Harry tried to cover with a quilt of humor all the
emotional hurt he had endured before we met, but I believe now that this
was a wound that never fully healed—one that always lay buried just
beneath the surface of his life, ready to open up and bleed whenever life
delivered yet another rejection or disappointment. I'm no psychologist,
but I believe his emotional baggage negatively influenced many of his
decisions, actions, and relationships with people, including me. He liked
a lot of people, but trusted few of them. He once joked with me saying,
"There are only two people in the world I trust . . . and I'm not absolutely
sure about you." It never occurred to me that he really *meant* this. After
all, he was always cracking wise, so I really thought then that this was
just another of his humorous quips. But now I'm not so sure.

A Widow's "Busy Work"

My priorities certainly shifted after Harry died. Four days after his death,
I sat down at the computer and built several web pages for him on my
personal domain. A couple of weeks later, I went to California to be with
my sisters for six weeks. Harry would have been pleased with the private
memorial service for him there that featured sister Mollie's beautiful
piano playing and the reminiscences of family members and relatives.

After returning from California, I created a memory box of our lives
together, got a cat I named Charlee, cleaned house better than it had
been cleaned in years, and arranged a "Remembering Harry" luncheon
for several of his musician friends and school chums in the area.

For the next several months, I literally felt obsessed by the need to
bring together all of his voice tapes, his professional recordings, his
letters, scrapbooks, photographs, and personal possessions. Then I spent

countless hours going through his thousands of LPs, CDs, tapes, and books, pondering what I was going to do with all these things that had been so important to him, but not nearly as important to me. One day one of his friends remarked that I seemed to be in a "Harry frenzy," and I guess I was. I finally realized that I was not only making work for myself to avoid my real work on the Web, but also trying to hang onto Harry the only way I knew how at the time.

One might think that in writing this book I'm still trying to hang on to Harry, and that may be true; but at least now I have a totally different mindset and purpose for doing it. As I see it, the next best thing to living a good life is remembering it all over again.

My "frenzy" gradually evolved into a kind of quiet determination to do everything I could to honor and memorialize Harry's life and accomplishments. My last big "Harry Project" that first year—which took three months to finish—was the dubbing of over a hundred CDs of several of his voice tapes and professional recordings that I gave to family and friends for Christmas. I wanted the people who loved him most to have a special keepsake to remind them of his exceptional musical ability, but in doing this work I found I was also giving myself a very special Christmas gift.

Later, someone told me that what I was doing here was called "creative grieving." In looking back, I see that my grieving period for Harry was actually very short, because I quickly turned that period of time into a celebration of his life that will continue as long as I'm alive. It has been said that one of the best ways to ease an aching heart is to commemorate the memory of a loved one, and I believe that my intense focus on documenting and celebrating Harry's life and accomplishments immediately after his death, and throughout my first year without him, made a great difference in my ability to be content, even joyful, as I began to move forward in life without him.

Everyone always tells a widow she has to "move on," and although I certainly did that, I will never "get over" Harry, because he was a presence no one could ever ignore or forget. His absence in my life after so many years together left an enormous hole I'll never be able to fill, in spite of having many friends, countless interests, and enjoyable work I look forward to doing for the rest of my life.

I like what Molly Fumia wrote in *Safe Passage* (Conan Press 2003), a book for grieving widows: "Life will not go in the same way without him. If it were the same, we could only conclude his life meant nothing, made no contribution. The fact that he left behind a place that cannot be filled is a high tribute to the uniqueness of his soul."

I was also touched by a line Gene Hackman delivered in the movie, *I Never Sang for my Father:* "Death ends a life, not a relationship. It struggles on in a survivor's mind toward some resolution which it may never find."

I suspect I will forever be trying to understand what it was that bound me and Harry so tightly together for nearly 44 years. I cry now for all the extra happiness we might have had if life hadn't dealt him so many emotional blows. He deserved far more from life than he ever got, but I thank God for placing me in his life because I know I gave him a kind of happiness he could not have had with anyone else. I always knew that I was the only person in the world who truly loved him and understood his needs, and I'm satisfied that I did the best I could under sometimes very difficult circumstances, just as he always did.

I now believe I thrived on the kind of stress, challenges, and excitement Harry brought to my life. In fact, for awhile after he died, I actually wondered if I might not die of boredom without him to keep my fire lit. I still talk to him and about him to friends, so he remains a huge part of my life—especially now that I'm reliving our lives in this book. I wrote letters to him for a year, and I still feel his presence in every room of the house where we finally put down roots in 1989. I plan to stay here as long as I'm able to care for myself and the house.

I still ache to share my life with a healthy and happy Harry, and I will always miss the love and laughter he brought into my life. And yet . . . I am also content to once again be in total control of my life, able to live and work exactly as I please—much as I did before I met Harry—and do what my heart is leading me to do without having to defer to his or anyone else's wishes.

"When I'm gone, " he often said in our later years together, "you'll be able to do exactly what you want to do and you'll probably work around the clock, because 'work' is your middle name. *But you're gonna miss me when I'm gone.*"

He sure had that right.

No Ordinary Joe

As you've gathered from this book, my life with Harry was often filled with financial uncertainty due to his being a freelance musician and entrepreneur. But I didn't marry him with the idea that he should be solely responsible for our livelihood. I was fiercely independent long before I met him; always wanted to work and have a career of my own. I also instinctively knew that, given my lesser years and better health, one day I'd end up taking care of him.

If I had married an ordinary Joe with a steady job for thirty or forty years, I would probably be sitting now in a house fully paid for, with a lot more money in the bank for my old age. But would I have been as happy or personally fulfilled with a nine-to-five fellow as I was with Harry? *Absolutely not.* I was able to secure my home with a reverse mortgage that has given me a substantial line of credit I may never need. Meanwhile, I have everything I need for my personal happiness and physical comfort, and I wouldn't trade all those wonderful music and travel experiences I had with Harry for a million dollars.

It's nice to look back now and see how we balanced one another and needed each other to live our lives to the fullest. I gave Harry stability to balance his freeform way of living, and he encouraged me to loosen up and be more creative. Without his encouragement and you-can-do-it messages, I never would have found my true life's work as a writer. And it's not hard to imagine what a boring life we would have led if I had encouraged him to get a regular job right after we married, or how sad we both would have been in our older years as a result. Once when I was working on my cross-stitch embroidery, he suggested a saying I ought to embroider on a pillow to remember him by:

"He was always difficult, but he never was a bore."

I was always proud to be Harry's wife, and I'm even more proud now to be his widow, not only because he was such a good and loving man, but because he accomplished so much in his life. I'm proud that he was such a positive influence on the lives of so many other musicians, and that he worked with some of the finest orchestras and conductors in the world; proud that he played countless operas, ballets, and band concerts, and entertained thousands of people with his drumming in all those fabulous musicals at Melody Top and the Shubert Theatre. And I'm especially proud that he could conceive and pull off something as unique as the International Crafts Exposition in Williamsburg, which gave us two fabulous six-week first-class trips abroad and enabled us to meet and work with dozens of the most interesting people we'd ever known.

These were accomplishments any man should have been proud of. But Harry's biggest problem was that he was a perfectionist, and he always expected more of himself than he could deliver. Of perfection someone once said, "Demand it of yourself and you'll always be unsatisfied; demand it of others and you'll always be disappointed." As a young man fresh out of high school, Harry thought the world was his oyster, and he had every reason to believe that his extraordinary talent would insure that he would have a lifelong career as a symphony musician. But life doesn't always go as planned. Things change, and we're all changed by the people and things happening around us. Before we die, most of us will have to deal with the fact that some of the dreams we once had are never going to be realized.

I once heard a noted psychiatrist on TV say that life is a series of peaks and valleys, to which Harry remarked, "Yeah, but mostly it's valleys and I don't like it anymore." But the fellow went on to explain that if you didn't have the valleys, then you wouldn't have the peaks either, because to go through life in the middle of the two would mean that you would have no great highs or lows in your life, only an average run-of-the-mill existence, like a vegetable. It's hard to climb out of a valley and get back up the next hill in life, but it's always worth the effort, especially when you consider that it's in the valleys of life that we learn our most important life lessons and find out what kind of stuff we're made of. It is only when we have experienced the deep lows in life that we can appreciate the fantastic highs when they come, however far apart they may be.

Because I've lived this way, when I'm preparing to die I'll know that I've lived my life to the fullest and squeezed out every ounce of joy it had to give. If I've learned anything about life, it's that money is nice, but it can't buy happiness or friends. Even when you're down on your luck, you can find many things to be happy about if you simply open your heart to the possibilities and keep your sense of humor honed. I had myself pegged back in the seventies when I noted in my journal that I thought I was born for the unusual, the adventurous, and the excitement of not knowing where I'd be tomorrow. Perhaps my greatest frustration about life with Harry was being torn between wanting the best of both worlds— the secure one tied up with a neat blue bow, and the adventurous one always coming apart at the seams from sheer intensity.

And the latter was really what life with Harry was all about. We certainly had an unusual and mixed-up life as each of us explored new roads of discovery and found we each had talents we didn't know about before we met one another.

Thoughts about Love

Near the end of his life when he was home on Hospice and knew he was dying, Harry astonished me one afternoon when he suddenly asked, "Why did you ever marry me?"

It wasn't a time to get mushy with him, but perhaps I treated his question too lightly when I said I loved him because I found him completely irresistible, so humorous, so cute and good looking. He grinned, seemingly satisfied because he had always liked to hear me say that he was "cute and good looking." But I wish now I'd told him once again why I loved him so much, even in those times when he was so difficult to get along with and not at all likable.

I loved Harry because he had a kind, understanding, and generous heart; because of the honest emotion he could never hide, and his wonderful sense of humor that could brighten the grayest of days; because of his strength of character, determined will, stubborn nature, and his willingness to try anything once—and then again if he should happen to fail the first time.

During the dark days of our marriage when Harry gave me so much emotional grief, I loved him nonetheless because I always remembered the man he was in earlier years when life was going well for him. I could never forget the impetuous and ridiculously romantic fellow who always remembered anniversaries, birthdays, and the kind of perfume I loved, or the candy bar I couldn't resist.

How could I not love a man who used to come home from a job and, finding me sound asleep, would create a good-morning surprise for me on the breakfast table by building a castle of breakfast food boxes around my coffee cup? What's not to love about a fellow whose idea of a birthday card was a long trail of toilet paper from the bathroom to the kitchen with HAPPY BIRTHDAY and love words written in big red letters, or a huge "Happy Birthday, Barbara!" sign on a building he knew I'd see from the train on my way to work?

Most of all, I loved Harry because he looked into my heart when we first met and saw all the things I believed no man would ever try to know; and because he always made me feel I was the most treasured thing in his life, even when he was speaking hurtful words that suggested the opposite.

I'll never forget what he said to me one morning in the hospital after I'd been in that room with him day and night for four days. I knew I looked like death warmed over, so when he woke up I gave him a kiss and then apologized for how I looked, saying I needed to go clean up a bit. He melted my heart when he quietly said, "You'll always be beautiful to me."

At home, shortly before falling into a coma, Harry woke briefly. Although he could no longer speak by then, he seemed mentally alert. I asked him to blink if he could hear me, and he did. I talked to him a bit, once again saying, "I love you. Do you love me?"

And the old devil in Harry—the one with a sense of humor that just wouldn't quit—smiled impishly . . . and shook his head *NO*. I had to laugh because this was the same Harry who had said "Hell, no" in the hospital when I'd asked for a kiss. I always believed he would try to be funny right to the end, and this proved it.

Being a Witness to Someone's Life

Harry had no interest in reading any of my business articles, newsletters, or books because he simply wasn't interested in those topics. In fact, he once dubbed me "Agatha" saying that whatever I was writing was a mystery to him. He constantly encouraged me to write a book about something other than business, but neither of us could have imagined then that I'd eventually come up with the idea for a book that revolved around his humor and his life and times as a musician. As I wrote this book, I found myself envisioning Harry "up there somewhere" looking down on me and shaking his head and saying, "You've got to be kidding. Who's going to read a book about an old drummer and a home business writer?"

Well, I don't know. But writers have to write. I can relate to Isaac Asimov, who said, "If my doctor told me I had only six minutes to live, I wouldn't brood. I'd type a little faster." Like all men with any kind of ego at all—even one as carefully hidden as Harry's—I think he would have been downright tickled to think that my favorite topic to write about after he was gone was him and the dog we loved so much (my next book).

In closing, I want to leave you with these thoughts about marriage. There is a great message for everyone in the movie, *Shall We Dance?*, which starred Richard Gere and Jennifer Lopez. In one scene, the wife has just passed up the opportunity to have an affair with the detective she has hired to see if her husband is having an affair. After being politely rejected, he asks what it is about a marriage that holds it together. Passion, he wonders?

"No," she said. "It's because we need a witness to our marriage."

What she said next will forever remain in my memory. "In a marriage," she said, "you're promising to care about everything—the good, the bad, the terrible, the mundane things. All of it; all the time, every day. You're saying, 'Your life will not go unnoticed—unwitnessed—because I will be your witness.'"

If you've been long married, that should mean a lot to you, too; but if you're a younger person who is cohabiting with someone now, not willing to commit to marriage, perhaps these words will make you understand the difference between *auditioning* for marriage and actually becoming someone's witness in life and having someone witness your life as well.

I didn't realize it while Harry was alive, but thanks to a few lines of dialogue from this movie, I began to see myself as a witness to his life, and the only person who could tell his story.

To which Harry surely would have said, "You tell 'em, kid, I stutter."

In retrospect, I now see Harry's life as being a lot like jazz. He started with set notes, then began to improvise, going with the flow wherever music led him, playing one variation on a theme after another, always different, yet somehow the same; never perfect, always in the process of becoming a song that he never quite finished—one that still plays on in the hearts of those who knew and loved him. Especially mine.

Without question, Harry marched to the beat of a different drummer, and though his life has ended, the beat goes on.

"Our life is like some vast lake that is slowly filling with the stream of our years. As the waters creep surely upward, the landmarks of the past are one by one submerged. But there shall always be memory to lift its head above the tide until the lake is overflowing."
— Alexandre Charles Auguste Bisson,
French playwright and novelist

Encore! Encore!

You may forget the one with whom you have laughed, but never the one with whom you have wept.—Kahlil Gibran

REPRISE: *"Harry had the ability to move freely from one subject to another as easily as he could move from playing a circus one day to performing in the symphony the next. What he was really good at was making some smartass remark that fit the exact situation we were in at the time. His brain always seemed to be running a hundred miles a minute, and every conversation would have some humor in it because he would immediately take all the data, the environment, and the people there at the time, process it faster than the fastest computer, and spit out a humorous quip."* —Rich Sherrill

ollowing are a "baker's dozen" of short stories that illustrate how Harry made me laugh from day to day when I least expected to be amused:

Harry made a legion of friends in his lifetime because he was never bashful about introducing himself to anyone he found interesting, or just saying hello to someone with whom he previously had only a brief acquaintance. One day when we were shopping in Evanston, he spotted Mal Bellairs across the store. He said he knew him from his days of doing radio transcriptions at WBBM in the fifties, where Bellairs was a well-known broadcaster. He walked over to him, they shook hands, and the two of them chatted amicably for awhile and had a couple of laughs before shaking hands again and going their separate ways.

As we continued to shop, I said, "I didn't know Mal Bellairs was a friend of yours."

Harry gave me a cocky smile and said, "He is now."

～～

Both Harry and I were first-born children with all the traits common to this birth order. But I had sisters and Harry was an only child, which intensified his first-born traits. Both of us always wanted to be boss, and neither of us could easily admit to being wrong about anything. Yet we were always able to work through our conflicts because we had a rock-solid marriage based on both love and friendship, and of course we had a mutual sense of humor that often saved the day.

Once when someone asked Harry if we ever argued, he said, "No, we never argue. We just have knock-down drag-out fights."

～～

Harry and I agreed on most of the important things in life, but we quibbled a lot, usually about my total absorption with my business which denied him time with me, or something stupid, such as who had the TV clicker last and lost it, or how come I had time to talk to a friend on the phone, but didn't have time to dust the furniture. Once, in a fit of pique as he was going to bed, he took off his shorts and started dusting the furniture, adding that I might be a good cook, but I was a lousy housekeeper, conveniently forgetting that I was then writing ten hours a day to meet the deadline for a new book. That's when I put *him* in charge of doing the dusting and running the vacuum cleaner.

The next day, he began to parade around the house with a big sign taped to one of his drumsticks that read *BIGGER RAGS FROM BOSSY BAGS!*

～～

When Harry worked with me full time on the business, he handled much of our daily mail and often wrote funny notes to me in the margins of letters or advertising material. There was a flyer promoting a book of home-business ideas that read: "Selling dust from your vacuum cleaner is just ONE of the unusual moneymaking ideas in this book."

In the margin, in red ink—and with lots of exclamation points— Harry wrote: "BUY THIS!!! We have a fortune under our feet and don't know it!!!"

～～

In the car one morning on the way to the post office, I had the rubber-banded mail on my lap and my restless hands were fiddling with the rubber band on the top bundle. I twanged it, and it made a musical sound. I stretched it a bit more and the sound changed pitch. I got tickled and then began in earnest to twang the rubber band, saying to Harry, "Listen—I can make *music* with a rubber band."

He took the wind out of my sails by dryly saying, "That's stretching it a bit, dear."

〰〰

I guess I must have been worried about my high cholesterol the night I dreamed my "spigometer" (spi-gom'eter) was defective. Later, in checking the medical dictionary, I learned that a "sphygmometer" is a device to measure the pulse. I had probably heard it mentioned on the radio, and in my dream I was just spelling it wrong. When I got up that morning, I told Harry about the dream and asked him if he knew what a "spigometer" was. Without a moment's hesitation the man who always had food on his mind quipped, "Sure, it's the thing you put on your fork to see how fast you can twirl your spaghetti."

〰〰

When Harry and I were in Vienna on business in 1976, we visited St. Charles' Church, whose stained glass windows were the most beautiful we had seen anywhere to that point. As we were exploring the church, being the only ones there at that time, he was looking at one thing while I was elsewhere looking at a plaque dedicated to Saint Barbara.

I called out to him asking, "Did you know that St. Barbara was patron Saint to the artillery?"

My laughter echoed in the huge empty cathedral when he said, without a moment's hesitation, "No, but that explains why you think you're such a big shot."

〰〰

It was on this same business trip that we toured a magnificent palace outside the city of Warsaw. To protect the beautiful marble and inlaid floors, all of us in the tour group were required to put scuffs on over our shoes, which made walking hazardous because the floors were as slick as ice. Although most of us were fearful of falling and were shuffling along stiff-legged, Harry quickly developed his own method of maneuvering. He was leading the group as we started down one particularly long hall.

Donning a big grin, he placed his hands behind his back in Hans Brinker fashion and merrily began to skate to a rhythm that was unmistakably that of the "Skater's Waltz."

No one needed an interpreter to understand his message, and within moments the whole tour group was laughing and feeling much more relaxed. I was the only one in the group who knew that Harry's back pain that day was intense. But as he did throughout his many pain-filled years of life, he never let pain keep him from laughing or trying to brighten someone else's day—most particularly mine.

~~~

One year after a quiet Christmas vacation at home, Harry decided to end his holiday with a bang—literally. On the last day, a Sunday, he got up early to get the papers in the driveway because it had started to rain. I was still sound asleep, and the first thing I heard at 7 a.m. was, "Barb, I'm in trouble."

Even without my contact lens, I could see that Harry's head and clothes were covered with blood that was still pouring from some unknown spot. It took awhile for me to stop the flow and get the story of what happened because Harry was in quite a daze. He hadn't realized that the driveway was coated with ice until his slippers hit it, and when he fell, his head hit a broken section of concrete where the garage door butts the driveway. He cut a deep gash in his scalp that soon after put him in the emergency ward for four hours and seven stitches.

I was pretty calm while I was working to stop the bleeding, but when I went to retrieve his slippers—which had flown off during the fall—and saw all that blood on the sidewalk, on the garage floor, and all over the wall by the kitchen stairs (which he had apparently leaned against on his way up—he never did remember how he got from the driveway to the bedroom), I got weak in the knees. Later, when Harry was feeling better, I really gave him the devil for going out without me knowing it.

"You don't know how lucky you are," I said, suddenly realizing the possibilities. Harry sat there meekly as I continued to scold him. "You could have broken your hip or had a heart attack from the shock. You could have been knocked unconscious and bled to death—or *froze to death*—while I was peacefully snoring away. Harry, you could have *DIED!*"

Without missing a beat, my ever-lovin' quietly quipped ". . . and I could have sent YOU for the papers."

Harry's ability to always find the humor in any situation was just what the doctor ordered. I collapsed in a fit of laughter, which released all my stress, and soon we were both laughing and hugging and reflecting on how lucky we were. Aside from a big headache and lots of aching muscles, Harry was okay. I discovered that I had a cool head in a medical emergency, and we both learned how efficient our 911 service was. Best of all, we had a guaranteed laugh every Sunday morning for weeks afterward as soon as one of us said "... get the papers.'"

~~~~

When Harry had a colonoscopy one year, he saw everything in living color on a monitor and didn't feel a thing. On the sheet they gave him before the procedure, it said the sedative would "put him out" and he would have no memory of the procedure itself. Afterwards, when he was explaining to me all they did, I reminded him that he wasn't supposed to remember anything. He looked at me and said very seriously, "I remember it all, Helen."

Always the jokester. No wonder the nurses loved him.

~~~~

If you've been married for a long time, you probably tend to tune out your spouse from time to time, just as I did. It seems I've spent my life trying to do two things at once, and Harry often said that, as a result, I heard only half the things he said to me.

"Why don't you listen to me the way I listen to you?" he asked.

One night he was having a nightmare and, as usual when he called to me for help in his dreams, I said, "Harry, Harry!" so he'd wake up. Only this time he didn't, so I repeated his name twice again.

As if to prove that he always listened to me when I spoke—even when he was dreaming—in an exasperated voice while still dreaming, he said, *"What????"* before he resumed hollering "Help! Help!" I laughed so hard he finally woke up.

~~~~

We always watched *60 Minutes*, and one night there was a segment on Paul Simon, the singer who was the other half of the old team called Simon & Garfunkle. Garfunkle, it was stated, had quit the act to become an actor.

"I wonder what happened to Garfinkle, the actor?" I mused later.

"That's 'Garfunkle,' not 'finkle,' Harry corrected.

"Wasn't there a cartoon character with that name?"

"You're thinking of Garfield, the cat."

"No, I know the *cat's* name—wasn't there a moose called Garfunkel?"

"No, that was Bullwinkle."

"Would you mind repeating this conversation so I can write it down?" I said. "We sound like an old Abbott & Costello routine."

"It's a good thing you married me," he said. "No one else could figure out what you're talking about half the time."

<center>~~~</center>

Some people really do not have a sense of humor. Harry and I ran into one of them once while on vacation in northern Wisconsin. We had visited the fishing museum in Hayward where admission was charged. Harry presented $10, got back $5, and said to me as we entered the museum, "I think it's pretty funny, going to a fishing museum, giving them ten bucks and getting back a fin." Naturally I laughed at his cleverness.

On exiting, I thought I'd share his humor with the woman up front who had taken his money. After delivering the punch line, I was surprised to see the blank look on her face. She simply didn't get it. Worse, she became defensive, thinking we were questioning our change. Even after explaining the joke, I'm not sure she got it. Certainly she didn't appreciate it. I thought everyone knew a "fin" was five dollars. I remembered then that old saying, "He who laughs last probably had to have it explained."

<center>~~~</center>

I continue to find life curiously funny with all its unexpected pitfalls, twists and turns, dead ends, and side roads. I've learned that if we just keep going, keep giving life our very best and loving the person who's traveling that road with us, things have a way of working out in the end. I will never forget all the joy, excitement, color, laughter, and love that Harry brought into my life, and my hope is that his legendary humor—now documented for both posterity and ma's terity, too—will continue to enrich people's lives and give them something to laugh about for a long time to come.

Appendix

Harry J Brabec ~ Professional Background

Author's Note: Harry never had occasion to need a formal resume of his entire life's work experience, so I had a difficult time in trying to reconstruct his working life and music activities year by year. I began by pulling out all the bits and pieces of information he had shared in his nostalgic letters, added information from my journal notes and scrapbooks, and then turned to his scrapbooks, which included other letters and copies of work contracts. Orchestra archivists provided me with details about his tenure with the Civic, Chicago Symphony, and National Symphony orchestras, and I prevailed upon many of his friends to help me piece together his past before I met him.

I'm sure even Harry would have had a hard time coming up with the exacting details I managed to pull together here, and I'm just as sure that he quickly would have pointed out where I had erred in making assumptions about some periods of his life before we met. I also know he would forgive me for any errors I may have made.

• **Graduated in 1944 from J. Sterling Morton High School, Cicero, IL.** While in school, Harry performed professionally as a marimba soloist and as a drummer/percussionist at community functions as a member of the school's bands, its concert and symphony orchestras, and as a jobbing musician in the area.

• **Chicago Civic Orchestra** (Chicago Symphony's training orchestra), 1944–1945; and Grant Park Orchestra in the summers.

• **Chuck Foster Orchestra,** February 1945 to May 1946. (May have gone back to the Civic as an extra playing timpani; perhaps played Grant Park in 1946 as well.)

• **National Symphony Orchestra,** Washington, D.C. Premier percussionist (June 1946 to April 1949), working with conductor Hans Kindler during the regular seasons. During the Symphony's summer Watergate season, he worked with conductors Richard Bales (1947) and Howard Mitchell (1948).

• **Grant Park Orchestra and Lyric Opera.** In the off seasons of the National Symphony in 1948–1949, Harry played with the Grant Park Orchestra (June and July) and the Lyric Opera in Chicago (September-November). He continued to play with both orchestras off and on until the mid-eighties.

• **Wayne King Orchestra,** 1949–1951. Toured with the band and played *The Wayne King TV Show*, broadcasted from Chicago.

• **NBC Studio Orchestra,** Chicago. On staff part-time in 1949–1951 when not working with Wayne King; on staff full time in the latter part of 1959–1960 until Studio closed. (During these periods, also apparently did extra percussionist work with the Chicago Symphony, Grant Park Orchestra, Lyric Opera, and some jingles and recordings at Universal.)

• **Chicago Symphony Orchestra.** Section percussionist (1951–1952); principal percussionist (1952–1956), working with Rafael Kubelik, Fritz Reiner, and many guest conductors; extra percussionist (1957–1965). Assistant stage librarian (1966–1968), and stage manager (1968–1971) who also performed as an extra percussionist during this period.

• **Activities unknown,** 1957–1959. This is a blank spot in Harry's musical life. Depressed after the loss of his Symphony job, he put down his sticks for awhile to do menial work of one kind or another; also worked as a salesman for Proctor & Gamble for about a year.

• **Full-time jobbing musician in Chicago,** 1961–1965. Did recordings, worked as an extra man with the Chicago Symphony, Grant Park, and the Milwaukee Symphony; played the Lyric opera, the ballet, and other entertainment events in the city, plus the Shubert and Melody Top Tent theatres (1962–1965) before going back into the Chicago Symphony in 1966.

- **Teaching in Chicago area** (percussion classes and private instruction): North Park College (1963–1966); Maine Township North and South High Schools (1964–1965); Northwestern University (1966).

- **Walt Disney World Marching Band** and drummer in other Disney venues, 1971.

- **Freelance musician and teacher,** Orlando area, 1972–1973; taught percussion classes at Valencia College for these two years and had a few private students as well.

- **Silver Dollar City,** Branson, MO, (1973–1974). Coordinator of the City's annual fall "National Festival of Craftsmen." On the faculty at the School of the Ozarks for the 1974 summer term.

- **Independent crafts show producer.** Produced Busch Gardens' "International Crafts Exposition" (1976–1977); and crafts festival for Marriott's Great America Theme Park (1978).

- **Freelance jobbing musician,** Chicago area (1978–1982).

- **Springfield Symphony Orchestra,** General Manager, 1982.

- **Barbara Brabec Productions** (1982–1995). Office assistant and manager of the company's mail order division.

- **Freelance jobbing musician,** Chicago area (1984–1995). Member of the Windjammers Circus Band (1981 to mid-nineties), and performed regularly with the Bensenville/Wood Dale Concert Band (1982–1992). Retired from performing in 1995.

Harry J. Brabec ~ Known Recordings

As documented in the text, Harry made countless recordings through the years as a jazz drummer or percussionist with various big bands, radio and television orchestras, symphony orchestras, and other groups. This is merely a listing of a few recordings on which his playing can be heard today, and the instruments he said he was playing.

National Symphony Orchestra

Harry was in this Symphony from 1946 to 1949 with Hans Kindler, conductor. The Orchestra made several 78-rpm recordings for RCA while Kindler was there, so Harry would have been playing on some of these recordings. Regrettably, none of them found their way into his record collection.

Chicago Symphony Orchestra

The following list includes only some of the many recordings the Chicago Symphony Orchestra made during the years Harry was in the Orchestra or performing there as an extra percussionist. As he indicated in one of his letters, ". . . refer to any of the Chicago Symphony recordings made from 1951–1956, in which I am usually playing play snare drum or mallets."

During the sixties and seventies, Harry acquired a small collection of Chicago Symphony recordings on vinyl that he made with Fritz Reiner or Rafael Kubelik in the fifties. After dubbing some of these albums to tapes for me and friends, I asked him to tell me what instrument he was playing in each recording. Given his steel-trap memory, even after so many years I didn't doubt that he remembered exactly what he was playing in each of the recordings documented below.

NOTE: Many vinyl albums lack any reference to the date or even the year a recording was made, but I have included dates I was able to verify through Web research or album notes. (Pictures of some of these vinyl album covers can be seen on TheDrummerDrives.com website.)

Reiner/Chicago Symphony (RCA LSC-2214)

Dvorak: *New World Symphony* (Recorded in 1956; Harry on triangle in the 3rd movement)

Reiner/Chicago Symphony (RCA VICS-1424)

• Weinberger: *Schwanda, the Bagpipe Player: Polka and Fugue* (Recorded in 1956; Harry on snare drum)
• Dvorak: *Carnival Overture, OP. 92* (Recorded in 1956; Harry on tambourine)
• R. Strauss: *Salome, Op. 54: Dance of the Seven Veils* (Recorded in 1954; Harry on snare drum)

Reiner/Chicago Symphony (RCA Victor LM-1934 Red Seal)

Bartok: Concerto for Orchestra (Recorded in 1956; Harry on snare drum)

Reiner/Chicago Symphony and the Sauter-Finegan Orchestra (RCA Victor LM-1888 Red Seal)

• Liberman: *Concerto for Jazz Band and Symphony Orchestra* (Recorded in 1954. In a letter, Harry said he was playing "legit snare drum" here, with "Mousie" Alexander doing the jazz drum solo.)
• R. Straus: *Don Juan* (Harry on bells)

Reiner/Chicago Symphony (RCA Victor LM-2201 Red Seal)

Mussorgsky: *Pictures at an Exhibition.* (Harry playing triangle, gong, and chimes)

Reiner/Chicago Symphony (RCA VICS-1025 Stereo)

• Tchaikovsky: *1812 Overture.* (Harry on snare drum)
• Liszt: *Mephisto Waltz* (Harry on triangle)

Reiner/Chicago Symphony (RCA VICS-1042 Stereo)
Strauss: *Ein Heldenleben* (Harry on snare drum)

Reiner/Chicago Symphony (RCA VICS-1068 Stereo, 1964)
- Tchaikovsky: *Marche Slav* (Harry on snare drum)
- Moussorgsky: *Night on Bald Mountain* (Harry on chimes)

Kubelik/Chicago Symphony (Original recording on Naxos label; reissued on Mercury SRI 2-77006)
Kubelik made many recordings with the Chicago Symphony on the Naxos Classical Archives label during Harry's tenure with the orchestra, but only this album, recorded in 1952, found its way into his LP collection:
Smetana: *Ma Vlast* (Harry on snare drum)

Kubelik/Chicago Symphony (Recorded 1952)
A reference to this album on the Web listed all the percussionists who made it: Harry Brabec, Allan Graham, Lionel Sayers, Otto Kristufek, John Morgando, and Sam Denov.
- Stravinsky: *Les Noceso*
- Mendelssohn: *Fingal's Cave Overture, OP. 26*
- Brahms: *Symphony No. 3*

Solti/Chicago Symphony (London CSA-2227)
Mahler: *Symphony No. 6—Songs of a Wayfarer* (Recorded in 1970, this album has a beautiful picture of the Orchestra, with Harry on bass drum.)

Gould/Chicago Symphony (MCA DPLI-0245 Stereo)
Fischer: *Chicago* (arr. Gould). Recorded June 18, 1966 in Orchestra Hall, this album features Benny Goodman on clarinet, with Morton Gould conducting; Harry is playing snare drum. (Titled *Chicago,* this album includes nine other works and other conductors. Selections were recorded over a period of years from 1940 to 1976.)

Classic Percussion Albums

Percussion in Hi-Fi (David Carroll, Mercury Records SR60003)
Recorded at Universal Recording, Chicago, 1956; percussionists

were Dale Anderson, Hubert Anderson, Harry Brabec, Bobby Christian, Sam Denov, and Frank Rullo.

Harry is playing chimes in "Hell's Bells"; bongos in "Maleguena" and "Jungle Drums"; bells in "Quiet Talk"; and one of the snare drums in "Flamenco."

An email on the Web from Brian Phillips comments on this classic album, saying, "This is a fantastic album and not just because I enjoy drums. The tunes are great ('Jungle Drums,' 'Discussion in Percussion,' 'Malaguena') and the arrangements are lively. The recording is indeed impeccable. If you see it and pass it up, imagine Dick Butkus. In a dress. Singing. And then tackling you."

Re-Percussion in Hi-Fi (David Carroll, Mercury SR60029)

Recorded at Universal Recording, Chicago, 1956; percussionists were Dale Anderson, Hubert Anderson, Harry Brabec, Gil Breines, Bobby Christian, Sam Denov, Norm Jeffries, Morrie [SIC] Lishon, Ed Metzenger, Jim Ross, Frank Rullo, Dick Schory, and Bob Tilles.

Harry is playing chimes in "Bells and Little Bells"; vibes in "Dizzy Fingers"; and snare drum in "George Washington Slept Here."

Big Band Recordings

Chuck Foster and His Orchestra (1945-1946)

From one of Harry's letters: "I made one album with Foster that included performances from August 13, September 27, and October 18, 1945 . . . all done at the Hotel New Yorker in New York. I may be on the 1945 broadcast from the Blackhawk, too."

Wayne King Recordings (1950)

In a reminiscent letter in 1999, Harry wrote that a friend of his in a recording studio had sent him copies of the LP recordings he did with King on November 12, 1950 at the Edgewater Beach Hotel in Chicago. No other details are known.

Other Recordings

Walt Disney World Band (Vista STER-3337)

This souvenir album released in 1972 by Disney World includes a collection of recordings made on different dates between the park's opening and the album's release. Harry is playing bells in "Seventy-Six Trombones" and may be heard in the marching band as well.

Bensenville/Wood Dale Concert Band

All concerts of this band are recorded live, and many recent concerts can be heard on the band's website. When possible, MP3 downloads of the 1986 "Circus Ring Concert" and selected numbers from concerts that feature Harry's drumming will be offered on TheDrummerDrives.com.

Heritage of the March (Vol. 71–J. Pecsi–E. Stolc).

Recorded in 1981 by Foeller's Illinois State Alums and Friends with George Foeller directing the band, this album includes several marches of Josef Pecsi and Emil Stolc.

This particular album came to my attention only because Harry's picture was on the cover, along with his old friend, Boyd Conway, plus other musicians who made the recording. Harry often played with "Foeller's Easter Bunnies" through the years and may have been on other Heritage of the March recordings in his collection (which numbered about 200). This was a series of band music albums created and funded by Robert Hoe, who traveled the world in search of marches. The Navy Band (Washington, DC) made the first Heritage series, and the Naval Academy Band recorded four. A number of universities and other service bands made recordings as well. Apparently many of the vinyl albums are now available on CD.

Original Harry Brabec Quotations and Other Quotations He Clipped and Saved

Did you ever stop to think about what clipped quotations say about the person who collects them? You can tell a lot about what an individual thinks, believes, and yearns for simply by studying the cartoons and quotations he or she clips and saves. In reading all the quotations Harry had either written in his own hand or clipped from the many publications he read, I suddenly saw how he felt about things we never discussed. This got me to thinking about why we all like quotations so much. I believe it's because the fine writing or inspirational thoughts of others often express feelings we're having at the time that we simply don't know how to convey to others.

Following are the quotations that were on Harry's bulletin board when he died. The first nine were written in his hand and are believed to have originated with him (since they can't be found anywhere on the Web).

"You're not that good and you are never going to be that good. But console yourself. Neither is anyone else."—Harry

"Some people come to a concert just to hear mistakes."—Harry

"Always be very smart or very nice."—Harry

"A man's decisions are no better than his information."—Harry

"That which is escaped now is but pain yet to come."—Harry

"One cannot think of the past without the pang of loss."—Harry

"If I had never met you, think what I would have missed."—Harry

"If life had been meant to be fair, there never would have been such a thing as a proctoscopic examination!"—Harry

"There are still a lot of books to read and a lot of fish to catch." —Harry

Other quotations on Harry's bulletin board that spoke to his heart or sense of humor:

"You are what you eat, said a wise old man.
If that's the case, I'm a garbage can!" —Victor Buono

"The more you've got to lose, the more nervous you are about losing it." — Vince Lombardi

"Screw up your courage—you've screwed up everything else." —Anon.

"There is no failure except in no longer trying."—Elbert Hubbard

"Fear saps more men than most anything else."—Wm. Wrigley Jr.

"The essence of youth is believing things last forever."—Eric Sevareid

"The longer I live . . . the more beautiful life becomes. The earth's beauty grows on man. If you foolishly ignore beauty, you'll find yourself without it. Your life will be impoverished. But if you wisely invest in beauty, it will remain with you all the days of your life." —Frank Lloyd Wright

Harry's bulletin board also included a copy of the "Showman's Prayer," a Glenn Miller Festival button from 2004, a BIX LIVES button from a festival in Iowa, and several other quotations he had clipped from magazines.

The Drummer Drives Website

*I*f you liked this book, you'll also like its companion website at www.theDrummerDrives.com. It features articles and other content that could not be included in this book, all illustrated with rare photographs and music memorabilia from the Brabec scrapbooks. While on the site, be sure to subscribe to the mailing list to receive announcements whenever new content is added. Featured now or coming soon:

- MP3 music downloads and video clips
- Many photos of bands, orchestras, and musicians
- The rare photo of five Russian composers
- Articles and music remembrances by some of Harry's friends
- The "Inquiring Camera Girl" column quoting members of the Chuck Foster Orchestra at the Blackhawk on courting girls
- More of Harry's letters
- Another of Harry's amusing and fictional New Year's Eve "Concerts" at Soldier Field
- A backstage view of Georg Solti's 1970 Carnegie Hall Debut
- A rare issue of the *Drums Unlimited* newsletter published by Bill Crowden in 1969
- A collection of Harry Brabec "Art"
- A caricature of "Light-Fingered Harry" at Disney World
- Photos of Barbara as a marimba entertainer in the fifties
- Pictures of autographed LP album covers and programs
- Programs from various concerts, Broadway musicals at the Shubert and Melody Top theatre, and other entertainment events

ALSO: Links to websites whose content relates to topics discussed in this book, from musicians, entertainers, and percussionists to bands, orchestras, and Chicago's music history.

Contact the Author

*I*f you enjoyed this book and want to tell me that, **I'd love to hear from you** with your comments about the book as a whole, or any part of it that was especially meaningful to you. I'd particularly like to hear from anyone who knew Harry, studied with him, or worked with him professionally.

Since nothing helps to sell a book like positive comments from other readers, *I would be especially grateful to receive reader comments that I might publish on the book's REVIEWS page in the "What Other Readers are Saying" area.* Or, if you like to submit book reviews on Amazon, posting your comments there would be particularly helpful to me.

Contact me at **Memories@theDrummerDrives.com** or by telephone at **630-717-4188** during business hours. Visit my personal website at **www.BarbaraBrabec.com**.

When you contact me, I'll add your email address to my private, permanent READERS DATABASE, and you have my word that *I will never share or sell your email address to anyone.* Being on this special mailing list means you will be given an opportunity to buy my future books at a special prepublication price. Several are now being planned on a variety of topics related to LIFE.

To be notified when I've added new content to the website, also **join the mailing list on the website,** which is totally different from my book buyers mailing list above.

My next book (planned for publication in 2011) is tentatively titled *Pawprints on My Heart—Lessons Learned from a Dog Named Ginger.* It's about the dog Harry and I loved—how we rescued her from certain death in the wilds of Missouri, then trained her, taught her to communicate with us, and traveled all over the country with her. It's also a story about how she enriched and changed our lives and the life lessons I learned from her.

Index

LaVergne, TN USA
07 December 2010
207714LV00002B/9/P